Acclaim for

THE JOURNALS

OF

Spalding Gray

"*The Journals of Spalding Gray* tells an important story that is painful to read but hard to put down. They bring you into a mind that is original and uncensoring even as it careens off the rails into deep destruction. Gray's complex moods, dark imagination, and wit are often disturbing and deeply moving." —Kay Redfield Jamison, author of *An Unquiet Mind*

"[These] journals allow us to see the unreconstructed Spalding Gray. . . . The book has been superbly edited and annotated by Nell Casey; she also provides an excellent introduction. . . . Full of panic and despair, leavened with boyish misbehavior and dry wit . . . and lit with a kind of disembodied lyricism that honors even the blackest perceptions."
—Daphne Merkin, *Bookforum*

"One of the most disturbing yet insightful aspects of reading *The Journals of Spalding Gray*, Nell Casey's distillation of Gray's unpublished, personal writing, is learning how magnificently and artfully Gray constructed his appealing onstage and onscreen persona out of his own obsessions, neuroses, and troubled history. . . . These journals are perhaps most useful in helping one to understand the healing and purgative power that Gray and no doubt many other troubled artists have found in both writing and performing."
—*The Boston Globe*

"The brilliant, tormented performer mesmerized audiences with his autobiographical monologues, but most revealing are these diaries leading up to his suicide in 2004."
—*O, The Oprah Magazine*

"The journals in [the years after his car accident] record a harrowing descent into madness, when he turned one of his greatest talents as a storyteller—his ability to find connections between disparate observations and events—against himself." —Nathaniel Rich, *The New York Review of Books*

"The publication of *The Journals of Spalding Gray* is a significant event in American arts and letters. If Walt Whitman was our great chronicler of American life toward the end of the nineteenth century, Gray was his ironic, darkly funny counterpart. He did more than anyone else to record what it was like to be human—achingly human—in the urban America of the late twentieth and early twenty-first centuries. This is not only a great book, it's an important book."
—Michael Cunningham,
Pulitzer Prize–winning author of *The Hours*

"*The Journals of Spalding Gray* . . . reveal a daring melancholic (he committed suicide in 2004) who mined his chaotic inner life, troubled relationships, and tragic family history to create sterling works onstage anchored by his signature desk, water glass, notebook, and microphone." —*Elle*

"*The Journals of Spalding Gray* reveal someone who was at once addicted to the rush of self-exposure and yet was also deeply private. Brooklyn-based journalist Nell Casey has edited Gray's literary anatomy down to a readable package. . . . As Gray's journals show, he honed his craft carefully, tweaking and adjusting his stories for maximum narrative torque." —*The Globe and Mail* (Toronto)

THE JOURNALS

OF

Spalding Gray

SPALDING GRAY was born and raised in Rhode Island. A cofounder of the acclaimed New York City theater company the Wooster Group, he appeared on Broadway and in numerous films, including Roland Joffé's *The Killing Fields*, David Byrne's *True Stories*, Garry Marshall's *Beaches*, and as the subject of the Steven Soderbergh documentary *And Everything is Going Fine*. His monologues include *Sex and Death to the Age 14*, *Swimming to Cambodia*, *Monster in a Box*, *Gray's Anatomy*, and *It's a Slippery Slope*. He died in 2004.

NELL CASEY is the editor of the national bestseller *Unholy Ghost: Writers on Depression* and *An Uncertain Inheritance: Writers on Caring for Family*, which won a Books for a Better Life Award. Her articles and essays have been published in *The New York Times*, *The Washington Post*, *Slate*, *Elle*, and *Glamour*, among other publications. Her fiction has been published in *One Story*. She is a founding member of Stories at the Moth, a nonprofit storytelling foundation. She lives in Brooklyn with her husband and two children.

THE JOURNALS

OF

Spalding Gray

listening to [some one]
[&] at night — watchi[ng]
[the] importance of sponta[neity]
[ou]t of you ... the m[an]
[we] can all do it but [the one]
[w]ho carries it off .. I [wonder]
what it must be lik[e]
[wi]th a horn, a camer[a]
[br]ush — tools for t[he]
[...] himself. We li[sten]
[b]ecause we feel he [...]
[...]y.

[a]fter reading Ch[...]
[I] was very happy, and [...]
[f]eel to get back to [...]
[...] can once more shar[e]
[...]nds I have. I feel [...]
[...]an ever before. I ne[ver]

THE JOURNALS

OF

Spalding Gray

EDITED BY NELL CASEY

VINTAGE BOOKS
A Division of Random House, Inc.
New York

FIRST VINTAGE BOOKS EDITION, OCTOBER 2012

Copyright © 2011 by Spalding Gray, Ltd.

All rights reserved Published in the United States by Vintage Books,
a division of Random House, Inc., New York, and in Canada by Random House
of Canada Limited, Toronto. Originally published in the United States by
Alfred A. Knopf, a division of Random House, Inc., New York, in 2011.

Vintage and colophon are registered trademarks of Random House, Inc.

The Library of Congress has cataloged the Knopf edition as follows:
Gray, Spalding, 1941–2004.
The journals of Spalding Gray / edited by Nell Casey.
p. cm.
Includes index.
1. Gray, Spalding, 1941–2004—Diaries.
2. Dramatists, American—20th century—Biography.
3. Screenwriters—United States—Biography.
4. Actors—United States—Biography. I. Casey, Nell, 1971– II. Title.
PS3557.R333Z46 2011
812'.54—dc22 2011010257

Vintage ISBN: 978-0-307-47491-9

Book design by Maggie Hinders

www.vintagebooks.com

I HAD BEEN brought up to look forward to heaven then began to think of heaven as history, that I would lie old and forever in the arms of someone while they accounted my life. That no matter what the pain, it would all have distance when it was recounted at another time. Told as a story in front of a fire through a very long night, left with a slight memory of it in the morning. This was in a way what I came to see as hope. Hope was a fantasy of the future and now with age the future has shrunk and so has the investment of hope in that future. What was there left to do but to report to myself the condition of the world that is out there, as I saw it. What was there left to do but to ask you to listen?

SPALDING GRAY
(1941–2004)

CONTENTS

A WOODEN DESK, a glass of water, a notebook, and a microphone—this was the stage setting for a Spalding Gray performance. Gray, with his long patrician face and habitual plaid shirt, sat alone before an audience for the first time in 1979 and, in his distinct New England accent, told stories from his life. It was an ancient notion—the history of confessional storytelling is made up of a group as various as Saint Augustine, Jean-Jacques Rousseau, Sylvia Plath, and Richard Pryor. Yet Gray's work transformed the theater world, creating an autobiographical genre that has since been so widely replicated it is hard to imagine the daring it took to come first. Until Gray appeared as himself, the monologue implied a performer inhabiting another character or characters while roaming the stage, such as the theatrical portraits Ruth Draper premiered in 1920 or Lily Tomlin in her 1977 Broadway show, *Appearing Nitely*. Gray, on the other hand, absented his body, always sitting calmly at his desk, speaking nakedly about himself: the formative wounds of his childhood, his repressed WASP upbringing, his tangled romantic life, and the intriguingly neurotic way in which he viewed the world.

Despite his natural ability to tell a story, it took some time for him to discover the monologue as his form. Throughout college and his early twenties, Gray acted in traditional theater but soon found that he did not want, as he once wrote in his journal, to "go on the stage every night and fake emotions." (And yet he was not ready to be himself either. "I wanted to be a not-be," he later remarked of his acting at this time, "all the glorious imitation of life.") After moving to New York City in 1967, at twenty-six years old, Gray became passionately involved in avant-garde theater, where he took on roles that hewed closer to his own personality.

He also began to cast a wide net for inspiration; he devoured all forms of theater and literature. He studied the works of an eclectic range of playwrights and writers and philosophers—Eugene O'Neill, Virginia Woolf, Jerzy Grotowski, Robert Lowell, André Gide, and Ram Dass, among them—all of whom offered him a more incisive sense of himself and therefore a new way to conceive of his own story.

In 1970, he became, along with his girlfriend at the time, Elizabeth LeCompte, a member of the experimental theater troupe the Performance Group; later, they co-founded the theater company the Wooster Group. In 1975, in collaboration with LeCompte, Gray began developing a trilogy of ensemble plays, exploring his childhood and family, called *Three Places in Rhode Island*. In the second piece, *Rumstick Road,* he stepped forward momentarily and addressed the audience as himself, thus beginning his career—and his particular cross to bear—in offering his life as art.

Gray premiered his first solo show, *Sex and Death to the Age 14,* in 1979. And he was off: he presented six monologues in quick succession over the next three years. These monologues—and the ones that followed—were a strenuous exercise in memory. From the start, Gray worked only from an outline for his shows. He tape-recorded his performances in order to play them back and edit the story in his mind; he would alter the piece to make it, as he explained in a 1999 interview, "more dramatic and funny by juxtaposing a little hyperbole here and playing with it a little bit there." As a result, he began an ongoing creative relationship with his audience—tweaking his stories based on their reaction, what he called a "dialogue"—that he would rely on for the rest of his career. "I start wide open and want it to come down to something set organically," Gray explained. "I never memorize my lines. I'm trying to corral them every time. It's like bushwhacking—I hack my way up the hill each night until eventually I make a clear path for myself."

In 1983, Gray debuted an early version of his one-man show *Swimming to Cambodia,* an artful blend of personal and political history, telling stories from his life and from his experience acting in the Roland Joffé film *The Killing Fields* while also narrating the Cambodian genocide that the movie depicted.

Swimming was Gray's watershed monologue. The piece was met with near-fanatical critical praise and, in 1987, was made into a well-received film directed by Jonathan Demme. Consequently, Gray was invited to perform his next solo show, *Terrors of Pleasure,* largely about the disastrous experience of buying his first house, at Lincoln Center in New York City. With this move, he further broadened his audience, extending it from his cult downtown following to the well-heeled theatergoers of uptown Manhattan. He made appearances on *Late Night with David Letterman* and *The Tonight Show with Jay Leno.* Three more of his monologues—*Terrors of Pleasure, Monster in a Box,* and *Gray's Anatomy*—were turned into independent films, directed by Thomas Schlamme, Nick Broomfield, and Steven Soderbergh, respectively. He wrote a novel, *Impossible Vacation,* published by Knopf in 1992. He began appearing in Hollywood movies—Garry Marshall's *Beaches,* which starred Bette Midler, and John Boorman's *Beyond Rangoon,* among them—though never as a leading man, typically as a side character spun off of the persona of his solo shows. He even played a recurring role as a therapist in *The Nanny,* a television sitcom starring Fran Drescher, starting in 1997. All the while, Gray continued to present his monologues at Lincoln Center as well as tour them in the United States and abroad. Throughout his twenty-five-year solo career, from 1979 to 2004, Gray pulled off the fine trick of portraying both the beautiful and the terrible aspects of his life while simultaneously allowing his audience to feel understood. He had, after all, just spoken the difficult truths for them. Gray had become our preeminent theatrical confessor.

.   .   .

The details of Gray's death are now nearly as well-known as his oft-performed life: He was in a serious car accident in Ireland in 2001 that left him with a broken hip, a limp, and a titanium plate in his head; he struggled with brain trauma and severe depression afterward; he was institutionalized several times for psychiatric care; and finally his dramatic life came to its surpassingly dramatic end. On January 10, 2004, Gray threw himself, it is believed, from the Staten Island Ferry into the dark, freezing water of New York Harbor. The feeling of public devastation that rose up after his death came in no small part from the fact that the decision to end his life—and the act itself—were so private. Gray, by virtue of the ongoing autobiography of his monologues, had promised to tell his audience everything. His story was our story. But his public narrative, despite his seemingly having always whispered it in our ears, was masterfully composed.

These journals—which begin when Gray was twenty-five years old and end just before his death at sixty-two—illustrate a teeming under life that the performer only hinted at onstage. Gray was not only surprisingly capable of keeping parts of his life to himself; he was able to skim these parts, shaving just the top layer of a secret and offering it up as a convincing whole. "The well told partial truth to deflect the private raw truth," Gray himself observed about his monologues in his journal.

This is not to say that Gray wasn't compelled to publicly confess. He was. This need—as well as the release and redemption he felt in confiding to an adoring audience—was possibly the greatest driving force of his life. But as his career evolved, as he grew older, as his interests and desires and relationships became ever more complex, his aim to continually tell his story became more difficult. Gray could not reveal everything, not only because he knew the best stories were lively distillations, but also out of the fear that too bold a truth might alienate his followers. He craved the love of his audience—and his audience wanted only a representative of Spalding Gray, a spokesperson for truth.

This dynamic made Gray increasingly introspective, ever aware of his public, even as he was simply going through the day. The audience became the witness without whom he felt as if he didn't exist. "The description of a memory makes a new reality," he wrote in an undated journal entry. "Am I more real in front of an audience?" In 1991, he wrote simply: "THERE IS NOTHING PRIVATE LEFT." As long as he considered everyone and everything as material for his story, there was little room for "real," or unself-conscious, life.

These journals make up the rough draft of Gray's adult life, the version he sought and often felt he lost once it was crafted and brought to light in his monologues. Here is the raw material—the wrenching emotional breakdown he suffered in 1976 following a trip to India, his time in Thailand making *The Killing Fields*, his jittery first marriage—that Gray later reproduced with swift, literary hindsight in his performances. These pages show how the monologuist intuitively shaped his narrative, as well as the character of "Spalding Gray," with a penetrating eye and a soothing bit of self-deprecation, for his audience. In the journals, he frequently comes across in a more extreme way, his anguish and needs not tempered by his perceptive charm.

And yet the themes of Gray's life as they appear here are consistent with those of his monologues. His story, and this book, begin and end with suicide: that of Gray's mother, Elizabeth Horton, and of Gray himself. From early on, Gray writes with eloquent precision about the ways in which depression and suicide felt like an inheritance to him. He articulates the obsessions and vulnerabilities that he suffered, and fought, as a result of his mother locking herself in the family car one night in 1967 and gassing herself to death.

By his own analysis, Gray was always looking to satisfy the longing that his mother's outsized personality, and tragic end, had instilled in him. He traced many of his problems back to her, reasoning that she, and his distant father too, had left a part of him arrested as a needy, self-indulgent boy throughout adulthood.

"The new fear was that mom had not only killed herself," Gray once wrote on a scrap of paper, "but had also laid the groundwork to kill me." He drew the parallels often between his mother and himself, emphasizing not only their similar emotional fragilities but also their vivaciousness. He frequently cites their shared love of the ocean. (Water, in general, has a constant and eerily foreshadowing presence in these journals.) He mythologized her life, particularly at the end of his own, obsessing about the ways in which he had replicated her circumstances for himself. Gray felt that his mother, more than anyone else, was written into his genes.

When he later became romantically involved, Gray constantly

thrashed and bucked within the confines of commitment. This pattern plays out with the three women involved in the major relationships of his life: Elizabeth LeCompte, Renée Shafransky, and Kathleen Russo.

Gray writes searchingly about these women, each one overlapping with the last, each becoming involved in his work in a crucial way. LeCompte was one of his most influential theater directors as well as the first person to suggest that Gray speak to the audience directly. Together, Gray and LeCompte developed a revolutionary model of theater with the Wooster Group, whose work not only broadened the scope of theatrical imagination but also endures as a powerful cultural force today. Shafransky was his muse, appearing as a character in his monologues throughout the eighties and nineties, as he rose to fame. She also became Gray's first wife—and the backbone to his successful career, eventually assuming the role of manager, producer, and director for many of his professional endeavors. Russo, who gave birth to Gray's first child while he was married to Shafransky, became his second wife and had another son with him. She was the subject of his last monologues, in particular *Morning, Noon, and Night,* a tribute to the unexpected pleasure he found in his late-blooming family life and his relationship with his stepdaughter, Marissa, and two sons, Forrest and Theo Gray.

These journals account for Gray's artistic history as it shapes—and reshapes—itself around each of these women. A portrait emerges of a restless performer, with hungrily self-destructive instincts offstage, whose talent and ambition were focused by the commanding women in his life. Gray chronicles his long attachment to alcohol, torturous and beloved, and the way he used it as a magic carpet ride out of the strained reality of intimate life. He also expresses guilt about his selfish impulses and his inability to see past them. "I lay sick in bed and told Renée that I felt I used her as a nurse to get famous," he wrote in 1991. "Just used her to keep me afloat." But in the free fall of loss and regret after their breakup, a more appreciative Gray emerges: "The image that constantly tears my heart, the image that rips at me is of Renée on her red bike with the fender rattling and her in her brown shorts and we are riding together down to the ocean to take our morning walk and I am there but not there. A kind of be here then sort of guy and she is looking back at me with love in her gaze and I respond."

Still, even while in these long-term relationships, Gray maintained a fluid sense of his sexuality. He analyzed—and upended—every role assigned to him sexually. He speaks of feeling like a woman after sleeping with an aggressive man in a gay bath club in Amsterdam, describes the lure of the young as he grows older, details the scrutiny with which he fought off intimacy, criticizing every woman he loved for a particular physical aspect. But Gray was never able to fully integrate his shifting sexuality into his stage persona. His only public mention, for example, of his involvement with a man was in his 1981 monologue *47 Beds*—and he denounced it to comedic effect. After he became famous, he continued to experiment with men on occasion, but he did not explore homosexuality in his work, except for a fictionalized account of his assignation with the man in the Amsterdam bathhouse in the autobiographical *Impossible Vacation*.

If these journals unveil the shadow story—the plot that hovered outside his monologues—then the question emerges, would Gray have wanted them published? He never stated explicitly to Russo that they should be made public after his death, although he did once suggest it to her in 1991, after reading a review of *The Journals of John Cheever* in *The New York Times Book Review.*

It is possible that Gray kept this record as a promise, or a hope, that it would someday be read. He refers more than once to "you" in these journals, speaking specifically to a reader—whoever that might be. There was a time when the "you" might have been Shafransky: Gray occasionally worried she would read his journals—he said as much in his 1996 monologue, *It's a Slippery Slope,* and also wrote about this privately. Yet he continued to address "you"—the unnamed reader— long after his relationship with Shafransky had ended. In 1990, he offered this explanation for why he should confess in a diary: "What am I doing? I guess I'm telling it to myself or to you, the reader." Five years later, he plainly asked: "WILL YOU READ THIS?" In 2000, four years before his death, Gray came as close to saying that the journals were meant for the public as he ever did: "Back in N. Y. C. for an interesting meeting with *[film director]* Peter Greenaway where he asked me who I wrote for when I did a journal . . . my audience of course. It is not enjoyable or easy for me to have a non-narrated private experience and I've always known that."

Still, publishing these journals poses a question that echoes Gray's own moral quandary: What is worth revealing? It seems, throughout his career, that Gray wanted both to be known and not, to seek the truth and to create it. And yet this book is an endeavor made in the spirit of his mission. More than once in these journals, Gray quotes a line from the book of Job, spoken by the messengers delivering the news that Job's children and servants and animals have died: "I alone have escaped to tell you."

We have lost Gray, but there is still more for him to tell us.

Nell Casey

June 2011

WHILE I WAS working on this book, the entirety of Spalding Gray's notebooks, videos, and audiotapes were housed in many cardboard boxes in the New York City office of Glenn Horowitz, a rare-book dealer who specializes in selling literary archives to scholarly institutions. (Gray's papers have since been acquired by the Harry Ransom Center of the University of Texas at Austin and currently reside there.) These boxes were neatly labeled—"Journals 1970s and 1980s," "Journals 1990–1995 and Misc. Personal Material," "Notebooks and Performance Notes," and the like—but it seemed at each visit I made, another cardboard box would materialize with sketches Gray had doodled, audiotapes of therapy sessions, short stories, videotapes of performances, and scraps of paper with fascinating one- to two-line glimpses into the performer's mind. Gray apparently wrote notes on every bit of ephemera that passed through his hands: hotel stationery, an Amtrak napkin, a Breast Cancer Coalition pamphlet. Every time I entered Horowitz's office, it felt as if I'd fallen down a rabbit hole into Gray's phantasmagoric vision of life.

Once, in the summer of 2009, when Gray's widow, Kathleen Russo, was packing up the last of his personal papers for the archive, I stood by in amazement as she rifled through the remaining fragments of Gray's life. "This is interesting," she would say, and then hand over a cryptic drawing he'd done as a young man or a letter his therapist had written to him. The papers piled up on a table before me, and as I began to root through them—unfolding wrinkled pages, opening long-forgotten, tattered notepads—a Tampax insert fell into my lap. Somehow, it had made its way from Gray's home into his papers and had been earnestly tucked away in his archives. This was, it seemed to me, not only a fitting tribute to Gray's career of ushering private life into public view but also an excellent symbol for the intimate chaos of this project.

Gray's notebooks—he wrote in a variety of diaries, from marble composition books to spiral notebooks to date books (every page filled to the brim with notes running straight through the "Earnings & Withholding Tax" page)—range from 1967, when he was a twenty-five-year-old doing regional theater in Texas, to the days just before his death, at age sixty-two, in 2004. All told, Gray left behind more than five thousand pages of his private writing. While most of these books contain his day-to-day musings—alternately written in tilting cursive or loose capital letters—there are also notebooks he used specifically for his monologues. These typically contain a list of plot points, targets Gray wanted to hit while telling a story, with changes and adjustments made in red pen. On occasion, Gray also tried out ideas here before committing to them. One such book, for example, is labeled "Mourning, Noon and Night" with the *u* in "Mourning" crossed out, offering a glimpse of the kind of revelatory fine-tuning he did with this monologue before he first performed it in 1999. There are also occasional intrusions of daily life: a babysitter's number is scribbled across the top of one page and, on the bottom of another, a list of things Gray wanted to remember from a trip he'd taken into New York City from his home in Sag Harbor, Long Island.

Conversely, the "regular" diaries often include the first version of stories before they were transformed for a monologue, perhaps before even Gray knew that he would offer these details to an audience. Because the "performance notebooks" were more skeletal—they are largely made up of outlines and lists—I primarily drew from the day-to-day journals for this book. On the rare occasion that I did use something from the performance journals—when I found something that added an interesting glimpse into Gray's artistic process—I made note of it.

In addition to giving me access to everything stored at Horowitz's office, Russo offered many other crucial elements from Gray's life such as letters and faxes he'd sent or saved, drawings, family photographs, publicity stills, reviews and press clippings for his shows, medical and psychiatric paperwork from the last years of his life, and an audio-tape he recorded—the last one he ever made—a month prior to his death. I mostly used these materials to help me better understand Gray and to fully represent his life through his journals. When I did include material in the book other than the journals—quoting from a note on scrap paper or a letter exchange—the source is identified. Toward the end of his life, when Gray was physically and mentally compromised and did not write in his journals as frequently or as coherently, I relied more heavily on supplementary materials such as hospital records, let-ters from this time, and Gray's last audio recording. When psychiatric records were not available, Russo provided me with names of hospitals and dates drawn from a timeline she kept at the end of Gray's life. I also conducted many interviews with Gray's family members, friends, and colleagues. I quote from these conversations throughout but do so more extensively in conjuring Gray's last years.

My greatest challenge as an editor was to cull the entries and shape a history from the vast array of fascinating personal documentation Gray left behind. I read everything available to me and then set about trying to portray the story of Gray's life while also abiding the gaps and idiosyncrasies of the journals. With the exception of 1977–1979, when Gray seemed to write every day, the diaries have varying breaks in time, though he didn't tend to let more than a few weeks lapse before return-ing. There are a few intervals, nonetheless, when Gray disappeared for longer. The most striking example of this is from 1984: In the year when Gray was first touring *Swimming to Cambodia* and his solo career began its steep ascent, he left behind few entries, with almost no mention of his work.

Throughout his journals, Gray sometimes drew boxes around cer-tain words and arrows pointing from one passage to another. He occa-sionally used other modes of emphasis: underlining words or sentences or using question marks to indicate his loss of words to describe something. In the hope of reproducing the feeling of the original journals, I have left these intact where possible.

For the sake of a coherent account, I have included my own narration in italics throughout the book, mainly at the start of each decade and at the end of Gray's life, when his writing became more diffuse. There are also brief clarifications, in italics and brackets either beneath the date or within the entry, that aim to orient the reader when Gray refers to an event, person, or story that requires further explanation. At times, I note when something from the journals later found its way into one of Gray's monologues or when there is an interesting discrepancy between how he told a story in the journal and how he presented it later in a monologue. But I did not note every instance in which a piece of his life made its way into his art.

The narrative provided throughout is meant to place the entries in the broader context of Gray's life, though this is not a definitive biography, which has yet to be written. This book is devoted solely to Gray's point of view; I asked for others to provide not counter-perspectives but rather a more complete sense of the story.

There are certain insights—such as his feelings about his growing fame during that seminal year of 1984—that left this earth along with Gray and remain mysterious. Along these lines, LeCompte told me she possessed two of Gray's journals from their time together as a couple, but later said she was not able to find them. Thankfully, for the most part, Gray left behind such a large trove of his reflections—in interviews, monologues, recordings—I was able to find clues and passages to draw from in order to fill in the blanks. (Russo also gave me access to transcripts of everything in Gray's archive. A small number of entries in the book are drawn from these.) At times, I quote Gray himself; this material was gathered from the journals, letters, television interviews, and newspaper and magazine clippings as well as Gray's monologues or other forms of his writing, both published and not.

I have not noted where there are missing passages—either between entries or within them—as I found trying to mark these lapses with ellipses riddled the page with a bewildering code of disclosure. The ellipses that appear in the entries belong to Gray.

One of the great pleasures of reading journals is to see the untidy origins both of the author's reflections and of his writing habits. As such, I felt a keen responsibility to keep these journals as close to their original form as possible. Gray, however, was dyslexic and made frequent misspellings and grammatical errors. Where there seemed to be a significant struggle for him to get a word right—such as a 1968 entry in which he wrote "now things are really difficult (great fears about ~~alchhol alcha~~ drinking I keep wanting to drink)"—or where the misuse of a word seemed to represent the way in which dyslexia actually heightened Gray's originality, I did not fix it. Similarly, I occasionally kept Gray's peculiar grammar and quirks of punctuation when they seemed to make their own statement about his creativity. That said, where the mistakes were plainly mistakes, I made corrections; there were so many misspelled words throughout these pages that leaving them would have served as a distraction for the reader. If a word within an entry was not legible, I signified this with a blank line.

Gray also had a habit of crossing through his words and starting again, refashioning a thought midstream, as well as suddenly writing in ALL CAPITAL LETTERS, as if he'd just realized how short and urgent life really was. He also used erratic indentations throughout certain entries, perhaps to heighten their poetic impact. These all seemed to be conscious decisions on his part and helped to reveal something of his feelings and intentions as he wrote—I left them as they were.

Gray did not always date his journals. Where no date appears before an entry in the book, there was no date to be found in the diaries. Undated entries have been placed in correct chronological order to the best of my knowledge. Otherwise, I have, for consistency's sake, given the date—in as complete a form as possible—on the upper-left-hand side of each entry. I also kept Gray's own descriptions of the date when they offered further—and occasionally revealing—description, as in "April One April Fools Day. I'm the fool," which he wrote in 1995. Gray also sometimes wrote in his journals twice in the same day. Under these circumstances, the two entries appear with the same date.

As one would expect from a journal, Gray frequently referred to people, institutions, and events by one name only and without description beyond the immediate entry. I was often able to track down full names and/or their roles in Gray's life and offer this information. When it was not possible to do so, however, I simply left the name with no further explanation. I also corrected the spelling of certain names. It is worth noting Gray misspelled even Kathie Russo's name—alternating between "Kathy" and "Kathie"—throughout the time they were together.

In a few places, I've changed the names of people in order to protect their privacy. In these cases, the name appears with an asterisk by it at its first mention.

Upon Gray's death, his legacy became Russo's responsibility, and the decision to publish these journals was hers alone. I am not sure, in relation to this project, that she always relished this role—acting as curator for Gray's eternal memory—but I think she felt it was an alternately consoling and necessary one to take on. This book not only allowed her to remain in the presence of Gray but also gave her a chance to participate in a work, the chronicling of her husband's life, that might have otherwise been taken up without her permission. She struggled at times with the decisions that went into making this book but was admirably willing to allow for the rawness of character that a person's journals invariably expose. Russo also endured seeing herself rendered by Gray, as flawed and criticized as any other of the intimates described here. She remained, as perhaps a wife of Spalding Gray must, unflinching. She did, nevertheless, request that certain entries be removed out of sensitivity to her family. Her children had already suffered the very public suicide of their father, and, out of respect for them and Russo, these entries were removed from the final manuscript.

Such restrictions—the finite number of pages in which to express a life, the discovery that a piece of the whole is inaccessible, the protective instincts of family members—are the particular challenges of editing journals. And yet, despite these limits, it is my hope this book captures the exceptional scope and meaning of Gray's remarkable life.

the sixties

SOMEWHERE THERE WAS A WAR going on and back in
Rhode Island, my mother was having her second nervous
breakdown. Perhaps she was having it because of the war.
I couldn't stand being around her anymore. I didn't know
what to do. I'd try to read to her from the Alan Watts
book *Psychotherapy, East and West* but it didn't make
sense to either of us. What she needed was something else
no one could give. My father sent her to a psychiatrist but
that didn't help because she was a Christian Scientist and
didn't trust doctors so she wouldn't talk to him. But she
did call her Christian Science practitioner and he gave her
some phrase to repeat like, "God is all loving and I'm His
perfect reflection." Then she'd hang up the phone and pace
the living room while repeating that phrase over and over
while tearing the hair out of the back of her head. There
was a ratty bald spot there. Then, afraid that my father
would catch her in that demented state and pack her off
to yet another institution for more shock treatments, she'd
begin to try to pull herself together by starting to make the
evening meal. Mumbling to herself over the frozen peas,
"Oh God, don't let him see me this way. Oh God, help me
get through another day." I just watched it all like a very sad
and confusing performance. A crazy show; I didn't know
what else to do.

UNDATED

Spalding Gray—or "Spud," as his family called him—was born in Providence, Rhode Island, on June 5, 1941. His mother, Margaret Elizabeth "Betty" Horton, was a homemaker, though she'd attended Rhode Island School of Design to study painting before dropping out to marry. His father, Rockwell Gray Sr., was first a credit manager and later the treasurer and secretary at Brown & Sharpe, a precision tool manufacturer, in North Kingstown, Rhode Island. As portrayed by all three of the Gray brothers, he was a distant and forbidding familial figure. Spalding Gray was the middle child of three sons: Rockwell Gray ("Rocky"), the eldest, was born in 1938, and Channing Gray ("Chan") was the youngest, born in 1947.

The family lived in a renovated nineteenth-century farmhouse in Barrington, Rhode Island, an upper-middle-class suburb of Providence, where Gray's mother herself had grown up. There were no liquor stores, no movie theaters—it was "a lily-white town," as described by Channing.

"It was a lovely, peaceful, safe, aesthetically appealing environment," Gray's older brother Rockwell recalled, "with a yacht club where we went swimming in the summer and where Spalding learned to sail even before high school."

Gray's father's mother, Gram Gray, as she was called, lived with the family as well. Gray's mother's parents lived down the street. Gray was close to his grandparents—with the exception of his father's father, who left when Rockwell senior was a boy—and made an effort throughout life to maintain close relationships with them; family intimacy was important to him despite his sense that it was nearly impossible to achieve.

Gray's mother, a petite and attractive woman with a pixie haircut, was a Christian Scientist. She held the religion's belief that people could heal themselves by prayer and the belief that illness was "error," a false construct of the material—as opposed to the spiritual—world. Throughout his childhood, Gray was rarely sent to see doctors. More often, his mother called Christian Science practitioners and asked them to pray for her son to get better. Once, when he was fourteen, Gray passed out next to a radiator in the bathroom. When he woke, he lifted *his arm and saw, as he later described it, "this dripping-rare, red roast beef third degree burn." He ran to his mother, who advised him to put some soap and gauze on it, dear, and "know the truth."*

Despite her fierce conviction that illness could be avoided by deny-ing its reality, Gray's mother struggled with her own emotional health, suffering her first nervous breakdown when she was thirty-six years old; Gray was ten. As a boy, Gray would hear her, as he told it in a CBS television interview in 1999, "shrieking, crying out to Jesus, in distress, like she was being attacked." Gray's father never spoke of his wife's episodes—he was conservative by nature, and there was little professional or cultural knowledge of mental illness in America at the time. "No one would say 'Is that your mother?'" Gray said, describ-ing his experience of listening to his mother's screams coming from elsewhere in the house. "It was like a ghost."

Over the years, Gray's mother spent time in various psychiatric institutions. After her first breakdown in 1951, she was sent for sev-eral weeks, as Rockwell remembered it, to a Christian Science home in New Jersey to recover. Later, when Gray was fourteen years old, his mother told him that Jesus had come down on a shaft of sunlight into the living room and touched her hands and she felt better.

After a second major breakdown, fifteen years later, she went to Butler Hospital, a private institution in Providence, where she received electroconvulsive therapy. "After she had her shock treatments—I think she went a couple of times—she would come back feeling bet-ter," Channing, the only son who lived at home during this period, said. "I remember one time when she came back saying how great it was to be alive again. But it was only a few weeks before she went back into a depression."

Still, there was always great affection between Gray and his mother. Betty may have been a religious fanatic with a turbulent emotional life, but she was also the life of the party, "a cutup and a hot tamale," as her son Rockwell described her. She could be funny, ebullient, outra-geous.

And she understood her middle son's particular talent. "Spalding began to elaborate very colorful stories quite early," Gray's older brother explained. "The grown-ups pooh-poohed it: 'Oh, Spuddy, he's always making up stories.' My father always treated it like silly busi-

ness. But my mother was interested because she had a rebel streak herself." Gray frequently spoke of the intensity of his relationship with his mother in his monologues and in interviews. *"Mom and I dated right up through college,"* he often joked about their attachment to each other.

And yet his mother was also the one on whom Gray later hung his romantic troubles, concluding that her devouring need, particularly during her breakdowns, obliterated his sense of self and his ability to make a lasting connection with a woman. He also blamed his distant father for instilling in him a sense of longing. In a 1991 recording of one of his therapy sessions, Gray complained too that his father had "indoctrinated" him into drinking, by the example he set with his "controlled alcoholism." Like his father, Gray turned to alcohol to enliven daily life, but his relationship with it was more combative. *"Drink was a land to my father,"* Gray once wrote on a scrap of paper, *"but produced the emotions in me I saw in Mom."* In holding on to these claims, even cherishing them, Gray remained, in large part, his parents' child—their sad, yearning boy—throughout his life.

At fifteen, Gray was sent to Fryeburg Academy, a boarding school in Maine, in an attempt to bring his grades up and straighten him out. Gray was dyslexic—though, in 1956, he was simply considered slow. He had never been a good student, failing most of his classes at the public school in Barrington while wandering about with a group of wayward local boys who drank too much. But things changed for him at Fryeburg. His grades improved, he became captain of the soccer team, and in his final year there he discovered acting. As a senior, he was cast in The Curious Savage, a play written by John Patrick that takes place in a mental hospital.

"The character I was trying out for had delusions of grandeur. Not only did he believe he was Hannibal; he thought he could play the violin, but he couldn't," Gray recalled in his 1980 monologue A Personal History of the American Theater. *"When I read [for the audition], I read relentlessly, the way I perceived the text, one word at a time. And I got the role because they thought that I was doing this really effective reading."* Gray even credited this play with giving him his first hint of needing an audience. In his Personal History monologue, he also told the story of opening night: there was a rug onstage that had not been

there during rehearsals; when Gray saw the squares in the pattern of it, he was inspired to hopscotch through them. The audience fell into uproarious laughter. Gray was delirious.

After Fryeburg, Gray briefly attended Boston University. Upon learning in the first semester that he would not be allowed in the theater department because of his lack of experience, he transferred to Emerson College. There, Gray played his first leading roles, in Molière's Misanthrope and William Congreve's Way of the World. He also discovered that due to his dyslexia, he could learn more from listening—as opposed to reading—and began to borrow Shakespeare's plays on records from the library. He continued this habit throughout life, checking out recordings of his favorite writers from the library and listening to them at night.

Over time, Gray outgrew the notion that he was "slow" and not a good student, labels that had been assigned to him as a child; he became passionate about theater and books, especially those that broadened his understanding of himself. "The intellectual turn-on for him happened when he entered Emerson," his brother Rockwell explained. "A lot of it was fueled by the excitement he felt in getting a hang of the theater . . . He was reading really major, rich stuff in literature and psychology and philosophy. Norman O. Brown, Sartre. Ambitious reading. It was a changing image of him, so it took me time to realize it . . . It's touching to think back on it, his openness and curiosity and his desire to be helped or given leads to get into something."

After he graduated from Emerson, Gray got a series of different acting jobs. He was the resident actor at Smith College in Massachusetts. He performed at the Theater by the Sea in New Hampshire and the Orleans Theater on Cape Cod, among other places, and in 1965 he landed a role in John Ford's 'Tis Pity She's a Whore at the Caffè Lena in Saratoga Springs, New York.

Elizabeth LeCompte, known to friends as Liz, was a twenty-one-year-old waitress at the Caffè Lena—a coffeehouse with an adjoining loft that served as a theater—and a student at Skidmore College in Saratoga Springs. In addition to waiting tables, LeCompte helped out with the theatrical events. She worked on lighting and appeared occasionally in a performance that required an ingenue. LeCompte met the twenty-four-year-old Gray at the Caffè Lena, and they soon began a romantic relationship.

LeCompte would become the first great love of Gray's life. He once described a fictional character he'd based on her as "the kind of woman who, in the old days when everyone got married, would have made a very beautiful bride." When Gray was fifty-four, nearly twenty years after he and LeCompte had parted ways, he recorded a series of dreams he'd had about her in his journal. "The image that stuck with me was of how strong, young and beautiful Liz's face was," he wrote upon waking from one of these dreams. "It was tight and angular and had all that courage in it that I was once so attracted to."

As Gray was becoming involved with LeCompte, his mother was experiencing her second major mental collapse in Rhode Island. In 1964, in order to be closer to his work, Rockwell senior had sold the family house in Barrington and moved, with his wife, to a house in East Greenwich, Rhode Island. In doing so, they moved to the other side of Narragansett Bay, a setting that Gray's mother, who had lived by the water her entire life, was deeply attached to. She was an excellent swimmer and relied, in many ways, on the views from their old house that looked out on the ocean.

While in East Greenwich, Gray's mother lost her footing and was never able to recover it. She was on the phone often to her Christian Science practitioner, repeating the mantras of the religion to herself in an effort to keep hold of her mind. Gray stayed with his mother for a time during this period, throughout his early twenties, when he was home in between various theatrical forays. She threatened suicide, even asking Gray if she should take her life by locking herself in the car and leaving it running.

"Somehow in the middle of all this, I managed to get myself to New York to audition for the Alley Theatre [in Houston, Texas] and some voice, perhaps a voice of self-preservation, told me to go and I went," Gray once told an audience at his alma mater, Emerson College. "My first flight on a plane. A Delta night flight. Before I went, Mom had some coherent farewell. She wished I were acting in Providence—so she could get to see me—and not so far away in Texas."

At twenty-five years old, Gray went to work at the Alley Theatre with the hope of getting his Equity card. Meanwhile, LeCompte was in her last year at Skidmore. The couple, Gray and LeCompte, made plans to meet in San Miguel de Allende, Mexico, once they'd finished their respective obligations.

MARCH 1, 1967

[At the Alley Theatre, where Gray appeared in small roles in Arnold Perl's World of Sholom Aleichem *and Friedrich Dürrenmatt's* Physicists, *among other plays]*

Many thoughts about growing old, older women and Liz. . . . the back of my arms are smooth and white like a young boy's . . . the sky is a spring sky and we are moving . . . moving the raw air dances. The time goes by without me realizing it. It may be that I've gone so far into dwelling on myself that I'm not hip to anything that goes on around me. I remember how that happened to mom. I know that I'm still alright because I still love, and have, the sky, the seasons, the ocean. If things get any worse, I can go to them and they will take me in. As long as someone can do this, he's free from suicide.

Although I'm still very much involved with problems of EXTREMISM and one track mind. . . . fears about not being able to act again once I see mexico. . . . fears that any contact with the "real" world will turn me away from theatre, I'm not sure. There is a chance that it could bring me closer in the sense that theatre is only a portrayal of all life. If it's the hide away acting bag you want, then that's one thing but if it's the stage of life . . . people-theatre, that's another thing . . . you can go anywhere. I'm still trying to filter too much out of life. . . . be selective, but be openly, and thoughtfully, selective . . . what do you like. . . . what do you want and take it.

I'm coming more to the conclusion that I must pursue my acting because I really don't know where I stand talent wise, and it is not now a problem of getting acting "out of my system" as much as it's a question of finding out how capable I am.

Also, be careful when considering N.Y.C. What is it I want there, and what do I believe in. (Perhaps the essential item that brings us through this life is: a sense of humor) Thoreau says that what all men really want is what is real—but I'm not sure that this is true. I'm also not sure that I know what is REAL. I think it has a lot to do with the ocean, the stars, swimming and dying. It's not reflected upon—it is just done.

One of the things I've discovered about my acting (which I like) is my not jumping right into a role and infecting it with all sorts of preconceptions but rather letting the role teach me a bit first. Come on to it slowly and not make a big display of preconceived ideas. You grow to it and let it grow to you.

What really upsets me in these past days is the problem of extreme elation—it's the extreme part of it which is hard to endure, it is exhausting and I hope that it will soon pass and not leave me at the bottom of a well. I see so much in everything I see or touch. I just can't get enough of life. The sky tonight was ~~life~~ like the end of the world—the dinner tasted so good—I will explode. . . . I want to embrace the whole world. I don't know if I've ever felt this way before. It makes me somewhat afraid because I know its not lasting. I long to get on some level ground. I can hardly carry a conversation with anyone because I am so distracted by all that's going on about me . . . the smallest things GAS me. They overcome me (the cat being caught in the curtain, this yellow flower in a glass on my table, the air mail envelopes, the Morton Salt shaker, the blues and yellows) I don't want to call it a trip but. . . . I feel like I'm on a roller coaster and there are all these levels of reality, all these realities that I'm riding through and what a fantastic ride. There must be a time for it to stop . . . I must pull myself out—I must be the driver.

I see so clearly the potential of joy and horror in the same object, or being. As I sit here looking at my kitten's face, I see and realize what fantastic cubistic distortions it can take or horror blocks of some wild and fevered cat woman. All things contain this potential. I may select them.

I have an idea for a play
"THE DRESSING ROOM"
tape a series of dressing room conversations and then try to stage it—after they go through all their chit chat and make up, have them step out to no audience. The end of their world is the beginning of another. As I take off my make up, life begins.

I didn't sleep much had many pleasant visions of dogs and cats (my kitten slept with me). Strange dreams like "Juliet of the Spirits" [a 1965 Federico Fellini film]. I was wandering through a large home smoking grass, and avoiding people. Suddenly I realized who the people were that I wanted for friends. Things seemed warm and good. The other dream was about bill and I in bed. Marie walked in on us just as he was screwing me (good pleasure) I said to him—oh no, Marie has walked in. Soon the cries rang through the halls and people ran to stand around our bed, to ~~taunt~~ scorn us. A lot of dumb young tough kids were there along with Mrs. Watts who kept howling with laughter. As bill and I lay in bed (side by side) I realized that I was right and the others wrong. I gave Mrs. Watts a great speech about being a Humanitarian and not laughing. Then I turned to the boys and said that I was not interested in them and if I happened to have a liking for bill, that was my business. I did not feel ashamed.

MARCH 7, 1967

I'm coming more and more to the conclusion that I could never go on the stage every night and fake emotions—if I had another life it would be another thing.

But I regret to say that I have only one life to give and will not be given exclusively to the stage. I want to teach and have my summers off. I want to give and take. I cannot see how actors can be normal . . . goddamn that's madness . . .

It could be that theatre is just a vehicle I've used for coming into consciousness.

It strikes me that the big "made it people" in theatre and business, make it because they have learned how (NOT ENDURE) to turn themselves off to compassion. If one has second thoughts about compassion he may "lose out" . . . Mr. Gray—watch yourself because you, yourself do not yet know how to live with people.

While in college, I led a very <u>narrow</u> life and now that I'm out, I've discovered I'd like to find out more about other people in other worlds and I just have not had the time to do it. That's one of the reasons I'm so frustrated and plan on staying in New York next year.

suddenly had a most important flash—that I have nothing to do with my parents—they will pass just as I will—we will all pass into nothing.

If I could do a perfect thing. . . . to take time for perfection—in photography, one can perhaps perfect an imperfect world . . . make form out of chaos . . . a good feeling to make and create the perfection of an image YES. . . . I shall go after this with all my being. It will be my single stand.

Good God!! now that I'm leaving and look back at that experience with the Alley, I know I can never ever. . . . NEVER spend a season in regional theatre again. I've been in prison for a year and because I've had no time to do (have had time to think, more than enough) yes TO <u>DO</u> there has been no action in my life. I feel now like a vegetable and can only hope that my Mexican experience will bring me out of it. I do not know how these womb seekers do it here. They have to be very sick. I'm not so fed up with theatre as an art form as I am with the way it is carried out.

Gray left for Mexico in the spring of 1967. Having grown restless and frustrated with traditional theater but still grasping for self-expression, he decided to study photography—he was interested in taking portraits of children—and write poetry. "It was really a dreadful summer," Gray said, remembering this period of his life during his talk at Emerson years later. "I was really running away from my mother. I should've been back dealing with her nervous breakdown . . . my father was kind of left to handle the whole thing."

[Gray's journals are not dated from this time]

My dear Familia,

This country is beautiful! There's no way that I can put it into words: only to say that the faces of the people have a sense of peace, that they sing and smile. Yesterday a friend and I, while driving back from Patzcuaro, drove through these wonderful mountains, a great grey rain storm on either side of us and the sun setting in front of us. The landscape! I hope to have some good pictures for you because I'm now working with two cameras, one black and white, the other, color. Also, I've decided to stay in San Miguel for at least a month and have registered at the Instituto Allende where, beginning tomorrow, I'll be taking a course in Spanish and Photography. Please send all mail care of Instituto Allende DR. HERNANDEZ MACIAS SAN MIGUEL de ALLENDE The night is brushing in from the hills and the town is ringing goodnight.

[This letter is written into Gray's journals, suggesting it was not sent.]

that the first time you know about love and how it feels to love is in the HOME I ~~how~~ now KNOW

Oh yes, I write a letter or two to my parents but what I say to them is not me but a reflection of all they've underneath persisted and desired for.

Spalding Gray, a bunch of experience with no roots no "who you ares" Spalding Gray in Mexico—but what is he, who is he and why has he come so far from Boston and Saratoga?
     I know now, more than ever, that I must get back to the east and root myself in something that has meaning to me, or I'm lost.

*What a pleasure it is to stop time with a camera.

Around a corner, a gust of wind and whoosh there before you is a fantastic brown girl against a yellow wall!

              Yes, I think I may want to become a photographer.

          TO MAKE A FILM is important to me.

That was it. . . . the disappointment about my mother's nervous breakdown—I guess I really wanted to believe she had something "going" for her. . . . something that would stun others—you know. . . . just make it
     just making it through life on your own juices (and a large bit of faith)

Last night I had the mild realization that I'm beginning to live more and more on the "middle road"—i.e. less tortured fears of the turbulent poet, one who was great but alas went mad—perhaps Hemingway and H. Crane saw their death in their life. . . . I'm coming to believe that I am like many people—an ego not quite so big. . . . . I think now that I want very much to live.

In an essay Gray wrote about this time, he described an experience he had in Mexico, before LeCompte arrived, when he smoked marijuana with his neighbor Olaf, "a drifting Norwegian who was always playing 'Ruby Tuesday' top volume on his stereo." Afterward, Gray looked at the fire that was roaring in Olaf's fireplace and had a vision. "Right in the center of the highest flames and being wrapped and devoured by them," Gray wrote, "was a terrified woman sitting straight up in bed."

AUGUST 8, 1967

August 8 after arriving home from Mexico—

have been told that my mother has killed herself my father asked me to pick up her ashes at the post office tomorrow—"a box," he said, "Would you pick it up, because it's probably your mother." . . . . . .

I could go mad too. . . . in the ice box I found green jello made by a woman who was my mother and is now dead. . . . but she would come to the car in the morning and keep him, make him twenty minutes late for work. . . . he could not get rid of her. . . .

MY MOTHER—gone

"Your mother would always complain about the butter"

but the gasoline bill was the ~~bloody~~ end

the end!

but didn't you hear her tossing and turning at night upset enough to walk out and do what she did. . . . how many days or years, will pass before I realize what has happened. . . .

Chan standing in his pajamas in the drive. . . . dead

dead

and I thought
her heart
had broken

Dear Liz,
    I want to see into you and touch you while we still can or else all,
all is fucked
up. . . . done
                lost

The thing which I cannot get over is that everything is in order from the
green jello to her paints

I MUST keep the outside me alive!

to LIZ

In the old days she smelled like lemons
lemons in her hair
and her flesh flushed
clean like the backside
of a ~~fall day~~ October (my new
hope) our lady of the leaves

*The following passage, a continuation of the undated entry about his
mother's breakdown quoted in the epigraph, has a more formal, lyrical
quality to it than Gray's typical journal entries. Though the story is a
seemingly true account of how Gray found out about his fifty-two-
year-old mother's suicide, there are a couple of minor discrepancies
between this version and the one in Gray's journals. Here, for example, his father presents an urn with his mother's ashes in it, whereas
in the entry above Gray describes his father asking him to pick up her
ashes at the post office. This indicates he took some of the liberties of
fiction in the passage below. Gray also included a slightly altered version of this story in his 1992 novel,* Impossible Vacation.

I hadn't given much conscious thought to my mother's condition. In fact, while in Mexico I never wrote to my parents and because of that I don't think my father knew where to write me. I phoned him from the La Guardia airport and asked him to pick me up at Hillsgrove, the Providence airport.

It was a hot August day and I sat outside the airport on the parched lawn. I drank some leftover tequila out of a brown paper bag while I waited.

Dad pulled up in his air-conditioned LTD and gave me one of his wiry greetings, a kind of uptight embrace without really touching. Our bodies on the verge of coming together. Me getting the vague impression of his body as being held together by bailing wire . . . He smelled the booze on my breath and said, "What, have you been tying one on?" He put my bags in the trunk and we got in the car together. The air-conditioning was a relief. We rode for a few miles in a sort of uncomfortable silence and then I popped the question, "How's Mom?"

"She's gone" was all he said and he began to cry a horrid, wheezy, sad, dried up, crackle of a cry. I just sat there frozen like a statue. I didn't reach out to him. I suddenly saw that dry August landscape go flat. The other cars passed with all their windows closed and all I could think was, she's gone, she's gone; died of a broken heart like in fairy tales, she died of a broken heart . . . Died of a broken heart. We rode in silence, Dad weeping over the sound of the air-conditioner. The broken, hopeless landscape passed and went flat suddenly without color.

When we got home to Shady Hill, Dad fixed us drinks and then opened up and told me all about it. Mom's condition had grown worse and he was running out of money. He couldn't afford those fancy private homes that gave all the shock treatments. He was getting ready to send her to a state institution. Perhaps she had picked up on that and decided to end it all. In the middle of the night, one night in July, Dad woke to what he thought was the sound of the refrigerator but then realized it was the car running in the garage. He got up to find her slumped in his LTD. He called the rescue squad and they came quickly but it was too late.

We drank some more and then he went on for the leftover proof that it had all happened. First he showed me the gasoline bill from Al's Gulf. He had replaced the gasoline she had used to kill herself and he showed me how much. He also showed me a bill from the dentist. Mom had had a lot of dental work done a week before she killed herself. A strange hopeful sign. Then he showed me all the sympathy cards set up on the mantle of the fireplace where the Christmas cards usually go. He pointed out that her Christian licensed practitioner had not sent a card. He was furious that her practitioner refused to recognize her death after all the prayers he had paid for. And, at last, he showed me a plain, brown cardboard box that contained the urn that contained her ashes. The box sat close to his bed on a little night table. Closer now to his bed than my mother had been in years. (They always had single beds close together but towards the end he had gotten further and further away and now sat as empty testimony at the far end of the room but her ashes rested close to my father's head.) They would stay there for a few weeks until my father could go out with my Uncle John in his powerboat and scatter the ashes over Narragansett Bay. Over the water she loved.

We went back to the living room to have more drinks. Dad began to talk about the future. How now that Mom was gone he was going to have the driveway asphalted. She had wanted to keep it gravel but the spring rains always turned it to mud and Dad's car always got stuck. Now it would be asphalt.

As the evening went on Dad got drunker and drunker until he fell down on his knees and then helped himself up using a chair or chest of drawers as support. I never got up to help him. I drank as much as he did but it didn't seem to affect me. I sat there like a statue. I sat and watched it all go by.

After returning home from Mexico, Gray moved to New York with LeCompte. They lived, along with LeCompte's sister, Ellen, and another friend, in an apartment on Sixth Street and Avenue D, on the Lower East Side. Gray took the occasional odd job—as a stock boy, for example—and collected thirty-two dollars a week in Texas unemployment while LeCompte sold postcards at the front desk of the Guggenheim Museum in order to make ends meet. The following journal entries are written shortly after his mother's suicide, and yet there is little mention of it. Later, however, the tragedy would become the centerpiece of one of his first works of theater—a collaboration with LeCompte in the early seventies—and be explored in many of the monologues he performed afterward.

SEPTEMBER 28, 1967

I've not written for a long while. . . .

So now, living here these evenings, I do feel somewhat at peace with Liz and her friends, taking the days as they come but outside me now (as my ~~mscels~~ muscles turn to water) I feel the sweeping steaming hiss of competition! And I think how easy it is to live in the country and not be tempted by money and things but here in NYC it is ALL, seems wherever you look to be all. . . . but there's something missing here. It's like a boat sinking.

OCTOBER 16, 1967

I believe with Liz in time.

—Liz gives me a FUTURE! she <u>GIVES</u>

I take!

JANUARY 6, 1968

It was sometime in my 8 or 9th year at 66 Rumstick [*address of Gray's childhood home in Rhode Island*] when I realized that the swing in the back yard made me think of a set—a stage or perhaps a TV set but we didn't get a TV until I was 11 years old—anyway, I wanted to put on a show. I didn't know what kind of show but I knew the area needed it. For some reason it was not complete in itself. I needed to comment on it. It has something to do with time and death—the swing being there then was not enough. I now have mind photos of it. And most of all—if someone were to ask me, "Would you take one complete and happy pump me up to the sky swing on that swing—<u>or</u> would you rather have a life long photograph memory—correct artistic interpretation of the swing—

    goddamn it I'd take the art

Art is not life but the living's realization and creative reaction to the termination of life.

    I'll take art and try to stop the clock.

In 1968, Gray was given his first acting role in New York City. In March, he was cast in a production of Tom Paine—*an experimental play by Paul Foster recounting the life of the political pamphleteer and one of America's Founding Fathers. Gray danced throughout the production—directed by Tom O'Horgan, at La MaMa, a well-known avant-garde off-Broadway theater. In May, he performed in Robert Lowell's adaptation of Nathaniel Hawthorne's* Endicott and the Red Cross *at the American Place Theatre. By this time, he and LeCompte had moved to a new apartment—a railroad flat with a shared bathroom in the hallway and a bathtub in the kitchen—at Ninety-third Street and Third Avenue, on the Upper East Side of Manhattan. The rent was low enough for the two of them to afford it while working only part-time. For a period, Ken Kobland, a friend of LeCompte's from college, lived with them as well.*

"Spald would come home, and he would tell us the story of his day," Kobland said of this time. "Those were the most extraordinary performances. The way he would put together a story of his day and his characterization of it and his ability to tell the tale where one thing here wound up connecting to something else later. He literally would torture you with pleasure." Kobland remained one of Gray's closest friends throughout life.

JUNE 10, 1968

The world is like a growing party to which I was invited late by my parents.

It's crowded now and needs much more sorting out. In time it will grow mad like any party and fall apart and purify itself.

in time TIME is the great purifier

I believe in time—long exhausting time is my god.

JULY 10, 1968

to be a good actor is to be good. . . . to love to be whole—not sick and selfishly out of it
    none of that shit about saving it for (saving life) ~~fore~~ for the stage.

in the most complete actor (not always the best) his stage art is only an extension of his <u>life</u> art.

    LIFE ART

a graceful and poetic

extension of self

OCTOBER 9, 1968

<u>The big come down</u> after "TOM PAINE" . . . it's hard I've been thinking about Fryeburg and what kept me going there and no doubt, a big part of it, outside of the security-escape aspect of it, was my "religious" conviction. . . . my faith in nature and man . . . the last long stretch of naïve boyhood and now things are really difficult (great fears about ~~alchhol alcha~~ drinking I keep wanting to drink).
    It's difficult to ~~me~~ BE with myself.
    Perhaps "theatre" is taking the place of my, no longer in existence, religious belief.
    THE GREAT NEED for a life form

I'm coming more and more to the enslaving realization that my "life" and "theatre" are so strongly integrated that I could never have one without the other.

I must . . . . I am a very religious person.

In 1969, Gray met Richard Schechner, an iconoclastic director in the downtown New York theater world. Schechner directed Dionysus in 69, *a play loosely based on Euripides' Bacchae, in which a live orgy took place onstage with actors inviting audience members to join, and which received critical (if astonished) praise, as well as an Obie Award—an off-Broadway theater award bestowed by The Village Voice—for Outstanding Play. Gray and LeCompte had seen the show together at the Performing Garage, Schechner's theater on Wooster Street, and were electrified.*

Later that year, Schechner put together an interpretive piece based on Shakespeare's Macbeth *called* Makbeth. *The actor meant to play Macduff quit only four days before performances were to begin. (He'd gotten a job traveling cross-country as Mr. Peanut.) Panicked, Schechner flipped through a stack of head shots on his desk in search of a replacement. He chose a photograph of a young man "staring out with eyes so far apart," he recalled, "he wasn't trying to look pretty, he wasn't trying to do anything. It was unlike any other résumé shot I'd seen."*

The eyes were Gray's; Schechner called him. Soon after, Gray attended a rehearsal where, as Gray later described it in A Personal History of American Theater, *Schechner, filling in for the role of King Duncan, lay on a banquet table and asked all of the actors to feed on his stomach. "[Schechner] had a belly like an orangutan and it was as hairy," Gray said. "I was on all fours. I was sucking, pulling out the hairs between my teeth, and he was going 'Suck harder! Harder!'"*

Schechner didn't remember it was his own stomach Gray was devouring but described the audition this way: "I had to do that scene because I knew [Gray] could probably act but that was one of those Schechner signature scenes—kind of sexy, kind of fun, kind of tyrannical and unusual. The actor had to really eat out somebody's stomach—it wasn't genitals, but it was on their stomach. He did it and I cast him."

Gray debuted as Macduff three days later. The play closed shortly thereafter—critics panned it, and it lacked the audience support of Dionysus in 69—*but Gray had made an impression. Afterward, when Schechner was in the process of re-forming his theater company— telling some actors he no longer wanted to work with them and seeking out others to come on board—he asked Gray to join. Gray became a member along with, among others, Stephen Borst, who'd also performed in* Makbeth, *Jerry Rojo, a set designer, and Schechner's wife, Joan MacIntosh.*

JANUARY 7, 1969

Have discovered two positive points about the "the workshop" (and that took some doing):

1) the yoga

2) that in order to relate to fellow actors one must find something in each one of them that you can love, accept and relate to. This is also true with a play.

It's one of the most difficult tasks in an honest approach to acting. It's really difficult to do with many of these "ensemble" people.

JANUARY 9, 1969

I feel so calm tonight so calm. . . . . so at peace that I feel I must be missing something.

I am beginning to feel stagnant yes, in one place too long it's the three month change that brings out the poet in me. (you may laugh but. . . .)

forced change is easier because it creates the change without me having to be active (an easy way out).

I feel like moving now but am a little afraid (a lot sometimes) of losing Liz.

I wish Liz could be her. . . . absolute . . . no change just the way she is forever "my goddess" (HA-HA) and I could come and go. . . . go and come.

The hardest and most bothersome thing for me is attempted recollections of childhood. I thought a lot about that today. I was trying to remember what it was like to wake up on Saturday mornings . . . . I'm thinking now that my upbringing was honest in relation with the world I was brought up in and that was a very dishonest world oh shit! but there were certain things that were allowed, without awareness, to happen in the child's world. . . . the smell of leaves burning. . . . . the sound of the Austins' great maple when all but me were asleep. . . . . .

JANUARY 12, 1969

new experiences are good just for the sake of putting one on new tracks of thought and reflective realization. Habit is a great deadener and so people make their way through an entire life on habit rolling like dumb snow balls.

(Good-god looking back at my writings. It's strange I didn't write much last year. I think I was too busy just doing. . . . which is alright I guess) ——→ more easily contented. . . . not really thinking about my relations with Liz or theatre, or N.Y.C. just looking for any acting work . . . which I got).

JANUARY 12, 1969

The only way I can judge the world is to live a lifetime in it as honestly as I know how. The theatre world can only be dishonest in retrospect.

I will do my best.

JANUARY 14, 1969

I'm sure the major reason for not being able to sleep last night is the fact and condition of opening up more to people, LIZ, experiences and I have this great fear of a nervous breakdown coming from having to "deal" . . . . . you see I feel that I must deal with these things.

Shit! how forced I still am. My whole mind is a running commentary on all that I do. I can't turn off the comments. . . . . walking through Central Park the wind. . . . the not too cold wind and the distinct shadows remind me of early spring (early spring and late fall are two of my favorites or should I say—late winter. . . . where the season is just ready to give itself over) I feel the wind in my face and I think I'll cry and I do and see. . . . . am aware of the way in which the first tear of out of my left eye has caught and rainbowed the reflections of the afternoon sun.

JANUARY 15, 1969

to be able to separate the object from its source. for a brief minute the light from the 23rd street subway was part of the tracks, the tracks were full of flowing light and for a wonderful few seconds I had forgotten about the subway (almost) the always being aware of not being aware.

such a ~~beautuful~~ beautiful day
sea-gulls like on a string in central park
sea-gulls: the freest most fantastic thing in the city, just that one cry of a gull could take me back to the sea because I do feel more open & free today. It has much to do with the weather I'm sure.

THEATRE SHOULD BE THEATRE—a "poetic" extension and enhancement of life. . . . an abstraction ABSTRACTION

let the actor and the script come closer. . . . let the script bend to the actor.

MARCH 15, 1969

I could end my life right now and also end the waiting
LOVE

dear Liz, you have now sense of my other side

I need Liz and I ~~muss~~ must make her realize that I need her and in all honesty I don't know whether I love her more than I need her ~~ore ore~~ or need her more than I love her.

Liz seems the only way and I sometimes hate her for it.
    could everything be blown out the window in one night?
WHEN I GO TO SLEEP I'LL CHANGE

MARCH 27, 1969

I sometimes see so clearly why people make films. . . . they are so gassed by life that all they feel they can do (perhaps to keep from going mad) is to record it. I want something else. . . . poetry I guess. . . . "life" and then something more. I guess one reaches a point where they accept all and sit back and watch whatever comes into their scope but one can go farther just at <u>that</u> point one begins to sing or dance or, I mean. . . . yes!

expression. . . . individual, and even group, expression. to make a film is to record expression . . . Theatre is so great because it is temporal and thus one gets closer to the immediacy of the action without the reflection on the action.

I discovered how much my camera was removing me from experience.

(film is a beautiful but expensive ~~sch sceth~~ sketch of ones life)

It's now ten o'clock and I've been up on this grass since two-thirty this afternoon and I can't stand all the thinking.

(I'm in a bad state tonight) I don't want to live a life through others, but rather, with them but I hardly feel <u>with</u> anyone. . . . way outside and not even getting along that well with LIZ but why should that MEAN so much? is she (or she and I) some sort of last stand in a world I hardly feel a part of. Just the two of us left. . . . looking out on all the strangeness.

dive in, the water's fine?

APRIL 2, 1969

In the end, I feel that nothing matters so why? . . . why art?

why anything?

APRIL 10, 1969

just realizing that my damned unemployment runs until october! If only I could cut myself loose from money. . . . the old fuckin' "money" that binds me like a big shit.

a joy for some but me I'm more anti-money and more pro-needs.

If only I could be SUBSIDIZED!

APRIL 12, 1969

(3:30 AM) After seeing the play at La mama, I want to get into every thing. I'm not content with just seeing (to be known by everyone. . . . to be known by everyone)

The big question is: do I want to be in a play more than I want to be in life? Or, do they (of course) become interchangeable a LIFE PLAY a playlife

lifeplay

in most cases, yes. . . . I admit it. I often get more joy and excitement out of the staged condensation, the poetic condensation of the playlife . . . of the play. . . . more joy out of the play than out of life.

It looks as though I have to stay in the city and exhaust all outlets.

APRIL 16, 1969

OPEN THEATRE WORKSHOP

[The Open Theater workshop was free and run by the actress, writer, and director Joyce Aaron and the playwright and actor Joseph Chaikin. "One day (Aaron) asked us to do an exercise where we stood up and told a personal history as fast as we could," Gray wrote in his preface to his 1986 book, Sex and Death to the Age 14, *a collection of his early monologues. "If we blanked out or ran out of personal memories we were to jam, like a jazz musician, on a particular word or phrase until a new passage came. To my surprise, when it was my turn I experienced a memory film, a series of rather mundane events that had occurred during the previous week. I had no trouble editing or selecting which material to use as I spoke. The images came into my mind in vivid frames and I was able to describe it all in perfect detail. When I sat down, Joyce said, 'Very interesting. Who wrote that mono-logue for you?'"]*

this judging in the mirror exercise has me worried. I really find my self into judging others and I hate this trait in myself. I don't think I can think of a worse (TRAIT) trate in me at the moment goddamnitshit-fucken

I think I have a need to judge because of an inferiority complex so that I must say: "ha once again, I'm in the right and she's wrong." It's some-thing worth giving a lot of thought to

I think it was *[Ingmar]* Bergman who said something about man free-
ing himself by getting past the (CHRISTIAN IDEA) of a man being
perfect. . . . . man's hope of perfection but I don't think I'm battling so
much with a perfection hang-up as I am with a basic. . . . a still basic
evil—or evils—I've felt in myself all my life, basic usings of people and
most of all judgings.

MAY 25, 1969

I still have little anxieties about the evil one in me and I know that the
little anxieties will not get close to great fears until I get closer to a recognition and confrontation with more of me. As Liz said in my feeble
plea that I was a driven man/she just calmly and honestly said, "You're
not driven." I love her for her honesty and it seems to make me stronger
because I'm not allowed the sweet, soft and foolish illusions of my past.

Accept yourself and move toward what you want to do. There is nothing else in the world but this. To be hung up on money, other people, better or lesser realities etc. is only blocking your freedom (once
again I'm giving myself a lecture). . . . MY freedom, only blocking my
freedom.

For me, freedom would be the overcoming of anxiety . . . and the stopping of thinking myself out of ~~reality~~ action. I'm becoming more and
more shocked with how dishonest I've been with myself!

MAY 26, 1969

an interesting dream last night—after being told by my . . . (I thought
mother) not to spoil my appetite ~~fo~~ before eating dinner by eating some
white fish—I took her by the arm and threw her across the room and
then returned to looking at ads of my mothers relatives. . . . magazine
ads. Upon waking, I realized that it was the "MOTHER" in me which
I was rejecting and tossing away. I felt good.

JUNE 27, 1969

It's all a matter of learning to give up these little parts of myself (giving
up my virginity was a big part and I suffered like a little school girl)

and much of my fear of acid comes out of the intense fear that I will see things in myself, and my still not so open relationship with Liz, that I'll not be able to face. And this is of course one of the reasons (perhaps) that I don't want to go home with her. . . . her parents may see worst of all worse than their lack of approval. . . . that we are not really arm and arm, lip and lip, cock and cunt in love (goddamit this is hard for me to write and it's throwing me into a real bad state of mind!)

ME and the nature of LOVE

> I feel very stupid and cheap
> not at all giving

I've held back on everything except perhaps the stage.

SEPTEMBER 1969

Labor day weekend 1969

I guess what bothers me most. . . . makes me drink before bed and wake at four or five in the morning is my lack of humanity.

Where are my loving friends? Where is love? Where are LOVE and joy? Why brood so much about things? I'm slipping back into those brooding days of Boston [at Emerson College] and yet this next to last day in August sits so heavy on me. Outside there's hardly a breath of air and Rod is singing folk songs in the room above me. I'm more estranged from my father than I've ever been. Liz is still some comfort but foolish and sad America keeps coming to mind and what can only be an outgrowth . . . a foolish and sad theatre.

DECEMBER 27, 1969

Sat.

just back from the Christmas stay in R.I. and wanted to record a dream I had night of the 24th

Ellen [LeCompte's younger sister] comes to an apartment I live in. She knocks hard on the door and I, at last, let her in. She comes in and she's on top of me. I am slightly aroused but not fully because of guilt I feel about Liz. Ellen gets up and begins to primp with her clothing. She is standing over my head so that I am viewing her from a strange angle.

She tells me that Liz. . . . came upon a dead body. Liz was counting uri-
nals so that her head moved exactly from one to another (like a machine
go stop focus etc.) and there was this corpse. As Ellen tells the story,
I begin to see it. . . . . I am there. We are in a thick deep, dark, grove
and there is Ellen Liz and someone like Ken. We see this dead woman.
Her flesh is white, full and beautiful. She is almost naked. She had
most likely been raped and beaten because she was mostly naked with
a dress covering the middle area (breast to thighs) but I only assumed
that she had come to a violent death there was no outstanding proof
of it although I kept thinking that I saw ~~bruses~~ black and blue marks
on her face. She was like a full beautiful Scandinavian woman. And the
Ken-type person was asking the corpse questions and moving her head
with his hands making an animated response with the body. Then he
lifted her up and put her in a wheelbarrow. The body was sort of out of
shape, legs and limbs in strange lifeless postures (not ~~they~~ THE way we
are used to seeing a dead body placed).

   And the next thing I knew was that Liz and I were out of the thicket
and on the flashing bright streets of some open clean city, perhaps in
Canada, and the wind flew flags, clouds, the sky, smiling people passed
and Liz smiled up at me and I knew all I had to do was to smile back
at her.

the seventies

I SUDDENLY FELT as though my life has been lived like a
man from the press. I'm always telling a story to myself or
someone else. I'm telling a story about my life.

MAY 29, 1973

Although Gray once felt great anxiety about the prospect of living in New York City, he was able to make it his home, literally and figuratively, during this decade. He and LeCompte bought a loft, a former machine shop on Wooster Street in the SoHo neighborhood of lower Manhattan, down the block from the Performing Garage, in 1974. "It was the cobblestones that first attracted me to Wooster Street," Gray wrote in a 1997 statement for the SoHo Community Council. "In those days, the streets of SoHo were empty at night. Our audience, many of them, would actually call the Garage before coming, to ask if it was safe to walk on the deserted streets. We, that lived there, loved those streets. For many of us, that was why we were there—for the beautiful old buildings and for the emptiness."

A community of artists formed in the neighborhood in the sixties and seventies, drawn by the raw, inexpensive spaces fashioned out of the upper floors of old factories. "We all knew each other, and so we all attended each other's events," Eric Bogosian, a performer and writer who rose to fame in the eighties, said. "People would have all kinds of impromptu performances in their own lofts all the time. Nobody cared about being a star. It was a hippie thing . . . Very extravagant things were going on in the art world down here. On Saturday afternoons, people would walk around and go to whatever art shows—Don Judd, Sol LeWitt, Cy Twombly. They were all friends. Or they'd go to performances at the Kitchen [theater] and there was zero interest, none, with uptown. All the cultural institutions uptown were seen as ancient dinosaurs. Whether it was the ballet or the opera—everything was old and stuffy, and we were new and exciting."

Gray came to know other emerging artists—Joan Jonas, Robert Wilson, Laurie Anderson, and Philip Glass, among them—while Schechner's reinvented Performance Group garnered attention and respect as an inventive theatrical enterprise. As Gray became better known in the downtown theater world, he grew steadily more confident in himself as a performer.

Throughout these years, he honed his sense of self in his work. In the spring of 1970, the Performance Group began rehearsing a piece called Commune. Created by Schechner and the members of the group, the show was based on "a whole hodgepodge of collected things," as Gray explained it in A Personal History of American Theater. "The setting was that we were a commune, also we were a theater group, and we were reenacting certain Americana Communal scenes culminating in the killing of Sharon Tate, supposedly by the Manson gang, which was a bit risky because it hadn't been proven that he was actually guilty." In Commune, Gray played the role of Spalding, based on how Schechner perceived Gray, an observer who would comment on the action. "That was my first move toward autobiography," Gray once remarked in an interview onstage at New York University with Schechner, "but I didn't realize it at the time."

In 1972, Schechner gave Gray the lead role in a production of Sam Shepard's The Tooth of Crime, a musical play about an aging rock star named Hoss who is desperate to maintain his fame in a changing world—in the end, however, he takes his own life. (LeCompte, who had first joined the group as an assistant to Schechner on Commune, also played a small role in The Tooth of Crime.) Playing Hoss, with his head shaved and wearing a green cape and glittery jockstrap, Gray confronted the audience once again as himself. "[In the play] I do a very long soliloquy . . . Richard said, 'I want you at the end of this . . . to drop your character. Drop all this character you've built up of Hoss, and just stand there' . . . surrounded by the audience," Gray explained. "I remember . . . feeling this onion of the character peeling away, peel after peel, and then standing there, looking at the audiences' faces. I looked at them from myself—whatever that was—which really felt quite empty. . . . And that was a really important space for me to go into every night, I really looked forward to that. It was a very powerful, beautiful meditation. It began to occur to me, what if I didn't rebuild my character? If I continued to stand here, looking at the audience. What might I say?"

By mid-decade, Gray and LeCompte had started collaborating—he as performer and she as director—on theater pieces, still as members of the Performance Group but without Schechner's involvement. This, however, was not an official break: Schechner, who encouraged others to direct within the group, knew that LeCompte and Gray were working on their own material. Over the course of three years, Gray and LeCompte created a series of plays: Sakonnet Point, Rumstick Road, *and* Nayatt School. *Together, these pieces were called* Three Places in Rhode Island *or, less formally, the Rhode Island Trilogy. Each play in some way reflected a piece of Gray's life. And each one brought him closer to offering his own story to an audience.*

Sakonnet Point *debuted in 1975. Gray described it as "a silent mood piece which represented the child before speech." Performers, including Gray, danced throughout the production while various recorded sounds including the trill of birds, children's songs such as "This Old Man (Knick-Knack Paddy Whack)," and Tchaikovsky's Piano Concerto No. 1—chosen by LeCompte and Gray—played in the background. Gray gave the other performers a very clear idea of what he wanted physically in the piece, which they improvised on. LeCompte then selected the movements that would remain in the show.*

Rumstick Road, *which opened two years later, in 1977, was an experimental exploration of Gray's family history and his mother's suicide. Many of the performers in the Wooster Group portrayed members of Gray's family. Ron Vawter played Gray's father and Gram Gray, among other roles; in one scene, Libby Howes played Gray's mother with a slide image of Elizabeth Horton projected across her face. It was a startlingly effective technique: Howes's face was completely transformed. The piece also used movement to evoke emotion—including Gray giddily chasing Howes across the stage and, later, Howes, again inhabiting Gray's mother, whipping her body back and forth repeatedly, from bent to standing, with her hair flying, a terrifying portrayal of madness. Then Gray, momentarily playing the narrator, stepped forward for the first time and addressed the audience. Excerpts from his interviews with his (reluctant) father, his two grandmothers, and his mother's psychiatrist about his mother's breakdown, electroshock treatments, and suicide streamed out from audiotapes across the theater during the show. "Of course, it's just a real mystery to me how she could've done it. We have no conception of what the mind can do," the frail voice of Gram Gray played from the speaker. "And how it could have turned that light-hearted, full of pep woman into what she turned out to be was just unbelievable."*

"I'd like to register a vehement protest about the morality of using private documents and tapes in this kind of public performance," *Michael Feingold wrote in a review in* The Village Voice. *"Gray obvi-*

*ously thinks he's found a terrific way to rivet an audience's atten-
tion . . . I feel cheapened by having been made to participate in the
violation of a stranger's privacy . . . to make a point of including dis-
honorable transactions like this in it is to brutalize the audience, impli-
cating them in the artist's pain instead of offering them a share in its
transcendence."*

Gray responded to Feingold in the following week's Voice: *"At the
time we made* Rumstick, *we saw theatre as a place to make the personal public. O'Neill quoted his family in* Long Day's Journey into
Night," *he wrote. "We live in a brutal time that demands immediate expression. By using private words and documents,* Rumstick
*employs the painful and 'exploitative' mode common to modern
autobiography."*

With the debut of Nayatt School *in 1978, "the monologue form
I'd been developing found its full expression," Gray wrote in the
introduction to his book* Sex and Death. *"Much of* Nayatt School *was
based on a deconstruction of T. S. Eliot's* The Cocktail Party, *and at the
beginning of the piece I performed a short monologue about my relationship to that play while sitting at a long wooden table." This piece
also included a re-creation of an Arch Oboler recording and an interpretation of* The Cocktail Party, *with ten- and eleven-year-old children
playing adult roles alongside Wooster Group actors.*

"A great deal is attempted [in Rumstick Road]: *to make memory
live not only for the rememberer, Mr. Gray, but also for the audience.
Feelings about one particular past are not merely described and portrayed but—or at least this is the attempt—also transmitted. Laza-
rus is not simply being recollected; he is being revived and made to
walk among us," Richard Eder wrote in a joint review of* Rumstick
Road *and* Nayatt School *in* The New York Times *in 1978. "[Nayatt
School] is a brilliant and engrossing work; one whose abstraction and
complexity are at the service of genuine emotion, and whose artistry
in execution is such that even its conceptual misfirings are splendidly
theatrical."*

*The critical recognition of the Rhode Island Trilogy and the ease
with which Gray fashioned his private self as a public persona delivered him to the art form he'd been searching for all along.*

On April 20, 1979, Gray debuted his first solo show, Sex and Death
to the Age 14, *at the Performing Garage. The show ran for a month*

and a half. He took the idea of using a wooden table from Nayatt School *but shrank it down to the size of a desk. "I sat behind that desk,"* Gray wrote in the book version of Sex and Death to the Age 14, *"with a little notebook containing an outline of all I could remember about sex and death up until I was 14 years old." He improvised the story for his audience, tape-recording each show, and adjusted his outline afterward. The story gradually grew from forty minutes to an hour and twenty minutes. "I was surprised that he was able to put it in this shape and it was such a success," Schechner said of seeing an early performance of the show. "I was surprised at how simple it was. I'd spent my whole life in theater, and I'd seen a lot of tricks—and this had very few tricks."*

With Sex and Death, *Gray was recognized as a performer in his own right with an original mind and voice. "He is one of the most candid American confessors since Frank Harris," Mel Gussow wrote in a* New York Times *review, "and his impromptu memoir-as-monologue could certainly appear between hardcovers, but the reflections take on added comic dimension in performance."*

But as Gray took these first steps toward his artistic breakthrough, his personal life began to deteriorate. In 1976, while traveling on his own in India after having toured there with the Performance Group, Gray had a sudden realization that he did not know how to make a decision for himself, that he had allowed himself to become so wholly identified with his theater work he no longer knew who he was outside of it. These thoughts continued on in a downward emotional spiral as he traveled from India to Amsterdam, where he stayed with friends, physically frail and consumed by a fever. He began to obsess on his sexual compulsions. He explored his homosexual attractions, making love to a man while others watched at a gay bath club in Amsterdam.

Ten days later, LeCompte traveled to Amsterdam to meet Gray. He told her about his distraught mood and confessed to her the experience at the bathhouse. Shortly thereafter, they flew home to New York. Upon returning to Manhattan, she saw Gray through his ongoing collapse—first, by urging him to rest at home, taking him to see a psychiatrist, and, later, by leading him back to theater work. As they began to collaborate on Rumstick Road, *Gray became calmer and more focused.*

Gray and LeCompte's personal relationship, however, did not weather this experience well. Questions as to whether they were well suited romantically had already arisen for both of them. The demands of Gray's breakdown and their theatrical partnership pushed these doubts to the front. "Liz and I tried to collaborate in creating theater and that put the relationship to the big test," Gray later explained in his 1996 monologue It's a Slippery Slope. "I began having an affair, which helped lead to our separation, but I think we really came apart over competitive-aesthetic differences. She went on to develop what became her theater company, and I went out on the road with the form of theater I chose to develop, the autobiographic monologue."

LeCompte also met someone else: a twenty-three-year-old actor from Wisconsin named Willem Dafoe who joined the Performance Group in 1978. And yet there was never a definitive split between Gray and LeCompte. It was more of a slow, relatively agreeable drift into friendship. In the journals, Gray observes LeCompte as she gravitates toward Dafoe romantically—at times with the chaotic sense of someone losing his center but other times with the affection and distance of a brother.

"Their relationship seemed to be mostly a professional relationship by the time I arrived," Dafoe recalled of Gray and LeCompte during this period, "but at the same time, I remember when we did the trilogy [in 1979]—I say 'we' because I helped put it up—I remember The Village Voice had a big article, 'Two Lives and a Trilogy.' But at that point they were no longer together so there was always that kind of weirdness."

In 1978, Dafoe moved into the Wooster Street loft with LeCompte and Gray. They put up a wall with a door in it, dividing the apartment so LeCompte and Dafoe were in the front and Gray was in the back. The door was left unlocked, and the three of them shared a bathroom.

Soon after Dafoe moved in, Gray met Renée Shafransky, a twenty-six-year-old, twelve years Gray's junior, who worked as program director of the Collective for Living Cinema, an artist-run cooperative and theater for experimental film in downtown Manhattan. "A number of us were at these places," Bogosian recalled. "At Artists Space, [the photographer] Cindy Sherman was sitting at the front desk, helping to run that place, and I was at the Kitchen theater with [the painter and sculptor] Robert Longo, and Renée was running the Collective."

Throughout his life, Gray offered varying stories of how he and Shafransky met. In It's a Slippery Slope, *he remembered Shafransky blurting out, after sleeping with Gray for the first time, "Excuse me, but I think I'm going to throw up." He recounted her uttering a similar line, though not on their first date, in his journals, but in a later television interview he recalled meeting Shafransky at Studio 54, where he was drawn to her "very open, soulful face." In this version, she did not return his feelings. He had to track her down afterward and convince her to go on a date. There is no record of their first meeting in the journals. Gray began writing about Shafransky in the early days of their romance, with the two of them ricocheting between a strong attraction and a reluctance to get seriously involved.*

FEBRUARY 21, 1970

I have this great feeling of sadness tonight and without the thought of Liz I don't know if I could pull through it so easy. I still feel very alone and find it difficult to come close to people who lay a heavy burden of emotional upset on me. It reminds me of the ~~huge~~ great problem I had being with my mother. . . . maybe all I had to do was hold her and just be there (what else was there but to reach out and love as much as you can) but I couldn't I guess because I was upset with her for breaking down (please don't let me see you go mad because it makes me afraid because I ran to your arms to feel safe and now you've gone crazy ⟶ how selfish of me)

APRIL 20, 1970

I want to see
    why?
    because seeing makes me feel more alive but at the same time it makes me feel that I could kill myself

all I have written in the past boils down to these questions

How much <u>truth</u> can a person take?

How honest will I be able to be?

JANUARY 10, 1972

how relation
    relationships
    become ART
    how relationships become art!

JANUARY 25, 1972

Tues

Woke with a headache, hungover and very out of sorts . . . the double bind of drink . . . not wanting it but needing it.

I feel great violence coming up in me . . . wanting to hit Liz . . . to be free of her because I allow her to think for me and become me. I fear that dependence, that crutch.

FEBRUARY 1, 1972

I am the story. The exercise is the articulation of the present me!

MARCH 7, 1972

[In Marquette, Michigan, touring with the Performance Group]

We've done *Commune* and it's snowing again. It's very beautiful.

It was a rough show tonight. I've reached the end of it. *Commune* needs to be put on the shelf. A show based on the "times" and words of us . . . was topical but doesn't hold up . . . it's dated for me and it's a drag to do.

I realize that the jig is up. This lazy in between: I've really got to come to terms with Liz, me, the work—who I am and what in hell am I doing with my life—without comparisons. I feel as though I'm reaching a large crisis point in my life . . . I can't turn away from it.

MARCH 18, 1972

Watchung, N.J.

Stopped in Saratoga, end of our tour: had dream of fucking Mary Powers a number of times. She was accompanied by a male homosexual companion. I was so excited to fuck with her that I sort of ignored the gay guy and jumped on M. with him watching. A second time I did it alone with a green cock. very confused about my bisexual feelings. This morning Liz and I woke early after a late night. (We sat up with Flip [McCarthy, a friend who filmed many of the Performance Group's plays] and Ken [Kobland, who also shot the Performance Group and continues to be a film and video collaborator with LeCompte] talking about the "end of the world.") What was most disturbing was Ken's pointing out to me that if I had feelings that I should be doing something else in the face of death then I was not living now. The old truth of that was brought home once again and then after waking early (also after a night of dreams about the very problem of these thoughts, of another existence, holding out for the "other life"), Liz accused me of not fully loving her, of dislike of women in general, and of actual desire for a man masked in the desire for young boys which I am safe from because young boys are such a taboo.

If I crave a relationship with a man, I am not aware of it. I think the problem is more centered on desirous search for the young . . . youth! Youth! Youth! The golden boys and girls of my fantasy.

But I don't know what to do about this problem of scrutinizing Liz and of dumping on her . . . it is, or seems, so deep rooted:
My fantasy
my supreme desire is to live each day in the face of death.

MAY 12, 1972

Liz said we'd love each other the rest of our lives. I thought she was right . . . it just hit me that she was right and it made me feel good/ almost overwhelmed but I'm really at odds and ends with myself.

AUGUST 1972

I am me . . . I am a human being . . . I can live without my father's approval (but I must tell him that I have to feel that happen). It is so hard trying to figure out how to deal with my father . . . just the thought of him makes me . . . almost angry then confused.

I may . . . I will not ever be able to look deep into my father's eyes but will that stop me from looking deep into the eyes of others?

SEPTEMBER 7, 1972

Thoughts of Richard, Liz and group being my super-ego. dream of group giving me permission to have homo relations and me trying to make up my mind (Ken?)

MARCH 16, 1973

Friday

After our first meeting on Thursday March 15th I felt a very strong, sick feeling in my stomach. And it came on me when Richard said (I'll try to make a rough quote) "I would like us to do one more piece together before we break up."

Who is talking about breaking up? Richard? How could he be so far into the future if it wasn't already happening now.

The most important thing . . . what I felt and what I want to confess is me as the first class cynic (my manipulation of Richard? I don't know but here goes . . .) I saw myself as a cynic because somewhere in me I saw Liz and Steve and Jim [members of the Performance Group] trying to get their feelings out to Richard about how they wanted the group to live and relate and about how they wanted the work to go. I saw Richard making the gestures of taking it in but all the time I felt him to be a wounded animal just treading water until he could get his attackers off his back.

Like a wounded animal, I see him able to sit it out forever until his attackers pass and for weeks he has been under various large or small attacks. So I'm in a limbo because the group means more to me than me means to me so I get afraid to rock the boat.

TOP Spalding Gray, second from right, at five years old, hamming it up
with his older brother, Rockwell, third from right, and two neighborhood
kids in Barrington, Rhode Island.
BOTTOM LEFT Gray, at age one, in Narragansett, Rhode Island.
BOTTOM RIGHT Gray's mother, Margaret Elizabeth Horton, 1955.

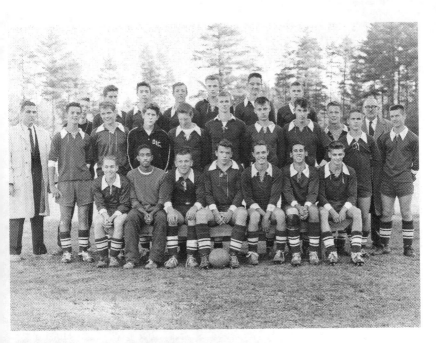

TOP A fourteen-year-old Gray,
center, with the ball between
his feet, at Fryeburg Academy,
a boarding school in Maine
where Gray first discovered
his love of acting—and the
audience.
LEFT Gray in high school,
undated.

TOP Gray's professional head shot from 1968.

BOTTOM The Albany *Times-Union* review of Gray's first performance at the Caffe Lena, where he met Elizabeth LeCompte.

At Cafe Lena's Gallery Theater

Robinson's Talents Virile, Magnetic in "Tis Pity . . ."

By ANNE MONAHAN

An actor of stunning ability now dominates the stage at the Caffe Lena's Gallery Theater. His name is Roger Robinson and his talent is a virile, imagnetic thing drawing the audience's attention among a large cast in "'Tis Pity . . .," the theater's current production.

Confusion marks the play and that confusion is still with the audience when the lights finally dim at act three's close. Is it a comedy or a tragedy? You'll wonder about it.

This 13th century story of incestuous love between brother and sister explores the conflict between strong passion and the range of restraints which can be opposed to it.

Kindly Friar

Religious restraints are represented by the kindly friar, played with sensitive understanding by Tom Varley, and the pompous Cardinal, played with stern demeanor by John Wynne-Evans.

Mr. Wynne-Evans' second season with the theater (he's artistic director and resident actor) gets a sterling start in "'Tis Pity . . ." Besides his role as the Cardinal, he cavorts with hilarious buffoonery as the foolish and funny Bergetto.

Certainly Mr. Wynne-Evans in this comic's role and Mr. Rob-

Spalding Gray takes the role of Vasquez the Spaniard in "'Tis Pity . . .," playing now and next week at the Caffe Lena Gallery Theater, Saratoga Springs.

inson in the very tragic role of the nobleman Soranzo married to the incestuous sister are each in their own areas, stars of the show.

Spalding Gray, like Mr. Robinson making his first appearance with the resident company,

is not to be slighted. Portraying the wily, sometimes-comic Vasques, Soranzo's servant, Mr. Gray does a fine job of delineating a difficult character.

Stig Liano's portrayal of Giovanni, the incestuous brother, is unfortunately uneven. In his opening scene with the friar, this reviewer was only able to catch the scene's gist from Mr. Varley's lines. Mr. Liano's words, when they could be heard, were too often delivered fast but faltering. He did, however, seem to gain in diction and stage presence with the friar's exit.

Trifle Too Coy

Passion-torn Annabella, the sister is skillfully drawn by Sue Bowlin. There were times when she appeared a trifle too coy, but then Annabella is in a pretty coy situation.

A grievous error in casting victimizes Thomas Behrens, cast as Richardetto, husband to the middle-aged noblewoman Hippolita, lustily filled by Lena Spencer. Young Behrens is ridiculously young for the role. If the casting was intended for comic contrast, it fails.

"'Tis Pity . . ." is an interesting experience in lively theater. It will run tonight and tomorrow night and next week Sunday through Thursday.

ABOVE Gray, far left, with his brothers, Rockwell, center, and Channing; this photo is dated "late '60s."
OPPOSITE Gray with then-girlfriend LeCompte.

TOP Gray and LeCompte in their Upper East Side Manhattan apartment, with a bathtub in the kitchen, 1968.
BOTTOM Gray as Hoss in Sam Shepard's *Tooth of Crime*, directed by Richard Schechner, with LeCompte playing the role of Keeper, 1972.

TOP Gray in
Sakonnet Point,
the first piece in the
trilogy *Three Places
in Rhode Island,*
with actress Libby
Howes, 1975.
MIDDLE Gray
with Wooster
Group members
Willem Dafoe (left)
and Ron Vawter,
rehearsing *Point
Judith (An Epilog),*
1980.
BOTTOM Gray at
The Performing
Garage, 1978.

Gray performing in Amsterdam.

Richard needs complete control. I don't know if he wants so much as he needs it and I see Liz bucking that complete control by being a woman that knows his mind very well because he is like her in many ways. They are alike in many ways.

MAY 29, 1973

Last night Liz and I TALKED about feelings and it got really scary for me. I suddenly felt as though my life has been lived like a man from the press. I'm always telling a story to myself or someone else. I'm telling a story about my life.

At this time, LeCompte and Gray informally split off on their own and worked on Sakonnet Point. *It opened at the Performing Garage on October 10, 1975. This was a crucial move forward for both LeCompte and Gray: it was the start not only of their theatrical partnership but also of their respective careers as director and solo performer.*

In December 1975, when Gray was thirty-four, he traveled throughout India with a production of Bertolt Brecht's Mother Courage and Her Children *put on by the Performance Group. While there, he suffered a nervous breakdown. The following is an undated entry—though it's clear that he is looking back on the experience— narrating the series of events that he would later come to call his "India breakdown." He explored this in his later work—in his 1979 monologue* India and After (America) *and more extensively in* Impossible Vacation.

My present difficulties have existed since I came back from India in June of 1976. We toured India with a production of Brecht's *Mother Courage*. I was in India for five months. We performed for three of those months and then had two months free for travel or doing anything of our own choosing. This was the first time I had had any long period of free time in ten years and I had the horrible realization that I could not make choices because outside of my identity as an actor in

our group I had little touchdown with who I was as a person. My whole
life had become a theatre and when I was without it I was completely
lost in a painful way. Nothing had any meaning for me and I seemed
without a will. I saw that I had given up my will to the group. I had let
the director and other more strong willed members make all the decisions . . . This whole situation became more and more complicated and
I began to feel that I could not go back to acting. That acting was not
good for me because it was too passive a situation to pile on top of my
already passive personality. It was in India that I decided that I must
begin to do my own work and that this work would be based on my
life. I would use myself as material. I was able to hold on to that idea
but I was unable to act quick enough. I was unable to will myself to
leave India. At last I made an arbitrary date to leave. The departure was
very painful. Elizabeth Le Compte (the woman I have lived with for 12
years and also member of the company) was with me and she stayed
behind to study yoga for a few weeks. I planned to meet her back in the
United States.

I had to switch planes in Amsterdam and I felt I would not go in to town
but just go right on through. When the plane landed I was exhausted
and decided to go into town to stay overnight with friends. Then a
number of things began to happen that broke me down even more than
in India. India had already taken its toll on me but Amsterdam put
me over the edge. On the way to my friend's house I came down with
a high fever and chills. At that time I was unaware of my weakened
condition and the fact that I had lost twenty pounds in India. When I
got to my friend's house I went right to bed for three days. Then I was
weak but had the strength to go out on the town. I began to drink beer
and smoke a lot of cigarettes. I was not treating myself well and felt like
I was on a kind of self-destruct spiral. I could not will myself to leave
Amsterdam and spent days and nights wandering the streets obsessed
with Bali and Greece . . . I could not make up my mind. America or Bali
or Greece. I started to get overwrought and just plain crazy. I began to
look for "signs" that I would try to interpret. An example of a sign: I
SAW a man from Indonesia on the street and I ASKED him when he
came to Amsterdam and he said 1941 and I'd try to read that. I'd try to
figure it out and make a map or structure out of it. Like: "let's see 1941

was the year that I was born and that means if I go to Bali that I'll be reborn." Then I'd think I was crazy. Don't go anywhere.

Then during this period I went to a homosexual bath club in Amsterdam and was "picked up" by this German photographer who was vacationing in Amsterdam. He was very aggressive and he made love to me like I was this beautiful woman. He took time with me with all this incredible foreplay so by the time he began to fuck me I was wide open and had this very intense climax. It was not a very private place and people were watching. This seemed to bother him but it did not bother me. In fact, it made it . . . intensified it for me. When he finished he acted real cool and just sort of got up and left. I felt somewhat lost. I mean I think I was on the other side for the first time. I was experiencing what many women feel when men use them sexually. This did not help my state of mind. In fact, it rapidly complicated things. It was not my first homosexual experience but I had never experienced one like it before. I had never experienced such a complete giving over before.

So, I had been in Amsterdam a week and I had an open ticket back to America and each day I would call and book a seat on a plane. I would call in the morning and then call in the afternoon to cancel. Then I found out that Liz was coming to Amsterdam. Her yoga class had not worked out for her and she was on her way back to America. She did not know I was still in Amsterdam and she called the place that I was staying at to find out if she could spend the night there. I was so happy she called and rushed to meet her at the airport bus station. As soon as she got off the bus I thought how ugly she is. She smiled at me and I thought she was ugly. I wanted to run but instead I stayed and beat her down with my "madness." Looking back on it I'm not clear whether I built this madness up to drop on her like a bomb. I was out of control.

I acted crazy or was crazy. I didn't know the difference really. I told her about the homosexual experience. Her advice to me was to go back to America with her and try to work things out there. I decided to do this but by the time I got to the airport I was a nervous wreck. I began to breakdown and went to the ticket woman just before I was to board the plane and asked if I could get my luggage off the plane and she said, "Yes." And I said skip it. I know I was crazy so I wasn't crazy (yet). For much of the flight Liz did not even know I was on the plane. I sat in the back and did not speak to her. The flight seemed an hour long. It was the first time I'd been on a plane without worrying about crashing. I really did not care if it crashed. My will was nonexistent. I was letting myself be thrown from situation to situation.

This condition got worse in New York. I could not sleep and I was very hyper. I would wake up early and roll on the floor and moan. I never stopped moving for the whole day. I felt this constant energy coming up from the base of my spine. I could not concentrate. My friends tried to help me out by finding therapists for me. I went to a psych friend and he said that I was having a major nervous breakdown and that I had to ask my father for money in order to go into immediate analysis. He sent me to a psychiatrist who said the same thing to me. He said I was psychotic and would have to come to him two or three times a week. This frightened me but I would not ask my father for money. Somehow I knew that would be a sign that I was really insane.

Liz took care of me. She brought me through. I don't know what I would have done without her. She stuck with me and was always there for me. I got into therapy once a week with a psychiatrist and he had me on tranquilizers. The hyper manic activity soon changed to deep depression and I slept about 18 hours a day. I could not stay awake. Liz told me to sleep as long as I wanted to and not worry.

Some friends, suspecting that I had hypoglycemia sent me to a clinic for a glucose tolerance test. I was diagnosed as hyperkalemic and was put on a special diet and given megavitamin therapy. That, combined with my seeing the psychiatrist, brought me back to a condition where I was able to work. It was then that I began to make *Rumstick Road*. I also began to have an affair with a young woman. Looking back on it I see myself as being totally destructive to Liz. It seems like she brought me through all that so I could run off with another woman. It's beyond me how I could have done this but I did it. And this is where it gets all confusing for me; this is where I stop being able to write about this experience. I feel guilty about this betrayal. I feel I used Liz. I feel I punished her for caring for me. I punished her for loving me. I resented her for helping me.

This is the part that's hard to write about. I have no distance on it. I'm in it now.

I am seeking treatment at this time because I am looking for some clarity in my life. I am torn between being an ARTIST and being "in the world." I feel I have to resolve this question now before I get any older, so that I can commit myself more fully. I feel I withhold. I sometimes want to get inside of it all. Even if it's only for a little while.

> India
> Lighthouse
> India
> Lighthouse

Cut out pages of *To the Lighthouse* and make a script where you read in between Indian stories.

JUNE 19, 1976

[From the journal Gray kept in Amsterdam (en route to New York from India)]

For days have had no energy, have just laid in bed and fantasized where to go next. The crazy compulsive sexual thing has got me in the pit of the stomach. I can't taste my food, can't feel my body, thinking about "love" narcissism—me as a sex object
    feelings that the whole idea of doing a solo piece is just a compulsive escape from ??

I woke up panicked and terrified again. I can't make any decisions because the action is all based on fantasy and I've let Richard and Liz lead my way for so many years that now I'm seeping and weeping the karma of being a baby. The little boy in me is sick.

Want to say how I view Liz even after these few days away. The memory most strong is of Daksum *[a forested walking area in Kashmir]*. After Liz had confessed to me all her fears about making it on our/her own in

N.Y.C.—under a tree. It was raining and I tried to listen but could give her very little support except that I thought she was a good director and that we shared some common vision. We went back to our room and I began to hint at splitting up and I kept pushing at it and I kept threatening. Liz said we'd have to sell the loft if we broke up. She grabbed her coat and ran out. I kept asking her where she was going and she ran out. I let her go. Thought that she was leaving for good. Those fears and wishes for total desertion. The image I remember strongest was of her running across the lawn toward the woods. She looked like a crazy lost child boy girl (when she tries to look like a woman, it doesn't work for me makes me irritated) but what I'm trying to get to was how Liz made me feel something like love and sorrow mixed seeing her running made me feel like "to the lighthouse," at base of all the impossible sadness—my inability to take pleasure in life (thinking of how she makes love to me like a child makes me angry). So I walk out to look for her and she is at the bottom of a big cliff sitting by the silver water like a lost boy. I watch for a long time. I think she may have been crying. I had the impulse to take her in my arms like a ? not like a lover but like a friend. I've never had a better friend and never loved anyone else before (fear of getting lost fear!) but I only walk down and we made our way home along the stream. The impossible sadness of it all.

Reading David Copperfield upset and threatened me—says we have to be revolutionaries finding out for ourselves what works—finding out about relationships. Working hard on our own. I lean toward Virginia Woolf because there is no sex threat no mention of sex—ships passing in the day—relationships never working. Brings me to the fact that there are at least two MES, two selves. One is the sensual sexual self that sometimes sleeps naked and the other soft old teddy bear man, old before his time—a joke. These two are in constant conflict. So now I want to explore the sensual self outside of my work—where does it go when I'm not working on theater. I think I equate sex (love?) with death. I know that there's a part of me so in love with death that I feel like I have already died and am looking at the living.

JUNE 25, 1976

[Back in New York]

Talked to Flip about relationships and also gay scene in relationship to quick object orgasm. I'm thinking a lot about orgasm and energy and directing sexual energy into my work. I told Flip that I feared I was a total narcissist and that I came back from India to make love to the other self that I saw dancing here. I could see this other me in my mind's eye. Now I realize, crazy as it sounds, that I was trying to get back to myself. What I haven't been able to integrate is the homosexual side of me and I know I have to face it here in New York with the me that's here. First, I have to do my work. But my "work" leaves no time for relationships so I have to answer that question, why not Greece?—a vacation makes it all too unreal. It's easy to have sex on a vacation. I'm trying to find it in my regular life, whatever that is. If things don't work out at _____ I can come back to N.Y.C. and start to face the music. How heavy life has gotten, how sad, how outrageously sad and lonely mere orgasm is, how I need both orgasm and relationship.

I feel as lost and desperate as the summer in Provincetown when I got out of college, not knowing who I am and ready to grasp at anything. Should I be this or that, here is what presents itself.

1. a world traveler
2. a Zen monk
3. a lover
4. a movie star
5. a dancer
6. a maker of a group to carry out my vision
7. a suicide victim
8. God
9. a family man just in love with Liz

UNDATED ENTRY

I'm back *[in New York]* and hit by the wave of sloppy materialism, all this concrete and pork chops and beer and the over stuffed Grand

Union. It's impossible for me to make any selection among the ten thousand cans and great fluorescent through of meat and meat people sexy meat people and not so easy to meet people.

So what comes into my head is wanting to sell myself. So, I'm trying out for the movies, porn movies or New York Gangster movies, any kind of movies and Liz is going to push me . . . going to manage me. I'm also trying to do my own work whatever that means sort of running around and going crazy based on some thoughts and memories of my mother's suicide.

Gray did, in fact, act in two pornographic films in 1976, when he was thirty-five. The first, The Farmer's Daughter, *was about three escaped convicts who storm a Pennsylvania farmhouse and rape a mother and her three daughters. The second, which Gray worked on for only one day, was called* Little Orphan Dusty. *Gray later wrote an essay called "The Farmer's Daughter," in which he describes the experience of not being able to sustain his erection for the shoot on the film. "I was beginning to experience my limpness as The Great Refusal, but all of this was at the expense of the production. But, fuck it, I thought, someone always has to pay. There is no place in this world that doesn't cost someone something," Gray wrote. "The director had a new idea. It would be a new configuration. Rick would ass fuck Alice while she sucked me off . . . The director was right, something about this configuration worked. I closed my eyes and stretched back over the bed as I gave myself to this newfound pleasure . . . In order to avoid premature ejaculation I ran the gamut of images, and at the same time, was careful not to choose an image so traumatic that it would lead to disengorgement and disengagement . . . I pictured starving bloated children in Africa. I watched god in his heaven stumble like a drunken bowery bum over his orange crate furniture. I saw Sissy Spacek with a wicked case of intestinal flu. And, for one terrifying second, I had a black webbing vision of cancer of the prostate. In short, I saw the end of the world as we have known it pass before my eyes, and breaking through these images I heard the director's voice as he strode above me, 'Make sounds, move around more, make it look like you like it. Moan, moan god damn it make some sound.'" In his journal, Gray wrote simply of this encounter, "I break down on the porno set because director gives me a hard time. I have tears."*

JULY 13, 1976

I dreamed that I made love to myself. I was in a big house and I walked by and found myself asleep on a couch and I was surprised and happy to find myself and I touched myself to wake me up then I climbed on to myself and began to make love to myself.

AUGUST 29, 1976

It's been ten years July 29th since mom's suicide and this is the Bicentennial.

[The actual date of Elizabeth Horton's suicide was nine years earlier on July 29, 1967.]

After returning from his trip to India, Gray performed Sakonnet Point *again from October 15 to November 13, 1976. According to members of the Performance Group, he seemed to be able to focus while working during this time, even though he was barely functioning in the outside world. On December 16, he performed an early show of* Rumstick Road *as an open rehearsal, with no set, for an invited audience. The show opened officially at the Performing Garage on March 25, 1977, and ran through the end of April. It ran twice more throughout the months of June and December.*

In 1977, at thirty-six years old, Gray made a vow to write in his journal every day. After discovering he was unable to make a decision on his own in India, he decided to keep a regular diary in order to take responsibility for his life. It was "also a more therapeutic way of splitting off a part of my self to observe another part," as he explained it in Sex and Death. *"It was the development of a writer's conscious-*

ness. I tried to write mainly about detail of fact and action, rather than emotions. This report became like a Christmas tree, the structure upon which I could later hang my feelings, like ornaments." As a result, the entries from this year, which are not excerpted here, often read like a police report—a recounting of the details of his day, including the weather, what he ate, whether he was hungover, and what time he went to bed.

The section below, however, is different: these are notes from a trip that Gray took from California to New York by car in 1977. On the way, he stopped in Las Vegas for the night only to find himself waking in jail.

SEPTEMBER 19, 1977

MONDAY

Hard driving through beautiful red hills straight on, flat out to Las Vegas. I drove 12 hrs. and came in to V. with "Tchaikovsky Piano Concerto # 1" full blast on the radio. I took the first motel I came to on the strip, showered, dressed nice and went out to see the town. Everything was an ugly plastic front. I got real depressed, had about three beers and I was headed home when I got into one of those dark "feeling sorry for myself" places—making sounds and what not when two cop cars moved in on me and I asked them Why had they stopped me (because I was feeling angry anyway) and they put the cuffs on me, took me in to the station, booked me, sprayed me with DDT, put me in prison outfit, finger printed, mug shot, put me in a cooler 15 x 15 with 24 other men. *[The police charged Gray with vagrancy.]* A pimp that had just gotten off a murder rap, a guy that had just beat up both his brothers out of love and a supporting cast. At 5:00 AM they took us down for breakfast then locked us up.

Gray was kept in jail for six days. On the fourth day, he was granted a phone call. He called LeCompte, but there was no answer. He convinced the guard to let him try someone else. He called Schechner; the line was busy. He was taken back to his cell. Finally, Gray managed to get word to LeCompte by asking an inmate who was paroled before Gray to contact her and tell her what had happened. LeCompte sent the bail money to the bondsman, and Gray was released. His trial was set for October of that year, but he never returned for it.

The following is a letter Gray wrote to his father while in jail in Las Vegas (and likely never sent, as the original was tucked into one of his journal notebooks).

Sept. 22, 1977

Dear Dad,

I've seen a lot of crazy things but this one takes the cake. I am a prisoner in Clark County Jail in Las Vegas. I mean, I would never have dreamed such a thing could come to pass. Someone in Santa Cruz loaned me a car to drive to New York, so I started by driving 12 hours straight to Las Vegas. I got in about 9:30 PM, Monday night, took a motel, washed up, and went out for a walk on the strip. I was dressed well with white pants and clean shirt. Two cops, in two different cars, stopped me. I did not have my ID with (a mistake I know) me, so they handcuffed me and ran me in. I spent the night in a detention "cooler" standing with about 24 men, all of us in prison outfits. They stripped me and sprayed with DDT, put me in a prison outfit, and photographed and fingerprinted me. All of this was like some mad dream. I mean I was stone sober. I had not broken any law I knew of, but I went along with it all . . . just played it cool. About five in the morning, they took us down in the basement for breakfast and then I was locked up in a cell with forty prisoners, some in for armed robbery, some in for rape, murder, trespassing, you name it.

Well, I just work at staying calm for the first two days. I mainly stayed in my bed and watched what was going on. It was all like a movie, but a little too real. On my second day here, someone stabbed himself with a wire and was taken away.

I find the only way for me to stay sane is to talk with the prisoners about their lives and that has helped, but what stories. I mean it's all like out of a movie. The worst thing that is going on is that the jail guards will not let me make a call to Liz to get bail money, and Vegas is such a rip-off town I don't know when my hearing will be. My bail is set at $250.00 which is not bad. I don't know what's happened to my car or any of my bags and money. They were all left at the motel and I don't trust them there either. Santa Cruz was paradise . . . full of love and Vegas is hell . . . full of hate and money mad zombies. It's a long story. I've tried everything to get out of here and feel like a helpless child.

So . . . I've had some time to do some real thinking. I've sort of gone over my life . . . kind of figuring out how or why I was here . . . how I got into this jam. One of the things I've come up with in thinking about my past—nothing to do with why I'm here—but having to do with our relationship, is that I've felt we have never been very close to one another. I mean, we've had some times in the past. I remember you helping me with algebra, and going frost fishing together, and you doing the stop watch while I ran around the block. These events are all part of a long gone past and I wonder what's happening now. I get so little time in Rhode Island, so we hardly have a chance to talk. I mean, it's not that I think you don't love me. Your helping me with the psychiatrist last winter made me feel that you still cared for me and wanted to help. Perhaps it's been a little one sided and I have not showed you that I care, but I want to take time now to thank you for that help last winter and I do remember a good visit with you at Christmas. I think I'm feeling age coming on me (you know all about that) and I want to have contact with you while there is some time left . . . not trying to be morbid but just realistic.

I guess I have some heavy questions. I don't want to get heavy like Rocky, but I often wonder how you feel about me and I don't mean just being nice . . . I'm not sure what I mean. I just feel strange about our relationship. I think that I did a lot of shutting down after mom's death, when we were together at Shady Hill, and that might have been a time together. Although, the visit in New York was good but I do feel bad about one past event. Shortly after mom's death, I was in the Robert Lowell play in N.Y.C., and you called to say you'd like to come down and I did not encourage you to do it because I was embarrassed that it was such a small role. After all was said and done, I was sorry I did not ask you down. Anyway, that's water under the bridge. I think it was a problem of false pride.

I am going through a lot of good and bad turmoil in my life now. I think it's change, and growing up, and part of it all, but I need to know where we are at. I don't feel we make contact, and that we are both uptight around each other. I'm sure a lot of it comes from not seeing each other much, but I can never tell if you want me at your home or if you are just being polite . . . doing what you think a father should do. I know you say you want me there but I'm missing the feeling. I think feeling is very important to me now and I want to feel where I'm at when I'm at it. I mean, I want to feel a little more. I've done all the thinking I want to do for a while. I've been so serious all these years and I had a good chance to loosen up in California (not in Vegas).

Anyway, why don't you write me a letter? I hardly ever hear from you by mail and would enjoy a letter. If all goes well, I hope to be back in N.Y.C. on October third. I don't want to go to Europe. I want to do a new work. There is a meeting in N.Y.C. about our European tour. It's tonight and I was going to call in my vote, but my jailer won't even lend me an ear. They just grin and say "Sure thing," "We'll see what we can do," etc. But I would like to hear from you. Nothing heavy, just some response. I feel I missed you somewhere along the line. Why do you think that is?

I worry about Gram and I wonder how she is. I want to come home for Christmas and hope to take three or four days off. Please send my love to Sis [*Alice Gray, whom his father married two years after the death of Gray's mother*], Gram, Chan, and Bianca. I don't have C&B's address, or I would have written them. I hope to be out of here soon and off to the Grand Canyon (if I still have a car).

Much love,
Spud

SEPTEMBER 1977

TUESDAY

At 10:00 AM they called my name and said the magic words, "Roll it up." I had been waiting for this so long that I could not believe it. I never thought it was bail. I thought I'd done my time. I got dressed. I was shaking all over and then realized that Liz had sent bail and my court date had been set for Oct. 3. I felt sick, just sick, but I left all the same. I wanted to get on the road so bad! The strange thing was, when I stepped out of jail I did not feel free.

The following are notes from one of Gray's journals that he eventually included in a short essay called "Natural Child Birth," about visiting LeCompte's pregnant sister, Ellen, just outside of Saratoga, New York, in October 1977. The excerpt below describes a conversation that Gray and LeCompte had about sex while on their way. They were waiting for their van to be fixed—after breaking down on the road—in a nearby coffee shop.

We ended up talking about sex.

Did it really exist? I brought up the subject because I had my doubts. I had felt lately that it was a sign for something else. That when I was in it I was never in it but felt like a puppet programmed by someone else. All the programs I had grown up with. The magazines, the movies. It was an old story. Sex was like everything else but I had used it as a last stand by. It had its power because it had been denied me for so long so I could never get enough of what I had never had from the beginning when it was there but not there. When it came up in me and then went back in circles and led to something else.

We both liked those upstate coffee shops. The waitress being right out front and overhearing people's slow conversations. Something about nothing. The slow morning, the watery coffee. The old thick white cups. Outside the leaves came down slowly. Made a hollow crisp sound when they hit. The way the man smoked his Pall Mall taking a long drag and exhaling the smoke straight up toward the ceiling away from the gal at the counter. Then slowly putting it back in the ashtray then folding his hand like a prayer, his big ass falling all over and off the stool, then slowly breaking to reach for his cup and sip again. The distant sound of a road machine. A jack hammer. What was it about sex? The way you could never have it really, not incorporate it, something like water. when you were in it, you were in it, when you were out, you were out forever. Like the dream I had had of this anonymous blind woman. I was trying to get her in the right position. I was in her but not in her. I couldn't get through. I couldn't really fuck her. Not lost not found but always in this place of expectation. Some feeling of mystery as though there was something on the other side.

Maybe like the way I had been brought up to believe in heaven.

Something I could not see or feel on the other side of all I felt and saw. Liz was across from me. Her steady eyes, her certain smile, the way I always come back to that. Home base and there were still times that we could be . . . what? Sexy together or was it like the machine again. The puppet. Doing it because we were together and not with someone else. The blind woman in my dreams. Who was that? Taken out of a closet when I needed her. Getting her in all the positions. Fucking her so hard. A kind of love. Go on say it. Love, love, dirty love makes the animal, the beast with two backs.

The following, from Gray's 1978 and 1979 journals, are, for the most part, undated. An asterisk indicates a new entry.

FEBRUARY 26, 1978

Sunday

Sometimes I see Liz running toward me with all that light and energy and I am happy and she looks beautiful to me and then, other times when I'm done, I try to bring her down.

Liz said something this morning that I too had in the back of my mind that is: sometimes she sees us as light lost people traveling around thinking we are artists while everyone laughs behind our backs.

        *

An odd kind of lonely Sunday. I think it's hard for me not performing. Its when I'm alone with a book or in front of the TV that I miss a family and community. We loaded up the truck in the morning. Liz and I had a quickie before we went over. After the load up, Ron [*Vawter*] came over to the loft and then we went out postering for the children's workshop. [*Gray and LeCompte ran children's theater workshops out of the loft.*] It was a very cold clear day and all I did was talk about sex and relationships and other women. I told Ron that things had changed because the guilt was no longer there with Nancy. I was sure Liz did not mind me being overnight with her and that changed everything. When all the neurotic little goodies disappear around sex there is little left but the act itself or the "movie" of the act—watching my cock go in and out of a new hole. I called Lane but she was not in. I called Jude and asked her out for dinner and she gave me such a "No" that I knew that one was over before it began. I thought I didn't mind but the old rejection got to me and I had a lot to drink and ate alone, in front of the TV. Sarah* [*a woman with whom Gray had an affair while he was in a relationship with LeCompte*] called and I listened to her talk (bored) while I watched TV then I asked her down (like a dirty old man). I knew she would not come. I watched "Cuckoo's Nest" and cried after he got the shock treatment—old left over drunken guilt for not having come back from TEXAS to help my mother die.

*

A beautiful cool spring day. I spent most of the morning in the loft puttering around—could not get started on any one thing and did not care. I think am only beginning to relax after the work on the trilogy. We all went down to the Envelope [*a theater next door to the Performing Garage that sometimes housed the Performance Group rehearsals and productions*] and read over some of Jim's new writing which I liked then spent some time talking about the space and I could not stay awake. Whenever Liz starts talking a lot, I tend to nod out to the sound of her voice. After rehearsal, Liz invited Willem back to the loft which made me kind of angry. I just did not feel like having him around. Liz and I went to see Irish ballet. The music was nice but we could not stand the dancing. Flip was there and we went to Joe Allen's [*restaurant*] to drink eat and talk. We got home about 10:30, watched Gore Vidal on the Cavett show, had another spat about Willem and what we should do. I get into these things where I feel I have to take some action against them.

*

A very record (94 degrees) hot day which made it difficult for me to function. I went to the gym and then sort of dragged around for the rest of the day. I just about fell asleep during warm ups and then we had a very slow reading with the boys [Gray cast some of the children from his workshop in Wooster Group productions, including Nayatt School and Point Judith (An Epilog), a play the Wooster Group produced in 1980 as a concluding piece to Three Places in Rhode Island]. At times it was hard for me to listen to Philip* because he read so painfully slow and it reminded me of him at his age and at the same time, I wanted to give him all I could. These boys bring this out of me although I do think it is short lived—at least in the case of David* when I could see him beginning to become that threatening MAN of the world (baseball and all the rest of it). It is just before adolescence when they are both boys and girls—that is what fascinates me. I walked home in the warm night. The city was alive with people all out in the streets swallowed up by the warm night. It was like India. I did not stop until I met John on his bike and I talked for a while. I drank beer and ate (against my will—NIGHT compulsion). Ray and Liz came home. After Ray left, Liz gave me a foot massage and told me that Ray did not like me because of my self-centeredness. He felt I did not see him. I only SAW MYSELF.

*

Willy and Liz act like a couple more and it's strange for me to watch but very necessary for growth in the form of knowledge. I see her treating him like a boy, like a child. . . . dressing him up, telling him to change his shirt or fixing his hair. I miss that from her but a big part of me doesn't want it anymore, doesn't trust it anymore. Liz is a mother and she nurtures well and then she moves on. In a way, she has nurtured me through the big crisis of birth after India. She got me on my feet for my own work—12 years, a very long slow painful birth. Now I see that Willem needs her and she responds to that need like any good mother. If I could see this more clearly. The most I can give her is to let her go. . . . let her do this and I also see that I have no choice. The FORCE is in motion. I put it in motion as much as she did. We are all in this chang- ing water together. I like Willem but it is difficult for me to listen to him talk. I like him for his natural way of existence. . . . his just being there for Liz. I think he is very good for her. A big part of me wants to see it work. I want her to be happy.

*

The old problem of doubt back on me again. Do I really have something to say or is it Liz who is saying it just like Richard? Am I just an actor, a vehicle through which other people's ideas pass? One way to avail that is the speaking of my own words and I have such a professional doubt of my intelligence. My mistrust goes deep but the intro *[for* Rumstick Road*]* works for me because I am speaking my own words. "Rumstick" is a sense of original language and the intro, my words.

I can't sleep so well because I am wondering what is left to be done. I don't just want to please my parent. PARENT = AUDIENCE. I want to get to it, what it (THEATER) was all about in the first place . . . the deepest needs of expression.

*

I went to Bloomingdale's to pick up my pants and buy another pair. After that I went to a porn film and then got rushed into the horrid Broadway Baths where this black ham sucked my cock for a long time, realized I was bored and would not let—did not want me to "come" and gave a long lecture on hedonism and how he lived in White Plains to keep his sanity. As I look back on it, it's funny but then I was depressed. I spent some time wandering around the horrid place, got man handled and sucked upon by gross men and at last let one finish me off. He was real good at sucking and swallowed my cock all the way then I got out of there fast and went to Sam Goodies to buy Brahms' 1 symphony and went home, talked with Liz a little before she went out with Joan Jonas *[a pioneer of video and performance art who came into prominence in the late sixties and early seventies]* and then had a few scotches—got a little drunk and had dinner alone in front of the TV.

*

I did not give up drinking today as I hoped.

Woke up late and so I was very uncentered—to the bank and then to Washington Sq. to start on cutting the Long Day's Journey script *[a seven-minute version of Eugene O'Neill's* Long Day's Journey into Night *that the group performed as part of* Point Judith (An Epilog) *in*

1980], to the bookstore and shopping and back about five and I was too early because I sort of walked in on Willem and Liz. I came in to the kitchen and started putting stuff away and Liz was in her closet hiding? (FROM ME?) getting dressed—strange feeling this looking across from the other side—Liz covering up and Willem stroking her hair, heavy vibes and all the rest of it. I went into the back and sat at my desk in a pout and Willem left and Liz and I had dinner together.

*

A long dream about a fascist commune (like Jonestown). I was kidnapped by them and could not escape (I wanted to tell Liz about it but I found her on the phone.) I was given one day of freedom to go home but I had to come back on my own or I would be killed by an assassin. Rich *[presumably Schechner]* and Liz (like parents) walked me up Chapin road from the harbor. I was crying and telling them I was going to be killed if I did not go back. Rich would not really listen to me (like DAD). It was during this kind of forced crying—like a child's tantrum that I had a kind of distance on it all and realized that a part of me longed to go back to the commune if they would choose a wife for me and take care of me and plan my life out for me.

*

Difficult adjustment to Willem and the movies *[this is in reference to Dafoe's small uncredited role in Michael Cimino's film* Heaven's Gate*]*— some jealousy. I want them to want me . . . fear of getting lost in some intellectual ART world—associations of Hollywood as being a working class world—theater for the people—fears of isolating myself in this little gay fancy SoHo world—looking at Willem as a FRESH meat and potatoes man. Another time of confusion for me. Willem going away brings it all up again—not so much the glamour but a theater for the people—working on the BIG American myth—repulsed by my subjectivism. I am stuck in this constant doubt . . . always reflecting and always in doubt. This doubt does not have a crack to seep into when we all work together but now Willy has made a crack in the boat. I made plans to go on with my solo piece; "Sex and Death up until age 14." I know I must keep working. When I don't—when there is no action, I am swallowed up in fear and doubt.

Have Liz or I or both of us been working under the grand illusion that we were individually artistic in temperament and that would not dry up even if there was no group supporting us? Willy's movie is now causing a fear and depression among us all. It makes it hard for me to work because I am constantly working under the knowledge of a sense of loss, also mad and sick fantasies that I could have been a "great actor" in the films.

*

Had a bad dream that it was the end of the world (a very real feeling so when I woke up I knew I had had a dream but I also knew it could be real). Children, who were plutonium polluted, were rushing at me everywhere and trying to touch me and I was dodging them and saying, or thinking, I was Christ and was charmed with some power of destiny and that I would make it through. When I got to the place I was going I realized that we were all going to die.

*

[In New Jersey visiting LeCompte's family]

A beautiful spring day. Liz and I got up early and had breakfast. I read some of my old College Philosophy text. Then went for a walk, not so relaxed, too much coffee. I came back and sat in the sun by the pool. I wrote a poem out of a coffee fit (who wants to hear it? I'm still the child. I can't go unheard—unseen. I am no Emily Dickinson nor was I meant to be—my private history shut up in a room—but still, I want to write my own material. I want to speak my own words.)

*

[Back in New York]

Chan [Gray's younger brother] came and . . . [we] went out for a walk about 3—up to Wash Sq. and back. Liz says Chan seems well. I would not know. So often I feel so involved in myself that I don't see others. I have to face what more seems to be the truth—that I could only love Liz to the extent that she was incorporated into ME, my work, my fears . . . all these years I've used her to PROP me up . . . to keep

me alive and now it's all being shaken and threatened by her relationship with Willem. Now I must be strong and take a good look at
it. I feel now like I'm re-entering that HELL that was before I met
Liz. I feel like a lost child again but before, I had my youth to go on
and now I only see loneliness and old age and then I think—let go of
it all—just give up on human love and put it all into ART and when I
think that way it all looks barren. I feel like I will die without Liz. The
worst thought is that Liz having our baby might save us. Oh HELP on
that one. I need distance? I'm just like all the rest. I'm in the WORLD
THAT IS.

On April 20, 1979, Gray debuted his first solo show, Sex and Death to
the Age 14, *at the Performing Garage. He followed it with two more
monologues in the same year:* Booze, Cars, and College Girls *and* India
and After (America).

*

There was a big audience for SEX and DEATH (over 70) which sort
of threw me off but I loved it—perhaps I played more for the laughs. I
don't know. I had some feeling that I was committing artistic suicide by
letting everyone get to know me so well.

*

Bill Harris called to tell me that I had won the SOHO Weekly [News,
an alternative downtown paper] award for best non-Broadway actor. I
was sort of surprised and happy but also felt a little empty (the difference between actual and symbolic power—my actual power is in my
work now and when that doesn't "come" then I feel empty). Liz and
I rushed off to see "Play It Again SAM" which was sort of sad and
hopeless but had some funny moments for me but I notice that I am
still not FREE with Liz—I often only laugh after she laughs. I wait for
her to give me direction and this frightens me. I identify with Woody
Allen's clumsiness when he tries to play THE MAN. I identify with the
little boy in him. I took Liz out for a hot chocolate after and we walked

home. It was a nice night and the city had been washed clean by the rain. The trees were very green.

*

Went over to the Garage to set up chairs for my 103 reservations *[for Sex and Death]*. It was a very full house and there were many people there that I knew and could play the show for. Yvonne Rainer *[experimental dancer, choreographer, and filmmaker]* was there and Elaine from Houston sat right in the front row with that old sad crazy face. I really felt like I talked to the audience and that felt good—kind of like a preacher, poet, comedian, all mixed together. With reluctance, I went to meet Renée at the Collective and when I got there, I was glad to see her. *[This is one of the first mentions of Shafransky in Gray's journals.]* We went for drinks and we got on well together and talked a lot. She is good looking and intelligent but only 26 years old. I would never have guessed it. We went back to her place. She lives in an office on John Street. We drank wine and talked then we went to bed and talked some about Willem and Liz. She, like so many other people, could not understand how I could live with it. These reactions make it hard for me to live with it. We got into some heavy fucking and she said, "Oh Spalding" and I said "yes" and she said, "I think I'm going to be sick" and at last she threw up. We both got very little sleep. I miss Liz.

*

A fire truck woke me up and I did not know where I was and for a long time, I had this kind of half awake repetitive dream fantasy, the siren on the truck was to be followed by a loud speaker proclaiming the FAME of Phil Glass and I but it never came up and a voice kept saying, "what if it never comes, what if they don't announce your fame?" and I said, "It doesn't matter."

*

I called Renée and got her and planned for dinner at her place. After dinner we had a long therapy session by candle light very New York, very intellectual, very romantic. She went through the old story again about how it would be masochistic for her to get involved with me as long as I was involved in an emotional love with Liz. In fact she told me no woman would touch me in the situation I was in. I began to fall for her and feel bad about myself. She told me I was in real bad shape but strangely enough I felt otherwise I felt at last I was beginning to live my life in a more honest way. What she told me should have made me feel depressed but it had a strange opposite effect for me. When I got home Liz was on the floor working on the script. It was good to see her. I felt warm towards her—like a real friend. I told her about my evening and she told me I played it real well. She said to be strong and hold out. I had 2 beers and went to bed. I did not feel any anger towards her. Hopeful.

*

I ended up staying up late with Willem and talking. He said he was angry about *Sex and Death*. He said I over dramatized my life, that I was full of a kind of hype and constantly made signals for help (the boy who cried Wolf—my mother's story) and that I did this to manipulate people into giving me constant attention particularly women (Liz) and he felt it was not fair. He told me that he was in love with Liz and that he could relate to her as a man to a woman and he wanted to know what I wanted from Liz. I told him that I wanted to work with her and to be friends but I felt weak and unable to let go of the hope of LOVE.

*

I'm coming apart and losing my center. At least I think I remember how to get back to it and will do it (can I trust myself to do it) when I need to . . . I do not like all the ACTING I do and that goes on around me. It feels like so much hype and I long to get back to a more simple state. I also feel a strong need to get back to writing and find no time at all for that now. I feel too much in the public eye. I love it but it eats me up and when I am left alone, I feel like a shell that always needs to be filled up by audience.

*

. . . Went up to meet Renée at 9 to go out to dinner at the Mitali *[an Indian restaurant Gray frequented in the East Village]*, which was crowded so we went to a bar on Second Ave. and talked and I even laughed some. It was good to see her. These long breaks are what help make it work and I refused to call that unreal. It is what it needs to be at this point in time. I paid for drink and dinner and we had a nice walk back to her place down under the Brooklyn Bridge and up Fulton St. It was warm and quite beautiful. She has a certain romantic way of approaching her life which I like. I think it is more than just her youth. It was a warm romantic night. The wind blew her white curtains. I felt cross-eyed with fatigue and then the old neurotic fears come back. I get afraid that I am going to jump out her window in my SLEEP AND WAKE ON THE WAY DOWN.

JULY 4, 1979

I am clearly unable to take direction from anyone but Liz and even that comes hard this is why I can't be an actor right now.

Problems with father tempted by the idea that all I do may be a reaction against my father—I look at his life and do all I can to live my life in opposition to this makes my life inflexible and rigid

How will I make money to live?
Work in a mental hospital?
That's the only fantasy I have left.

To be famous is to be stuck in an inflexible place.
But at least it is to be stuck with money.
Money is not everything but it is something.

I don't know where my identity lies now. What do I call myself when people ask—
I am not a father, a husband, a lover.
Maybe a performer.
Yes, maybe I am that.
I perform things in public
And right now I am doing these talking pieces.
So right now I have to hold on to that.

You can also work on your vocabulary; begin by taping words and their meanings.

Better ask Rich about a good dictionary.
He may have one.
Begin with the word—"indulgent"

The question for therapy?
Do I want to become a professional something?

And if so a professional what?

But I still think about being a child therapist and I can't get that fantasy out of my head understanding the child in me? I think I will apply to the clinics anyway and see what happens. One thing I did want to say about the idea and fantasy of my becoming a therapist is that I'm very able to act as a screen for people's fear and anger. I don't seem to get involved.

I sometimes feel like that; like I am this open conduit through which I let other energies pass. It started as an actor and the other energies were other people's scripts.

Now it is my life that is passing through me.

AUGUST 25, 1979

Debbie got out the zip code sheets and showed me that most of our audience came from the lower east side—people in transition, I thought. People that are working their way up to the ladder to a better lifestyle. I felt a slight feeling of loss and bitterness that these people were using me as their jester. Their poor entertainer who used his neurosis—his life for entertainment, that I was stuck somewhere as the poor artist that people came to see, to live off my pain and to say "there but for the grace of . . . go I" a kind of unhappy Christ figure—a Woody Allen Wasp that cannot love and cannot make a lot of money because the audience that identifies with me has no money. It was a black thought and I could not face it straight on—that I was a curiosity on the outside, that I was somehow lost.

DECEMBER 20, 1979

The shark's mouth eats at me, the reflection of white silver winter light on trees. I read about Dusty Hoffman in the SoHo News. Am I that? I could be just a well-adjusted ACTOR. Am I putting myself into the place where I will die? Who is the artist? Liz or I? I like watching what she does but who am I in it and could I function just as well somewhere else? I keep disappearing.

Gray and Dustin Hoffman acted together in Brendan Behan's Quare
Fellow *at the Theatre Company of Boston in 1964, three years before
the twenty-seven-year-old Hoffman would take on the iconic role of
Ben Braddock in Mike Nichols's* Graduate. *Later, in his monologue*
A Personal History of the American Theater, *Gray would describe
Hoffman as "very funny, he looked like a dog, a funny short little
dog." And Hoffman, according to Gray, would repeatedly say in the
dressing room, "You know, Spalding, you're strange. You know that,
Gray? Spalding's strange. Spalding, you're strange." Throughout his
journals, Gray taunted himself with Hoffman's more successful, more
commercial acting career—and perhaps a path not taken.*

DECEMBER 28, 1979

Middle of the Night
My art wants to bend around to meet my life, the arrow comes back.
I was telling Renée how I started to live when I started doing theater.
Now I am trying to bend it back.

the eighties

THERE IS ALWAYS a constant precarious balance between dark and light. The yin and yang. Civilization and its discontents.

Looking back on it after the fact, I realize that "Swimming to Cambodia" is an attempt to balance those poles. Like any work of art it is an attempt to become God out of a loss of contact.

An attempt to create a tiny, balanced universe. An attempt to play at being God out of a lack of contact with the real or imagined source.

And like life it is a fixed and imperfect text.

APRIL 1985

The eighties began for Gray with professional breakups. Schechner officially left the Performance Group in 1980. Gray and LeCompte took over, renaming the ensemble the Wooster Group, the title under which the company had originally been incorporated. "Liz began to do her own work—which was more formal than mine. I had a humanist impulse, and she was more radically postmodern," Schechner noted. "The actors were gravitating toward Liz's method. Also, they were more or less the same age, and I was a generation and a half older, I'd done it for fifteen years, so I didn't feel like fighting it out."

In 1985, Gray also stopped performing with the group in order to pursue his solo career. But even as he tried to distance himself emotionally from the Wooster Group and LeCompte, he continued to open his monologues at the Garage and live as a roommate of LeCompte and Dafoe in the Wooster Street loft. It was an eccentric arrangement in perhaps many of the ways that Gray himself was eccentric: boundaryless, contradictory, and embracing.

Even among this upheaval, however, Gray began producing his shows with increasing frequency. By late 1982, he had performed Point Judith (An Epilog), presented four new solo pieces at the Performing Garage, as well as an eight-monologue retrospective at the end of the year. Throughout, his work became more sophisticated in its self-revelation; he developed his own personal artistic stamp with his suggestive non sequiturs and sly comic timing.

Gray also challenged himself to try new work that would take him beyond the monologues. In 1981, he tried out an ad-lib piece called Interviewing the Audience while touring in Amsterdam. "I thought, I have to do something to spice up these performances," Gray wrote of his idea. "I can't do these old monologues anymore. So I decided to interview the Dutch audiences. At the performance, I asked audience members to write their names on little cards, and then I'd call them up [to the stage] and ask them what happened to them on the way to the theater. Either it would take off or it wouldn't." It did. Gray went on to refine and perform Interviewing the Audience throughout his life, making it a regular part of his repertoire.

"Interviewing the Audience was one of the works I loved most, and perhaps the one I saw most often," the novelist Francine Prose, who met and befriended Gray in 1982, wrote, "because it was always different, and always fascinating. . . . He had an uncanny eye for choosing people who had something exceptional and even startling to report, and he could (correctly, it seemed to me) discover the zeitgeist of an entire city or region of the country from the kinds of stories its citizens told, and their willingness to tell them."

Gray also began writing a novel, called The Father of Myself, in 1980, though it was never published. Six years later, however, he had begun a new novel—drawn, in part, from the work he'd done on The Father of Myself as well as from his own life—under contract from Knopf. (The Father of Myself, the novel described by Gray in his journals, was not among his papers, although there is a long poem in his archives with this same title.) "I never heard of The Father of Myself. But neither did [Gray] ever mention, 'Oh, I've got another novel too,' which would naturally of course have come up," concluded Gary Fisketjon, who edited Gray as well as such authors as Raymond Carver and Cormac McCarthy. "I'd almost bet my life that The Father of Myself became Impossible Vacation."

Gray worked on Impossible Vacation intermittently from 1986 to 1991, the greatest length of time he devoted to any single project; the novel was finally published in 1992. Throughout that period, Gray struggled mightily with the demands of writing fiction—the solitude (with no audience to look forward to at the end), the need to invent or bend material rather than pull it directly from life, the crippling doubts encountered when sitting down to the blank page. "My position was always, 'Why do you care about doing this?'" Francine Prose recalled. "He seemed to think that fiction was a superior form to what he was doing."

Gray also returned to traditional acting in this decade. In 1983, he was cast in his first major movie, one that would significantly alter the course of his career: Roland Joffé's The Killing Fields. Gray was taken by the politics and history portrayed in the film: the American bombing of Cambodia, beginning in 1969, and the genocide perpetrated by the Khmer Rouge. Gray himself admitted to being surprised at his own interest in the material. When Joffé first suggested that he audition, Gray said, "I'm not very political—in fact, I've never even voted in my life." To which Joffé reportedly replied, "Perfect! We're look-ing for the American ambassador's aide." Gray played the role of the aide—who is ultimately forced to flee Cambodia in anticipation of the Khmer Rouge invasion—with quiet passion. The experience of acting in The Killing Fields made a deep impression on him—and would later become the basis for his most celebrated monologue—and yet his total screen time in this film is less than three minutes.

On December 12, 1983, Gray premiered Swimming to Cambodia, Part One, at the Performing Garage. Almost two months later, he pre-sented Swimming to Cambodia, Part Two. By the fall of 1984, he'd brought these parts together and whittled them down to one show. Swimming to Cambodia was a kaleidoscopic account of his time spent on The Killing Fields: Gray's personal story of the Hollywood story of history. It was also in this monologue that Gray first famously claimed his search for the Perfect Moment, his hope for one simple, transcen-dent experience that would absorb him wholly, if fleetingly. The film version of Swimming to Cambodia, directed by Jonathan Demme, was released in 1987, catapulting Gray to a national level of recognition.

Curiously, this period in Gray's life is largely overlooked in his jour-nals. In fact, during this time, he wrote very little in his journals at all. There are scant entries throughout 1984 and 1985—and he rarely discusses his work with regard to Swimming to Cambodia. One can only guess why Gray, someone with such drive to document his life, wouldn't feel compelled to narrate such a crucial turning point as this one. Perhaps in the midst of it, he couldn't see it as such. There are com-ments in the later journals that would suggest this, when Gray looks back with the advantage of time and recognizes that his career shifted with the theater and film versions of Swimming to Cambodia. It's also worth noting that this was a period of both meditation and preoccu-pation for Gray in terms of his work; it is possible that he was often too busy performing and crafting the show to write about it elsewhere.

In 1984, Gray also met and signed with his lifelong literary agent, Suzanne Gluck. As a student at Brown University, Gluck had seen Sex and Death and edited an excerpt from it for the school literary maga-zine. Four years later, when she was hired as an agent at International Creative Management, Gray was the first client she signed. "When we met, I had been an agent for about thirteen seconds," she said.

"He came into my windowless office with no books and no shelves and didn't even think to ask me who else I represented—but I think he picked up on my passion that his work would translate brilliantly on the page. He was somebody who could experience the same boring thing as you and then spin a story from it that made you realize just how interesting it had all been."

Gray's career escalated further in 1986, when he premiered his monologue Terrors of Pleasure at the Mitzi E. Newhouse Theater at Lincoln Center. This move significantly broadened the scope of his audience. "If you want to see when he became famous, just look at whenever Lincoln Center decided to adopt him," Eric Bogosian said. "That is the peak. As they kept putting him out there as this brand name that we should all be familiar with, I think everything changed. He made a quantum leap."

Meanwhile, as Gray's relationship with Shafransky deepened, they also became entwined professionally. With the success of Swimming to Cambodia, Shafransky moved into the role of Gray's manager (later working alongside his booking agents at International Production Associates); she also served as a producer on the Demme film and directed the theatrical monologues of Monster in a Box and Gray's Anatomy. "It wasn't going to happen without her. They were co-creators," recalled Bill Talen, also known as Reverend Billy, a New York City performance artist and protégé of Gray's beginning in 1982. "She really was the one who made it happen with Jonathan Demme. They had other commitments in other directions, but she got everybody out of the way and said, 'This is the man. This is the person we want to work with.' She facilitated the editing of Swimming to Cambodia. That shift—Renée was all over it." (Shafransky also wrote screenplays of her own and produced the 1983 film Variety, written by Kathy Acker and directed by Bette Gordon.)

From then on, Shafransky became the backbone to Gray's career. She edited his writing, directed his monologues, and produced the film versions of his shows; their lives became a tangle of romantic yearning and professional enterprise. As their relationship haltingly moved forward, Gray's career soared.

Sustaining this success, however, came at a steep price: Gray promised his life to his audiences. Toward the end of the seventies, he had

had flashes of worry about the consequences of exploiting his intimate life and neuroses for his work. As his career gained traction in the eighties, this worry developed into a darker and more fixed sense of destiny, one that left Gray feeling trapped and afraid. This anxiety—that he had gambled his privacy for fame—would haunt him for the rest of his life.

This torment aggravated Gray's other neurotic vulnerabilities. Throughout these years, he worried constantly that he had AIDS, which had become epidemic in the eighties—and perfectly suited his free-floating sexual guilt and intense fear of death. (His worries were not unfounded: Gray frequented gay bathhouses, had affairs with women on the road, and didn't always practice safe sex.) He faltered under Shafransky's demands that they marry and have a baby. He drank too much.

Perhaps in anticipation of these deepening anxieties, Gray began his first long-term therapeutic relationship in 1981, less than a week after he turned forty. He started seeing Paul Pavel, a Czechoslovakian psychotherapist and Holocaust survivor and a dynamic character in his own right. In fact, in Pavel's obituary in The New York Times, *it was noted that two of his artist patients, Gray and Art Spiegelman, presented him in their work. Throughout the eighties, Pavel holds a striking presence in the journals as he helps Gray to address and shape the complex preoccupations of his character.*

And yet despite Gray's growing personal agonies, this is arguably the decade that brought him to the pinnacle of his career.

JANUARY 3, 1980

Renée had a dream that I had a big scar on my heart. She feels that I am not in touch with my feelings and maybe I should take a year off and go work on a fishing boat on the coast of Weather with all the men. She says I am controlled by the fact that I see everything as an image and cannot see beyond the image, that I always make up my own world. She is right but who doesn't. She seems freer perhaps because she had to fend for herself at an earlier age. She went with me while I made my food shopping rounds and then I went to work on Pt. Judith *[a multimedia pastiche of performance and video including the seven-minute version of* Long Day's Journey into Night*]* from 3–6:30. The Balcony *[Gray played the role of the Bishop in this Jean Genet play, the final Performance Group production directed by Richard Schechner]* was packed and I stayed around afterward and talked. People seemed to like it.

JANUARY 27, 1980

I met Renée at 2 and I had the idea we would just trot down to her place for a good screw. I get all mixed up about my body needs and forget that she has any feelings about it all. She wanted to talk. We sat on a bench by the city hall. Basically she feels that I am not giving enough. It is an old story I've heard before but this time it made me sad and I turned away and looked down at the grey stone walk under us. I look out to see the beauty in the object outside. A part of me wants to turn in and turn away to write and another part sees my salvation with people but never with one person—maybe only Liz. Renée thinks Liz and I may be together "forever" but R. *[Renée]* puts fear into me when she says that I may already be emotionally burnt out and that I am not in touch with my feelings in any direct way, that I am not simple and direct, that I am devious and that she does not trust me anymore. How strange because I don't trust Jennifer* *[a woman Gray was seeing at the beginning of his relationship with Shafransky]* but I do trust Renée. The sun went down and it got cold and we walked back to her place where I got more depressed because she said I was only in search for a nurturing mother who could stand behind my work. To some extent I think this is true. She says such people don't exist and those that do are sad lost and unhappy women. This is a sign of the times women and men in different places. We make good slow love. I go do a show and meet her at the Collective. We go to Magoo's for drinks. I eat a rare hamburger. We go back and make passion love in THE DARK.

FEBRUARY 17, 1980

Renée and I woke up at the loft, made love, got up and had lox and eggs and headed off for Central Park. It was a bright cold windy day and we walked up to West 4th to take the subway. We talked about whether or not she felt she could be away from me emotionally for 5 weeks while I am in Amsterdam. *[Gray performed* Point Judith (An Epilog) *in Amsterdam for most of the month of May in 1980.]* To some extent I welcome the break but I am not looking forward to being in Amsterdam for that long. I hope I can get down to some writing. It would be the only thing that could save me.

FEBRUARY 19, 1980

[Visiting his father and Gram Gray]

It was a busy day in Rhode Island for me. Each time I think that I can frame it in a poem I am bombarded by new real life images of pain and death. I was amazed at how clear and attentive Gram was. Her body is old and wasted, just ready to be burned but her eyes still go out to things or people. We did not have much to say and after we got up to leave after an hour, she began to complain about Dad never taking her for a ride in the wheel chair so I talked Dad in to letting me stay. He drove into town for some reason. He said to call Sis *[Gray's stepmother]* but I don't know. I took Gram for a wheel chair ride and she said faster. I gave a fast one but was afraid she'd fall out so I slowed down. Dad came back while we were looking at the tropical fish. The nurse was not there to help Gram out of the chair so I did it. Her arms were around my neck, I got her under her arms and lifted, she hung around my neck like a paralyzed body her spine all rigid. It was my touching her that made all the difference. She just lit up after that. I realized that Dad must never touch her. He can't—the fear on all fronts—just sits across and looks from a distance of 93 years. I kissed her on the mouth and looked into her eyes for the last time. It was hard to leave.

MARCH 2, 1980

[Back in New York]

I wrote a fast letter off to Rocky with the new found Wallace Stevens quote: "One's cry of O Jerusalem becomes little by little a cry to something a little nearer and nearer until at last one cries out to a living name, a living place, a living thing, and in crying out confesses openly all the bitter secretions of experience." The man came to fix the stove and then I went off to do our last picture call for Pt. Judith. The last show went very well and the audience seemed to be right with it. Joe Papp *[Joseph Papp, who founded the New York Shakespeare Festival in 1954 and, three years later, began offering free productions of Shakespeare in Central Park; later, he founded the Public Theater in downtown Manhattan]* was there with his wife and stayed after to thank Liz and I. I'll miss Pt. Judith but I'm glad it's over so that I can now return to thinking more about new work and the solo work.

MARCH 3, 1980

While watching TV I decided to do the History of American theatre *[this became the next monologue Gray would perform at the Garage;* A Personal History of the American Theater *opened in November 1980]* as an epic piece telling my life story around the plays no matter how long it takes—I feel a little nervous about it because I don't know where to draw the line but I think the piece is about sexual identity and that I must go into those things—that I want to do what Henry Miller did in print but instead being there and taking full responsibility and the whole idea turns me on. There is so much material it feels like an oral book. Renée called and said she needed me because she was feeling insecure so I said come at ten. Jennifer called at 9:30 to say she wanted to come to Philadelphia to visit me which pleased me so by the time Renée came my ego was all fired up and in a good mood. We went for a walk up to Washington Sq. then came back while I drank three beers and talked with Ken *[Kobland]* and Renée. By the time we got to bed, we had a fight because I was acting annoyed (like all those bad men) saying things like why can't it be like it was in the beginning when you were all footloose and did not need me all that much so she was angry that I could not accept her as needing me and as having all this emotional involvement with me. I'm just no good at it. I am so adolescent with her.

MARCH 13, 1980

I read in the tub and I read in bed and I called Jennifer and said no, I could not see her now but on Sunday and even as I said it I was trying to figure out how I was going to get to Joan Jonas's for her dinner party which I want Renée to come to. Jennifer sounded very disappointed but I think I know what I'm doing now. It feels right.

APRIL 30, 1980

[Traveling to Amsterdam with the Wooster Group to perform Point Judith (An Epilog), Sex and Death, *and* Booze, Cars, and College Girls *at the Mickery Theatre]*

Too much time in the airport, not a place to stay long. When we got to the X-RAY Renée took me aside to kiss me goodbye. I did not say anything, just kept smiling. I could not tell if it was the end. We sat in the plane for a long time before it took off, me so tired of waiting. Liz, Willem and Jim reading magazines and paper, seeming bored. No excitement? No holding hands on the take off and away!

MAY 3, 1980

Felt out of it and ragged. A nice day, went out for breakfast with Willem & Liz, telling my stories which always makes me feel good but I think Willem was bothered by all my chatter, they went off to the theatre and I went back to Ivan's to masturbate with little feeling and taking a long time to come—forced. Then walked over the theatre to see if Chan and Bianca had called. Feeling somewhat lost and alone reviewing my past relation with Liz where did it go wrong? We all ended up at B. Belly for a small expensive meal. How the money goes here so fast. I went back to the apartment alone, drank more beer and took another bath, relax and go to bed and asleep by one o'clock. I don't know if I can go on with these tours and fear that Frankfurt will be the same, more snacks and beer and being alone. I'm not at all sure that the work can sustain me anymore. Feel at the END.

MAY 7, 1980

I walked through Vondelpark *[park in Amsterdam]* and as soon as I
entered I began to think about what I would do for The Kitchen piece in
FEB. I thought about a long tape in the dark in which I would describe
all my sexual encounters. By the time I got out on the street I dropped
the idea. Why do it, I thought. How would it enrich my life? I don't
want to do something for my audience only. I need to do something
with more exploration in it and must trust that when the time comes, I
will know what to do on the spot. A simple structure like the I CHING
in which I frame where I am at that point. I spent some of the afternoon at the theatre working with Liz, W. and Ron on the intro to Pt.
Judith. Then back to my room for an hour sleep and to the theater for a
very good show but a small (31) audience that was silent so we played
among ourselves which worked well. Beers and talk after John read us
our first good review and I took Philip *[one of the boys who acted with*
the Wooster Group and performed in Point Judith (An Epilog)*]* to Red
Light District after he called his mother. He seemed very excited by it
and wanted to go see a LIVE show and the man said he would let him
in which surprised me. I told Philip we'd come back another time. We
all went to Mike French's room and had a great party. Philip telling
dirty jokes as he bounced up and down on the bed. It was a wonderful
family party.

MAY 11, 1980

Philip and I went for a long bike ride outside of town. It was a beautiful
bright clear day and we get on very well together. He takes pictures of
all the animals we see—sheep, cow, donkey, duck, swan. Like a Dick
& Jane farm book, even thinks of calling the sheep Dick & Jane but
decides on Mary & Joe. We stop to play CHICAGO pinball. He knows
all the streets on the game glass. We ride through a cow pasture toward
the dikes he always thought were lesbians, he thinks a mason sail is a
house before he sees it moving along the top of the dike. Bright sun blue
sky. I sing "The old row song" my mother used to sing. He likes it. We
ride back to AM. He is speaking fake Dutch most of the way. We find
our way back by five o'clock and rest and all out to dinner at a very
expensive and not so good Greek place, 50 guilders for my meal.

MAY 15, 1980

Writing in the park for a while and Philip, Marge and Kate *[members of the Wooster Group]* showed up and I had a nice time with Philip. We'd go for little walks and then write a sketch of what we remembered. It's not that he is all that intelligent it's that he has a lot of animal energy that is always bursting out. We walk back together about 4 and he asked me questions of sex the whole way. I felt a little strange talking to him about Renée but I could not stop myself. I liked the way it turned him on and to some extent it was like having that fantasy triangle in which a boy (me?) watched the man-me make love to Renée.

MAY 17, 1980

The sight of every beautiful lass makes me angry like a child because I can't have it and have pretty much given up trying. I did miss Renée today and thought about BEING with her and wondered what she was doing.

MAY 31, 1980

Got fast into writing about one o'clock, spin off fantasy writing now that gets me excited like masturbation but writing is so much like it if you are just going in that uncontrolled way and that's how it goes. It reaches a peak in which someone is shot (me) or someone comes, then it goes into that relaxed dreamy place where all gets calm again. Went out for a walk, bought some boots for 50 guilder then walked the shopping street having some . . . yes I find it is possible that I can have some private experiences without needing to share them with someone right away but for my enjoyment letting them die as they pass out of existence. It's those little deaths of those little precious moments that are hard still, can't accept life as FLOW. But I think I'm on to something in the writing and must give it a go or I will never know.

JUNE 4, 1980

I walked to the theatre with Pablo and when John said good news from New York I was sure I had won an Obie. What a surprise when I found it was Liz for best director *[for* Point Judith (an Epilog)*]*. After I got over the shock I was happy for her and wrote her a letter. I think I had six people for BC & CGs [Booze, Cars, and College Girls] and three of those were comps. Then I walked home to drink beer (too much again) alone sitting thinking letting it all come in thinking about the Obie and realizing how it's all a systems game and how they just plug in to a new name each year and how they were getting at Richard by putting Liz on top.

JUNE 5, 1980

[Gray's thirty-ninth birthday]

So my birthday and a good but confusing day a lot happening in the morning. Talked with R. about coming back [to perform in Amsterdam] next year which put me into a big upset thinking about the group, about my writing, about Renée, about my whole life but I could get away for three weeks but I don't think I want to go to Frankfurt but who knows. I'm not so keen on N.Y.C. now. What to do and always a crisis in Amsterdam! I thought all day about it and then went to Jules and Marion [the friends Gray stayed with in Amsterdam during his breakdown in 1976] for dinner. Talk of Liz and her relationship to Emma [LeCompte's niece] made me in tears. I had to hold back walking to the theatre. Hot day and went to that place where almost 4 years ago I met Liz off the bus, great sadness (don't look back). BC & CGs went well although a very sober audience. Over came GWENDOLYN and I must say I really fell for her. I asked her to go to bed with me and she said no so I let it all go and we played around some and she said, now I shall take you home with me. What a wonderful birthday present! She rode me on the back of her bike. She looks like a muse and a wonderful body and such a beautiful old loft, like making love in a barn. It was so good!

JUNE 6, 1980

My head is all mixed up. Gwen over for dinner and me making love with her still holding back because I think guilt for Renée even at this distance and then all the different women at the show. I'm trying to set up teaching dates and a dozen long stem roses from Renée which is my confession I leave at the theatre. Also she called me just before the show and I told her about the airline stewardess because I was already feeling hemmed in by the call, by the roses and I want perhaps to live out the rest of my years as this, wander, wander, wander but afraid to be alone.

JULY 6, 1980

[Back in New York]

Cool clear windy, best weather in a long time! We decided to go down to Battery Park so I called Liz and W. to invite them. We lay in the sun and talked then Renée bought tickets for the Ellis Island boat so we took the tour and it was very nice out there, fresh grass, wind in the Sycamores, healing clean air. We both got tired of the tour after we lost our cute tour guide and went out and slept on the grass, then back, me still looking for Liz, the "disappearing mother," flash memory of Liz waiting on the beach for me in India. We went back to R.'s, ate cherries. It was a good day. The other days have been difficult. I think often it is because I am not writing and then I think that all the writing is a fantasy and that in fact I don't want to be a writer but interested in Wallace Stevens' battle with solipsism and wonder often if that's what I have to go through. Kerouac died at about 47 years old. Ginsberg got religion. Renée says the religion came out of guilt. Guilt for what? I say and she says for fame and that rings a bell. My guilt for fame and money I MAKE.

On July 9, 1980, Gray and Shafransky left on a car trip across the United States ending in San Francisco, where Gray performed Sex and Death *as well as a story called "The Great Crossing," about the trip he'd just taken with Shafransky to get there.*

AUGUST 12, 1980

Woken from long Amsterdam dream, as Yvonne *[Rainer]* was whisper-
ing in my ear about what a scoundrel I was for sleeping with the different women, by a phone call from Bob Applegarth so I told Renée the
dream and she was very hurt and upset that I'd done it with Gwen—
someone I liked. So we spent a good part of the morning hacking it
out. She was calling me a cad and how she did not trust me but I was
"up" from the dream because in the dream I was able to stand on my
own and resist the somewhat sentimental and idyllic vision of nature-
harmonious GROUP vision that Yvonne showed me out the window.
She told me that this was how their group still was and I was able
to have distance on it and knew it was not true also knew that I was
changing. I also stood my ground with R. and said I would do it again
with a woman I like if the opportunity presented itself. Of course, she is
upset about me being alone in SF. By the time we got to the beach, she
had calmed down and we had a nice day there.

AUGUST 19, 1980

Renée thinks that I am both the boy and the mother. I want to be 12
again and also be the mother of myself and that I make women like
her and Liz into the father and punish them by obsessing on the boy
the way my mother did with ME and that I will only STOP doing this
when it causes me too much pain and disaster in my life. We made love.
Not so connected both of us realizing it was the end for awhile. R. and
I headed off early to the airport. I parked the car while she checked her
stuff then we went to the bar for a brandy. R. was very emotional and
cried a lot told me she loved me and that she had had a good time. We
went to the Eastern *[Airlines]* Waiting Room together and the plane
was late to board so we sat on the floor, my head in her lap for an over
long goodbye, then she was gone. I did not look back. Drove back to
Beethoven Leonora Overture to drink beer and read R. D. LAING'S
"The Facts of Life" then I went to bed at midnight, a little drunk and
out of it. Fast asleep.

AUGUST 28, 1980

[San Francisco; Shafransky has returned to New York]

Getting into the same routine now, working on the writing in the morning until too painful stiff to move and then started a tape to Renée out in the sun which was not so bright but warm enough, then for my shopping, walk down to Mission St. bought one trout at the fish store for $1.59, so light and delicate, I could eat them every night. My little nap in the afternoon. I was feeling a little lonely and missed Renée and admit the need of a "love" also was brought down by Bay Guardian review saying "Sex & Death" was not fresh material but it's true. Looked at the list of names *[of people coming to the show]* and saw Shepard, made joke that it was Sam and it turned out to be true so I sort of did the show for him. It got me thinking of old TOOTH *[The Tooth of Crime]* days and how close the material was. He sat center and I avoided looking at him most of the time. Often his eyes seemed to be closed with a slight smile on his face but it gives me good energy. I went with Adele and Ted to the Powell Grill to drink with Sam. It was good talking with him, serious Western Male that he was with son named Jesse of course. Ted and Adele left at 11 and Sam and I went on drinking and talking about writing, New York, Hollywood, Bob Dylan, Joyce Aaron, Boroughs *[William Burroughs]* = weak and dissident. Sam the moral Western man with two horses and a leather jacket and cowboy hat on the seat of his truck car. We drank Anchor Steam till 1:15, he put it on his credit card.

OCTOBER 27, 1980

[Back in New York]

Watching Renée get up, seeing her as beautiful and sexy and yes, I think yes, it's all connected. First woman I think would look good pregnant with my child (FEAR) and off I went to get my stuff and head up for R.I. *[where he would perform* Sex and Death*]*. It was a beautiful day. Dad and Sis were at the train station to meet me. I was surprised to be happy to see them and of course talked my head off in my nervous way. They wanted to know who my "new friend" was and what had become of Liz. Sis saying something at dinner about Liz having run my life for long enough. Me wondering how dad and sis had picked up on that. "Well, she never waited on you," was their response (but I tried to make her "WAIT").

OCTOBER 28, 1980

[Rhode Island]

Got up late and was a little rushed by dad to get over to see Gram Gray before eleven. She was very surprised to see me and I think she thought I was Chan at first. She had a lot of problems with phlegm and could not hardly talk and kept choking up her V8 juice saying "I hate myself," then she'd ask for her "little candy" Fig Newton's, which she said were her only joy and she kept eating them and choking on them. Dad wanted to go so I said to go along and I'd stay because Gram started to cry when I got up to go. I sat with her. There was not much to be said because she could not hear me and she could not talk well. I put her sweater on her and felt her old flesh and bone arms which felt good they were soft and still very strong. They had a kind of beauty to them like an old tree.

OCTOBER 31, 1980

Up around seven, could not sleep, all geared up I guess from the performance. Had breakfast and got down to Gram Horton's about 11:15. Felt agitated and bothered by her constant insults of my work but got more relaxed after asking her about her life. She looks very old now, hard for me to look at her mouth and she is nervous because she has lost her faith from creeping doubt and insists it is her fault. So strange to see this active guilt at 90 almost like it gives her energy, something to fight with, to come up against. She showed me pictures of her 90th birthday and I felt faint and a little sick. Everyone looked so old. We had a nice lunch of beans, rolls and breaded oysters, trying to avoid topics of old age and death, then I left and drove down to the river.

Everything seemed so small and in no way a threatening reality like as a child when I knew it as the only world. It felt like an acid trip.

NOVEMBER 10, 1980

[Back in New York]

Stopped to have my palm read on Bleecker Street. Long life, not much money, travel this year and three children, two boys and a girl. Cold night, nice to be in heated cozy loft, three beers and sitting, doing a little writing on book, short talk with Willem and Liz and to bed early. Beginning to read *[Virginia Woolf's]* The Waves again: "Everybody seems to be doing things for this moment only; and never again. Never again. The urgency of it all is fearful." It was good for me to be alone again. Come back to myself as CENTER.

NOVEMBER 19, 1980

Renée having trouble with her feet and is afraid she may need an operation plus more anxious talk about where we will end up this summer. We talked about looking to rent something cheap Upstate so we both could come in for unemployment and maybe I could keep it into the fall. We both want to be in one spot but I think she is worried about getting bored and not being around her friends. I think that I am longing to get in a place where I can write as a habit, I don't know. When we talk like this I see little future in our relationship together but I am writing a lot now and it gives me pleasure, also going through crazy regrets about why I did not go into movies and trying to get a clearer view of how I was in the early 70's and how I thought. This should feed into a History of Theatre. To bed alone.

NOVEMBER 26, 1980

Worked on a poem "Coming down from Berkeley Heights" which I really like sections of. It seems to me that I'm going through another crisis and that one creative way to follow it through is to stay with the poems. The book *[the novel* The Father of Myself*]* will come when it comes. I must slow down on the drinking.

A small audience but good I did it [A Personal History of the American Theater] as a relaxed show. Ken was there and very encouraging. He liked the name cards [with the titles of various plays that Gray had acted in throughout his life] and the way the stories played off the names. Back to the loft to drink four beers and feel so sorry for myself. I kept crying like the old hypoglycemia days. Wrote crazy passages and read about Freud in New Yorker—free association—don't sense or hold anything back. I wrote, "I am crying, look at me mom, I am crying" should be juxtaposed with "look at me mom" in the water—need for audience to prove to myself that I exist! "Look look over here" see me go to bed DRUNK and crying. SEE me weep for all HUMANITY.

From November 28, 1980, until February 8, 1981, the Wooster Group performed Point Judith (An Epilog) *at the Performing Garage.*

DECEMBER 7, 1980

Old Sunday, down day. Always miss Liz on Sundays and can't get around it. Renée and I go out to Market Diner and talk of Liz and what to do. She says I am still involved and she is right. I suggest that Liz and I go into therapy. Renée says you only do that when you want to get back together again. She says I have to propose that to Liz or break it off. I feel that it does not have to be so black and white. Liz and I are who we are and we are different. My biggest fear is that Renée will soon demand that I live with her and I don't know what I will do in that case because I don't want to leave the loft and I know she won't move in with me which I could swing if I had a studio and moving in would soon mean children. [Gray and Shafransky would discuss moving in together for several years before actually doing it.]

DECEMBER 8, 1980

Around midnight, just as I was grinding down to Wallace Stevens, Renée called to tell me that John Lennon had been shot and killed.

I was surprised she was not more upset. I did not know how to talk about it and I heard Liz in the bathroom and said hold it and opened the door a crack to tell her and it was like I had hit her with Robert Kennedy again. She looked incredulous (later in front of the TV with Willem she cried) but Renée got so upset that I reported it to Liz that she hung up on me which brings me to think Renée and I are almost through. She cannot accept the friendship I have with Liz. I had just had a long talk with Ken about that and how I didn't know how to go on with R. NO SLEEP. NIGHTMARES OF BEING STABBED.

DECEMBER 21, 1980

Gram [Gray] died last night at 12, full moon. A bleak cold and depressed Sunday. How do I get out from under these sad Sundays? They come each week and this one seems worse and is worse because of Christmas and Gram's death. Renée and I came over to the loft so I could catch up on my diary then went out for a walk on the lower east side. Dad had called me to tell me that Gram died and would understand if I did not come up. I got all confused and Renée cried all mixed up. I'm sure her tears were also much about my not coming to her Christmas party and oh the day got worse. We went to bed. She slept some and I read "The Waves" and then it was time for Pt. Judith which went very well. A big house and they loved it.

DECEMBER 30, 1980

Up at Renée's and off quick to meet Rock [Rockwell, Gray's older brother] at Cupping Room [restaurant in SoHo]. I slept late because of anxiety insomnia, fears of death and no money, wondering what to do for Poetry project. Rocky and I had a nice breakfast at Cupping Room. We shared a vegetable omelet then I went off to buy the *New York Times* with big headliner "Spalding Gray's Pt. Judith" which was an inflation to my ego but Liz burst into tears when she saw it and cried for a long time as Willem and I sat on either side of her. *[The review, by Mel Gussow, mentioned that LeCompte directed the play and then criticized the production but praised Gray for his "comic equilibrium" and his "intuitive style of storytelling and play-acting."]* Willem took her in his arms and said stop freaking out. She said it was like losing a child that she could have had TWO children and she did this work instead and now it was gone and I had received all the credit. I felt sick for her and very sad and depressed for the rest of the day.

DECEMBER 31, 1980

Woke late at Renée's, called Rocky, made love with Renée, went off to meet Rocky at Cupping Room for vegetable omelet then went out to get Voice for [Michael] Feingold review which was OK. Well written, at least. No one else around the Garage except for Meghan would read it as a sort of boycott to all the attention I've been getting. My back is still bad so I took a bath and did some work on the ball and then over to do Pt. Judith for an uptight intellectual New York Times audience, one of the worst we've played for. It reminded me of Amsterdam, no response. All that energy going backwards.

JANUARY 1, 1981

Thursday

Renée came over in a good mood. She is going to do loft cleaning to supplement unemployment. I took her out to eat at Eva's [restaurant]. And then we rushed over to the Poetry Project [an institution that has presented readings at St. Mark's Church-in-the-Bowery in Manhattan since 1966]. It was snowing and very beautiful but I could not enjoy it because too nervous. We got seats. The place was packed. As I began to hear all those poets do their stuff I began to think I should tell a story instead of reading. Then slowly I began to realize that Allen G. [Ginsberg] and the whole mob was there. I began to lose my identity. It was like a nightmare. When my turn came I got up to do a short thing on the death of Gram Gray but I was not centered nor was the room. I felt bad after. Renée said I was only half there. I'm afraid that I have gotten lost in the FAME DRUG, the need to be instantly GREAT without working at it. Back at Renée's we talked heavy stuff about me going away to Europe and how she could not wait. FOR ME.

JANUARY 12, 1981

Monday

When I think of that Doris Lessing idea that we've all been put on earth as an experiment makes me feel weird and ashamed. Everything becomes flat like a bad joke. Even the sea feels like a foolish puddle.

JANUARY 19, 1981

Monday

I went in to see Liz who was talking to Libby about some private matter and ended up getting the riot act read at me from both of them—how selfish I was and they only kept me around the Garage because of my talent so I got all dry mouthed and defensive and then just gave up and admitted yes I was selfish and self concerned. Ah, but I hate that word "selfish."

JANUARY 24, 1981

Saturday

Worked on one short section about masturbation in my book and then Willem came in acting like a little kid sort of embarrassed because Bob Holman [*a poet who curated a reading series at the Poetry Project*] had demanded to see the porn film. [*LeCompte shot a pornographic film in 1980 with Dafoe and other members of the Wooster Group to include in their play* Route 1 & 9. *The controversial piece combined excerpts of Thornton Wilder's* Our Town *with snippets of the porn film; the actors also performed in blackface, prompting many critics to condemn the play as racist.*] Then Willem told me a long dream he had had, sat on the edge of my bed like a little kid. For the first time in a long time I felt like a father to him because he was trusting me with all this personal material and I felt both flattered and a little uneasy. The dream was long and I only remember the image of him giving life to a male bust, a statue that he touched and it came to life in his hands.

FEBRUARY 6, 1981

Friday

Unemployment then rush here and there and up to Lincoln Center to see video of Rumstick with Dan and Morgan. Just before it goes on, Morgan tells me that his mother is suddenly dying of cancer and he has to go down to Baltimore. This puts an extra heavy feeling on Rumstick. I keep crying as I watch it. It's very strong but I know I am also sad that the video in no way captures the potential power of the piece. I have many sad feelings and ended up going out after with Dan and Morgan and I talk about the car keys and feel an old unanswered guilt come up. Why? When mom said to me that she wanted to do it with the car. Why didn't I hide the keys or tell Dad. Was I just so passive or did I think it would be better if she did it. This was a new and strong guilt that I had never realized was working there so strong before.

FEBRUARY 7, 1981

Saturday

I told Renée how Philip made my heart beat fast. She said she felt that for me when she first met me. Have I ever felt that for a woman like when I thought my heart would burst in Amsterdam for "love" of Philip? I tell Renée that I am worried about her growing old. I am attracted to the 10 year old in her.

MARCH 2, 1981

Monday

I have so much resistance to packing up and getting on the road again. There is part of me that would just like to settle down and write that book. Just get down to the material, to take a place on Staten Island and just write. I think I will try to do that next spring.

Gray traveled to Amsterdam once again in March to perform Nobody Wanted to Sit Behind a Desk, *a new monologue primarily about his cross-country travel with Shafransky, as well as* Booze, Cars, and College Girls. *This trip also marked his first performance of* Interviewing the Audience.

While in Amsterdam, Gray wrote "Seven Scenes from a Family Album," a thirty-page chapbook comprising seven very short fictions about a middle-class suburban family, which was released by Benzene Editions, a small independent New York City publishing house, in 1981. This is by far the darkest of all of his work—the stories include the rape and killing of a young boy as well as scenes of grim magical realism, such as one with a father taking a large bite of his son's body. Throughout, the language is rhythmic, playful, and sinister, with details from Gray's real life smuggled in. (Like Gray's mother and father, for example, the fictional parents were married on Halloween.)

APRIL 8, 1981

[Shafransky met Gray in Amsterdam, and they traveled together abroad]

Wednesday

It was strange to see Renée. I got freaked out about money when she said the train cost $50.00. On the boat we talked a lot, got caught up on New York, nothing much new. I babbled a lot to Renée. Was confused to see her. (Who was I or to me who). All the money! So expensive here! Renée has a bad cold. We make love and then I gush with confession babble about Aggie *[a woman Gray had an affair with in Amsterdam]*. Renée says sleeping with her was hostile act. Maybe it was. I don't know. Renée also says I look tired. I use her as my traveling analyst. We talk to 12:30 then have another fuck. It feels good. She says I get my money's worth at $50.00 a fuck. I laugh and think is that what she is to me? My whore. I talk a lot about my future. How I do not want to do another autobiographic piece. Will work with children for a bit. Maybe do some acting. Sleep at last.

APRIL 14, 1981

Tuesday

In bed late everyday, why-get-up-feeling roll around, make love. Slow mixed day. We get a late start and drive down the coast road in the opposite direction of Sligo. Very beautiful. Some sun. Small towns but I am beginning to get bored and feel a real need to get down to work which is what? I'm not writing. Just mulling over things in my mind. I do not miss THE GROUP. I miss Liz and Philip. I miss being the center of that group, old group family atmosphere. Here it is beautiful and a welcome time to unwind. We shop for food and I fixed up the lamb stew. We eat and Renée reads to me from "The Mandarins" by [Simone] de Beauvoir. I am also skimming through [Henry James's] "The Beast in the Jungle." The old egotist who could not love until it was too late. Liz speaks to me from the past in this story.

APRIL 19, 1981

Sunday

I woke fighting off my depression by acting like a spoiled kid which finally got Renée angry. I said something to the effect that I hoped all was well between Willem and Liz and R. said, "And if it isn't what does that have to do with you?" And I admitted that I might be drawn back. Old passive fear. At last Renée said and I felt she was right. I am a masochist to the extent that I mainly feel and express and identify with negative emotions. I would always drive Liz to a painful state before I could feel deep feelings for her. After breakfast we went for a walk on the beach and Renée suggested that if I do want to see a psychiatrist I should try [Paul] Pavel because she has heard nothing but good reports about him. I have decided to call him as soon as I get back to the city. It is being out and distant from it all that has made me realize that I must make a plan of action and try to follow it for the next year or so. Writing, work with children, the film and maybe some theatre work. We walked back and made love out in the garden in the sun. It felt good but ended fast, me coming as I looked up at the clouds. Yes, the spiritual aspect is missing with Renée. I had it with Liz in the WORK. That work was like our religion together. The spiritual aspect is very important for me. Renée says my HEART is elsewhere and not with her. With her

I am heartless. "Where is my heart?" I ask her. She says it is with my mother. I feel she is right.

The thought that my heart is with my mother makes me embarrassed and afraid. Also one reason for therapy is to get to the point where I can take responsibility for how I acted toward Liz. To cop to the fact that my behavior was real. That I did what I did for whatever reason. Renée says that my conflict comes between not being able to choose between a world of fantasy and a world of reality. She is right. She also says my world of fantasy is destructive because I have mainly destructive fantasy, i.e.: the corruption of innocence. I want to corrupt the child (in me, outside of me, in Liz, in her). The only time these fantasies became creative are in The WORK whatever that work may be.

APRIL 23, 1981

Thursday

I met Renée at the Dove. Beautiful pub on Thames. She talked about staying in the city for the summer and I said I would not. I shocked myself saying that. What did that mean? I was as much as deserting her and yet I know I wanted to do what I wanted to do. It was all coming back to the reason I left Liz, that willfulness and after a hard day it came up at dinner again and we almost split up. I said that I have never been able to dump all my emotions into a relationship (? perhaps early on with Liz I did?) and that she had the wrong man if she wanted to be a future oriented couple. I felt quite clear but also quite DRUNK.

APRIL 24, 1981

Friday

We both woke horny at six o'clock. I did it with my earplugs in. A way I like very much but after all that happened and was said last night—sex again. This false break-up only seems to increase the appetite. We ate breakfast and were off in a cab to Victoria Station. Renée asked me if all I said was true and pointed out that it was up to me as well to leave if I felt I was hurting her. She cried. She smiled. We said goodbye at the doorway of the train and I was off for a wonderful trip to Dover.

APRIL 25, 1981

Saturday

I got back to the hotel and saw the fun passports of Ken, Jim, Willem and Liz. What a strange way to see them first. Not knowing who was coming and to have such a pleasant surprise. I said something about Liz looking angry and then we all came together in my room (over Irish whiskey) for fast stories and gossip. It was strange to see Liz again. I realized that much of my missing her was in my memory of our past together. The PRESENT has changed and Willem is very much there (here) for her in a different way than I ever was.

JUNE 5, 1981

[Gray's fortieth birthday; back in New York]

Friday

Renée let me have a birthday fuck. I knew she wasn't into it but she let me do it to her. Like all those times with Liz when I would try to force it. It gets like a diet or athletics. A kind of escape.

JUNE 11, 1981

Thursday

Renée is not sure if I am the right one for her. She does not want to get too close. Get hurt. She knows that she wants to have a career and children. Maybe I am not the right one. I lay still and listened. She took off about 2:30 and I went into a semi-relaxed sleep. Relaxed for the first time in a long time. I was very nervous about seeing Pavel *[for Gray's first session]*. Started to cry when I saw Central Park. Long good session 9:15 to 11:00. I shall TRY it.

JUNE 27, 1981

Saturday

Renée said that she felt I had a real attraction to WASP women but could not deal with them on any sexual level. I also talked about going to bed with Bill in Athens and Renée got real scared that I might in fact be gay but I still don't think I am. At least I've never met a man I thought I could love in any whole way. It was a beautiful day, sunny day, so we spent a good part of it on the roof and then went for a drive. I discovered what that sound was on the tires and fixed it. It was nice. I felt like a real man just doing the work of changing the tires. It felt very good to do that simple task and I was reminded how good it felt to be out in the real world.

JULY 1, 1981

Wednesday

Pavel wants to know why I have to put myself down so and can't just go ahead and make good work and be a seducer without worrying about it. Says that the actor who plays Christ does not have to drive the nail through his hand.

AUGUST 16, 1981

[At his brother Channing's house in Providence, Rhode Island]

Sunday

Woke on futon Jap bed Chan's floor. Anxiety about my death. How I would die forever, no meaning. To escape that thought I began to count how many beds I'd slept in since March first. Over 40. Was amazed. Thought of a piece. 45 BEDS. Names on cards like "Personal History." I got excited. It felt right. I'll do it I thought.

AUGUST 18, 1981

Tuesday

Ron *[Vawter]* called to tell me that Liz's father had died at 10:30 last night. After I hung up the phone I sat down and cried. Lonely out of it feeling. I thought I had more feeling for Frank *[LeCompte's father]* than for my own father then realized how feelings came out during and after death. Somewhere deep in me I know that the real project would be to get my feeling going in the present. This could be a greater task than making a work of art even. But writing and acting could be in the present as well. I spent some time on the roof working on "47 Beds." Late dinner alone and met Renée at New Morning [a bookstore in SoHo]. She was upset. "47 Beds" would be a HUMILIATION for her.

47 Beds *became Gray's next monologue; it opened at the Performing Garage in November 1981. In it, he told the story of his one-night stand with a man in Greece while he was seeing Shafransky. "The next thing I knew I was in bed with him and so surprised because he was warm, his skin was soft like a woman's, his body had contours," Gray decribed it in his monologue. "At first I put my arms around him, but I couldn't deal with that at all and I just went right down on him. I kept thinking over and over: I am a homosexual, I am a homosexual, I am a homosexual. . . . Then this mad raving passion burst like a bubble, and I found that I was choking on what felt like a disconnected piece of rubber hose." Shafransky may also have found the monologue a "humiliation" because Gray spoke of looking for "romantic love" among the women on the nude beaches in Greece.*

AUGUST 20, 1981

Thursday

Up at 7:15 with a hangover and made love to Renée but could not get real hard and my cock felt numb because I kept thinking about Frank's death, old age and the coming funeral. I fucked her like a (god) dog and when I came, I felt it deep in my spine but my head did not empty out. I then realized that when sex was good with her it was very good because it was like emptying out my whole body and head as well. Kate, Ken, Ron and I drove out for the funeral. The wind blew the oak trees. We went to the grave sight. After reading from the bible the service ended. Some of us stuck around to see the coffin slam shut in the concrete marble.

Friday

Renée told me the heavy news. Her gynecologist told her that she should have a baby within the next three years because she might have to have a hysterectomy. When she told me this I felt a rush of excitement then I felt exhausted and had to lie down. She was not all that upset. She was glad to know the truth. She needs to get her life together. She wants everything (her friend Kit has cancer of the cervix and needs to be operated on). Renée is giving me the best years of her life. Do I want a baby? It would be fun for a while but the thought of it going on forever makes me exhausted. We tried to have sex together but I was almost impotent looking over at the sad light on my grandmother's furniture. The real hard world. Am I weak that I cannot cope with reality?

SEPTEMBER 5, 1981

Saturday

I called Ken to ask for a walk. We met in Washington Sq. The Park was a mad place with six kinds of music, all happening real loud. Ken and I went through the old issues. I told him about Renée needing to have a child within the next three years. He said take it easy, you have time to make up your mind. I talked about leaving the city and how I was thinking of applying to Berkeley for the child psychology program but I have this feeling I could not go back to school for five years and write all those papers when I'm trying to write a whole other style. Renée said if you are really interested why not go to school here? Renée and I had a nice wok dinner at the loft and I played tapes of what I wrote today. I agree with her that the writing is too dramatic and way over done. The images need to be cut down and simplified. I am so impatient that I can't wait and want to work all the time. It's hard for me to stay away from my desk when I am in the loft. I keep going back and changing stuff. I want to somehow make the pages live. I keep trying to breathe life into the page and it comes out like a dead thing. We went to bed early.

SEPTEMBER 12, 1981

Saturday

But I don't function well under pressure and the new one is that if I am to stay with Renée I need to give her a child. So, now I wake up thinking about that instead of death. Renée was so distracted from a new job offer that she could not come so she blew me and I came with the fantasy that I was a German WWII army officer and she was a 12 year old Jew. She asked me how I could still have sex if I was so upset about a baby? Well babies don't come from swallowing sperm and what a fantasy. When Renée came over at 6:30 I was still writing. We made love, showered, sat around and talked while I drink two martinis and told Renée of my idea for making a book about men who have had children.

SEPTEMBER 30, 1981

Wednesday

I was tired and unfocused with Pavel. We talked about my fear of strong women, about the ten-year-old in me, about having babies and growing up, about "Why Renée?" out of all women in the world. About how love is commitment. He asked me if I was building a house on a hill in the Catskills would I look over at another hill? Yes, always.

OCTOBER 5, 1981

Monday

Rushed to class at N.Y.U. [Gray had begun teaching a class in the Experimental Theatre Wing of New York University.] Had them walk around the block twice and report what they saw. Slowly it dawned on me that they saw what I saw and that we are all alike and that I've had some investment in being special and now I have to face the fear and realization that I am basically like all the rest; a lost confused human being and that my years working with Liz kept me feeling special. This feeling was even more enforced when they read their autobiographies because some of them were well done and made me realize that everyone had a life and could put it down on paper as well as I could. This left me quite depressed and on the way back to the loft I ran into Liz and walked with her. She told me she is quite sure she is pregnant and is going to have the baby. This colored the rest of my day and made me scattered and depressed.

OCTOBER 14, 1981

Wednesday

Everything is a rush and a blur. I feel descended upon. My knee hurts, my elbow hurts. I know now that I will—that I am growing old. What kind of subconscious fantasy did I have all those years holding on to the protected idea that I would stay young forever? Was it the group, was it Liz or perhaps just me in the way that I used Liz. In the way that I used the group. And it's an old story now and I have to face it. My constant fear of death. My wanting to hold things still so I can look at them forever. Not to be a part of this body that is growing old but somewhere in me seeking eternal life. The obsession with film being the immortalizing of an image. Going to Pavel and him blowing my mind telling me that he was a swinger and went to orgies with his wife. Somewhere along the line I did equate sex with death and still do and when he asks me to associate about why I can only feel and come by seeing my cock go in and out, I can't think of anything to say except that it makes me feel powerful. Wanting to overcome death. Suicide is power over death in that you do it.

OCTOBER 21, 1981

Wednesday

It must be some kind of Indian summer because we have had a long period of warm days. So what? Skip to Pavel. His wife is young and good looking. The apartment smelled of marijuana. Penthouse and Playboy were out for reading. I was titillated by it all. We talked about my father as a passive aggressive. How he would not respond to my mother's anger or to our anger. I told Pavel that I felt he was guiding me to settle down. He told me that was what he felt I was saying I wanted, I felt I had nothing more to say to him. I said it was all like looking for needles in a haystack. He said I knew what the needles were.

NOVEMBER 13, 1981

Friday

I feel like I cannot rest, or be at peace anymore and I often think it's because I am not with Liz. I think I'm also nervous about my reading and "47 Beds" which Renée is all upset about because her friends keep coming on her and asking her what she thinks of me doing this and she gets very defensive and I got angry with her asking her why she felt she had to defend herself or me. It made me want to go ahead with the piece all the more but I do feel more nervous than usual about expressing myself.

NOVEMBER 27, 1981

Friday

I had a good size house for 47 Beds and I was able to really go with it. I pulled out all the stops and DID IT!

DECEMBER 1, 1981

Tuesday

I'm not sure what set it off but I finished the scotch, had two beers and then had wine with dinner then had two beers at Renée's so was far gone by the time I hit the bed. Renée says it's a dependency and that I ought to look at it as a project to try to stop drinking for a while to see what is coming up. When I stopped drinking with Liz I had the affair with Sarah. Also, I had that anxiety panic insomnia where I woke up near dawn and could not get back to sleep again. It is so hard for me just to do something for myself like stopping the drinking that does not feed directly into my work. It seems that I need an audience all the time. That's a lot of why I can't get down to the writing. I have a great fear of getting well and normal lest I disappear. Become a grey washout. But I've got to give it a try.

DECEMBER 2, 1981

Wednesday

At therapy, I asked Pavel why he never had children. He told me the story of how he was shot in the groin and was given up for dead for two days until the Russian troops found him. Perhaps he was one out of five that lived from a death march of 20,000. As he told it I could see it like a vivid film in my head. Who needs movies with such stories? How he was wandering in the woods, escaped from his group and was herded into another group only to be shot. All chance and luck. A ¼-inch difference and the bullet would have hit an artery. I felt I had little to say after that and that I felt in competition with his experience. He asked me if I thought suffering ennobled and I said yes. It's a silly idea he said. He was already set before he went through all this.

DECEMBER 9, 1981

Wednesday

The only review [of 47 Beds] that came out was John Howell's in *The SoHo* [Weekly News] and that was good. I get so angry with *The Voice* that I called Erika [*Munk, a theater critic at* The Village Voice] and she said it was short and would be coming out next week. I don't know what happened to *The Times*. Spent much of the day over at the Garage. At last we had a run through of Joan's piece at 4:00. It was rather ragged but I can't think about it and I do know in spite of what Renée says that good art can't be made without a certain amount of tension and bad feelings. It just happens that way. It was strange and interesting being in her piece. At times I was in it and at times not because I knew Liz was outside watching it and that often took me out. I did not have the blessings of the MOTHER but I was on all the time and was able to improvise through with a broken prop. Cab to Pavel and as fast as I told my problems to him, I felt like my life was a stupid soap opera and I had to get through that. Problems with Renée. She wants time off.

DECEMBER 12, 1981

Saturday

The Times review came out and it was good. *[Mel Gussow described Gray as a "sit-down monologuist with the comic sensibility of a stand-up comedian."]* It's strange because all this personal success makes me feel more lonely and isolated. I'm getting large audiences but I miss the group warm ups and got back a little to that warming up with Joan. After my show I saw Willem and Liz came downstairs and Liz did not even look in to say hello. She looked to be in one of her angry fits which made me afraid and paranoid. What is she angry about now I wondered. Renée and I went back to my place and I read the Times review over and over. Yes I do exist.

DECEMBER 31, 1981

Thursday

Up at Renée's. Breakfast with her and Arthur *[Shafransky's brother]* then off for a not very productive day, still feel the sluggish Holidays upon me. Did a lot of agonizing about the house. Had a few drinks and at last called Barbara *[the real estate agent Gray worked with to find a house in upstate New York—she is mentioned in the beginning of his later monologue* Terrors of Pleasure, *about the crumbling house he eventually bought in the Catskills region of New York]*. She said if I wanted to offer $30,000 in cash that I would have to send a three hundred dollar deposit. We took a cab down to Camilla's* New Year's party. She was in good spirits and seems to have her life together. A big crowd. Nice food and lots of Champagne. A nice blue fish pâté. Liz and Renée talked some which I was happy to see. Liz looked quite elegant and Willem paid a lot of attention to her which was nice to see. Ken was not in a good mood. Renée and I walked home in the rain to my place.

JANUARY 26, 1982

Woke early from many dreams perhaps set off by the smell of Renée's bed. All the sweat, piss and come odors that have built up. I get horny just thinking about it but there were dreams of being by the sea and Renée and I had a child that looked like me and I thought for a moment I had lost the child to the sea and was running as fast as I could to find him alright and smiling. Also that I was given a big dinner in honor of me and Ping Chong *[avant-garde theater director]* and Yvonne Rainer. I was served a foreskin cake.

JANUARY 28, 1982

Got out my book and looked at all I have written. I feel now too paralyzed by the idea that I have to write a whole coherent novel. Who am I writing it for? For History? Who am I trying to please? I'm thinking now of doing a series of autobiographic fragments. Psychoanalytic fragments. Where I take the writings that I like and just print them up? Perhaps use "Sex and Death" as a structure. I'm all mixed up but I think it's good.

JANUARY 29, 1982

Renée and I got into a big heavy discussion about us breaking up because we have been fighting so much. She said I was CONFESSIONAL but not HONEST.

FEBRUARY 8, 1982

I met Renée in Phoebe's *[a bar in the East Village]* and she said she had to talk about moving into the loft, I said, please another time so she went ahead and she has really gotten what I call pushy—PUSH PUSH. She says she won't move in without a plumber and bathroom and she has found a plumber. She wants the space absolutely separate or she won't move in. *[Gray and LeCompte, after dividing the loft, continued to share a bathroom.]* I could not believe her brass. She said goodbye Spalding. It's been nice knowing you.

FEBRUARY 9, 1982

I know that I am not facing head on that Renée and I may have in real fact, broken up. Made a simple vegetable soup and settled in for what I thought would be a very depressing evening because I knew I could not stop thinking about Renée and what to do. Well, it was up and down. I was reading the authority book and got the impulse to write—to do the work—to go over what had been written and work on that. I worked until ten o'clock and then went out to buy three beers. Took a bath and got a little drunk on ice and whisky. Laid on the couch and regressed with the Walkman. CRIED AND CRIED ABOUT WHAT?

FEBRUARY 15, 1982

A combination of feeling very depressed and very hopeful at the same time. Everyday seems like a new beginning. Renée and I went for a slow walk together. It was like a spring day. We talked for a long time and I can't remember specifics but that these conditions in which, in the face of I feel paralyzed all foggy and ready to say—anything you want dear—or—if you say so. It feels like I have no mind of my own. It is like a muscle that has atrophied and she keeps telling me that I might rather be with a passive woman. We went back to her place and after much discussion we ended up going to bed together which felt real good for both of us.

FEBRUARY 16, 1982

Renée called all positive because she had a good session with Frank [*Shafransky's therapist*] and he said that he would see us together but that I should speak to Pavel first. Renée and I went out for drink. I could feel the flu coming on. A hyper tenderness in my skin. I walked Renée most of the way to her place and then went home alone. It was a nice date. She looked beautiful.

MARCH 30, 1982

Around 5, I heard Liz and Willem come in from Amsterdam and I got very excited. In fact I had not been able to rest after I found out they were coming back. I got right up to go in and welcome them back and Liz looked and said that Willem told her not to let me or invite me in. Liz came into the center alcove to talk with me and then Willem and Kate came in and he was obviously upset. I went off feeling like a rejected child started to cry and then decided not to indulge myself or let Renée know (save it for therapy). Pavel thinks I had to leave Liz because I had to find out about being a "grown up." He says that I am in a constant conflict between being a child and an adult. This both wears me down and gives me fuel for my work. When Liz could keep that conflict in "the work" it worked but not when it got outside, it overturned the balance. Stayed at Renée's and had a good night. Talked some things out.

APRIL 1, 1982

We got on the road early. It was a good bright sunny trip up but the car began to stall out again. We were at the house a little after noon. I liked the people we were renting from and I loved the house that was for rent. [Gray and Shafransky rented a cabin in Krumville, New York, from the novelist Francine Prose and her husband, the artist Howie Michels, who lived in the main house on the same property.] My fantasy of a summer house. The old original house on the property built in the 1700's. Renée got them down to $300.00 a month and I was happy.

APRIL 5, 1982

I cleaned up a bit and got a laundry done. Set up for copying my tapes and then had the last of the whiskey and headed out for the decadent uptown George Plimpton party where I didn't care to speak to anyone there. It looked like a giant Updike book. Knew if I stayed I'd just get smacked so I put down my scotch and headed out. And like when I stole all those glasses from my one debutante ball, I took a whole pile of wooden hangers on the way out. Took a cab over to the anti-nuclear rally at Symphony Space but the place was mobbed and I had given up all chance of getting in when I saw Renée up by the door and she said they had my name on a list so I was let in and also let in about six groupies with me. It was long and strange. A lot of flashing egos. I didn't get up to do a testimony because I felt I was too locked into my ego and was doing it to be seen. It felt like a big end of the world scene. I had such perverse mixed feelings about it all. My old stubbornness of resisting all movements coupled with a solid distrust of the performers ego. Back to Renée's at 2:30. She says I've gotten more negative over the past months. She wants to get married. She doesn't want to make love. I get angry and withholding. Help!

MAY 4, 1982

Ken and I took a long walk over to the river to watch the sun go down. Talk about Liz and how Ken sees her baby as a group baby and she is having it for the group. Also about how he can't stand the thought of how a woman's body is torn apart by having a child and how it never comes back to shape again. Talked about the fantasy around the woman and boy I saw on Sunday (at Pavel's)—how I had masturbated in the mirror after that. We talked it through for a bit and he sees it this way: Mom was openly seductive with me (in the tub and elsewhere). I could not deal with it so I turned it all back on my own body and there it got stuck. And I now make some area of womans bodies taboo (Liz = BREASTS, Renée = thighs). I accused Pavel of trying to make me into a family man and said he thought I was longing for that and that if I had a child I could manage some out of transference because it's the child I long to be.

MAY 20, 1982

We slept so late and then I had to work on "47 Beds." I find I don't enjoy working over the monologues in print because they are not writing but rather a reproduction of speech. I look forward to getting back to my book and feel very frustrated about being cut off from it. Spent the whole day in and was happy to have the Garage to go to at night. It is a wonderful physical outlet. Nayatt went well for me even though there were a number of technical slip ups but it was a full house, the audience seemed to eat it up. *[Gray reprised* Nayatt School *at the Performing Garage from May 6 through 23.]* We got two solid curtain calls. After the show Ken, Renée, Stokes *[Howell, writer and longtime friend of Gray's]* and I came across to my place and drank beer together. Got exhausted from the beer, the show and the hot weather and the fact that Dusty Hoffman is getting 4.5 million for his next movie.

MAY 31, 1982

I secretly see myself as a novelist but Liz is right when she says that I am missing the empathy to develop characters outside of myself. I think she's right. The characters come out as symbols—flat and intellectual. I am better at researching the actual details of what happened.

JUNE 9, 1982

Heard that Liz had gone into the hospital. No one called me about Liz so I called Jeff and he gave me the report. "A boy." 8 pounds. Red hair. At first I thought I should rush up there. Then I felt like crying but I didn't. Sick of feeling sorry for myself. Decided to wait until next day. Didn't want to be with the adoring group.

JUNE 10, 1982

At Renée's and off to a busy day of visit to the hospital to see Liz, Willem and the new baby. The baby looked good and healthy. The doctor even said it was a beautiful child. Liz was in a lot of pain because she was having contractions during the breastfeeding and this gave her pain because of the stitches. Then off to Pavel where we had our last session before September. He said I understood all that had to be done but that I just needed to develop the faith that I could do it. He thought it would take about another year.

SEPTEMBER 4, 1982

Willem invited Renée and I to dinner. I saw it as a great excuse to escape. I rushed out and bought wine and vodka. Maybe I should try to live as though the world was going to go on forever. Renée and I went to see [Richard Pearce's] "Heartland" but they would not cash my traveler's check and the line was so long I didn't want to go. I hate all those people except when they come to see me. We came back to my loft and I drank three beers. I was so keyed up from strong coffee that I could not sleep. There was no toilet paper so I could not plug my ears. I woke up at night to the sound of someone throwing up. I thought I was at Renée's. It made me think of those fat pigs I saw on the street. The fat man and woman and how she threw up right in front of us.

The world is horrid, barren and full of pigs. Hardly any people left. Our neighborhood is turning into a ZOO. The PUNKS are taking over and DEATH is coming again into power. All people witness as much of death as they do of life before they die. I think life is just a big party and nothing more.

SEPTEMBER 8, 1982

Bottled up and could not speak. I stood there like a statue in the rain. I had the feeling that if she moved in we would soon have a child and I would be stuck in a reality I had no control over. I told her that I needed time to think. She told me that if she lived with me she would not have to take a job she did not want. The thought of opening up my private space was a sad thought. The rain came down and she yelled and cried. At last we went into Spring Street Natural to get free food from Halle [a friend of Shafransky's]. All the beautiful waitresses existed like eternal responsibilities. We got soaked going back to my place. What a downpour. I took a bath. I got angry with her. I know I love her. I know I am not in doubt about that. At last she began to cry like a little ten-year-old. She said, "I want to go home" and then I felt deeply for her and held her in a loving way. It was that phrase—"I want to go home." I felt it too. I want a home. We both want a home. I can't deny it. Such a longing for that HOME. A place that was not a work factory but a home. It was a very sad, sad moment. I think it was very real.

SEPTEMBER 12, 1982

[Staying at Edward F. Albee Foundation—a residency for writers, visual artists, and composers—in Montauk, Long Island]

Renée and I woke at the Albee foundation. Not a very sexy place. We had a nice breakfast with some of the people here and then headed off to the beach. It was very hazy and warm. I went for a walk and stood on a cliff to wave back at Renée. As I raised my arms a big fog rolled in and covered it all up. The houses and Renée. It felt like a great magic act. We went for a walk along the beach and when we came back I went in and rode the waves and also taught a boy (about 15) how to ride them. I felt good when he was able to catch a few. When I told Renée about it she lightly accused me of lust and I got upset and told her that on one level it was always there but that it was coming from a different source this time = father and teacher who also had some attraction to the boy. We drove to look at the fishing boats. We had a fish sandwich lunch which I paid for and then looked for Tony's two tone blue boat.

SEPTEMBER 16, 1982

Up with no hangover. Guess I'm drinking just the right amount. A good work day. Did about 18 handwritten pages until the pen felt like it was pressing on bone and a big water blister grew. Worked on the Masturbation scene fast and furious then just put it away. *[Gray was still working on* The Father of Myself *at this point.]* I have no idea what it reads like. Went to the beach and took a long walk. Saw all women I had known and loved come at me in my imagination along the sand at the water edge where the big waves left foamy fans and just before getting the car I decided to go in for a swim. With some fat guy rode the waves and they pounded me down and spun me around and rolled me like a ball and like a kid again in the ocean. I was out of control. They say the waves are caused by a Hurricane off Bermuda. Went for a long run after getting back to the house and then a phone call from Renée telling me how much she missed me. Made me feel a little guilty.

OCTOBER 14, 1982

[Back in New York]

Woke up and made love and by the time we got it all together it was almost time for me to rush out and up to meet *[the film director]* Milos Forman who I liked a lot. I think because he reminded me a lot of Pavel and I didn't realize that Milos was also from Prague but I felt like I hit it off with him. I may be mistaken but once I got my elbows on his desk I felt like I had hit it and arrived. He smiled and I smiled back but on my way to the park to eat my lunch in the beautiful sun I thought I must be careful not to be taken in. Came back to the Garage and went for dinner at Eva's. I ran into Renée and we went together and I was surprised to find that I enjoyed the whole brief evening but it did kind of twist my head around in a delightful way.

OCTOBER 25, 1982

Woke to shocking reality and made love again and then had to face the reality of day and how Renée has planned for me to go to Frank with her and as I look around me and feel reality of being back rush in on me I panic and try to hold it back as it comes in on me like an ocean wave. I don't know how I can cope. It's an effort for me just to clean up or to put one dish away. A part of me wants to let it all go and just dive deep into the whirlpool of escapism. Had a long visit with Liz and Jack *[Dafoe and LeCompte's four-month-old baby]* who is getting real cute. I met Renée later to go to Frank's. He's an interesting old man and I did take to him. He pointed out that I don't tend to build boundaries or to make judgments on myself and others and that maybe I wanted to keep it that way and I said something about if only I was aware of choice. Perhaps I do those things and I'm not aware of it. I'm not sure what we came to except perhaps I would come back again but felt I had to discuss it with Pavel.

OCTOBER 27, 1982

Went off to Pavel to present my case and basically it's the old story about boundaries and how I'm afraid to be devoured because I want to be devoured. He called me an excitement junkie and said that I'd be over that in five years or so and would be left with a nice vitality.

OCTOBER 28, 1982

[From October 28 to December 19, Gray performed A Spalding Gray Retrospective *at the Performing Garage, which included eight of his monologues previously produced by the Wooster Group:* Sex and Death to the Age 14; Booze, Cars, and College Girls; India and After (America); A Personal History of the American Theater; Nobody Wanted to Sit Behind a Desk; 47 Beds; In Search of the Monkey Girl—*a piece he'd written about carnival freak shows in collaboration with the photographer Randal Levenson—and* Interviewing the Audience. *He performed a different monologue each night.]*

Another hangover and just plain nerves about opening "Sex and Death." Worked on it in the morning and talked some with Liz who was cleaning up the bathroom in preparation for a visit from Willem's parents and then went over to the Garage to check on all that seems to cry out to be taken care of. Tried to rest in the afternoon but could not really unwind. Listened to S & D [Sex and Death] tape, took more notes and then ate dinner alone. There was a good turn out for my performance and I was surprised and happy and a little thrown off. I went through it all very fast.

NOVEMBER 4, 1982

Booze Cars went all right. An audience of about 65 or 70. The weather is still very warm and humid. "Booze Cars" is still a little too linear for me in structure and I think I like the College Girls section the best. No one stuck around except that ex-student of Morgan's who I had interviewed last year. I sat around and talked with our new technician Hank Stevens and then Renée showed up and we went off to share a plate at the Bamboo Corner. We had a pleasant dinner and then came back and talked. I drank some beer while Renée fell asleep on the couch all exhausted from having taught all day at CW Post [Shafransky taught a film history course at the C. W. Post Campus of Long Island University in Brookville, New York]. We went to bed about 12:15. We're getting along better I'm sure because I've said that she could move in with me.

NOVEMBER 10, 1982

Renée, Arthur and I went up to see the Milton Avery show at the Whitney and I got let in for free because I was RECOGNIZED. Little things like that still make my day. Renée and I walked through the Park. A Silver Winter light. I went home alone to rest and on the way stopped at New Morning just to check and was surprised to find a short but good review by Robert Massa. Suddenly my depression and melancholy hangover was gone and I went and sat in a hot bath and read over it all a few times, "Gray gives almost no self analysis or self justification" and it occurred to me, while at Pavel's, that this could be developed as a style even though I was working on self-analysis with Pavel, I could keep that out of my work and develop a conscious style of writing or talking. Pavel was on to the old castration theme again. I told him I had nothing to say and then ended up talking about all these morbid images like the suicide and Gram Horton's body and the dreams of how my body was all bandaged and how I peeled them off and found my body had rotted away and I went to Dad to show him how my thigh was hollow. Pavel saw it as a castration dream and the bandages as protection.

NOVEMBER 16, 1982

Is my work no different than the *New York Post*?

NOVEMBER 28, 1982

Got up late alone and spent the morning listening to *[the WBAI talk show host]* Larry Josephson talk about me on the radio. Said that I was close to the edge of insanity when I performed. Plugged me a lot and then played about one half hour worth of "A Personal History" and ended his show with the short excerpt from "Booze Cars" which all excited me and put me way up. Went shopping and then to boring rehearsal of "Crucible." *[Gray rehearsed the role of Reverend Parris in the Wooster Group's experimental interpretation of Arthur Miller's* Crucible; *he left the play before it premiered. Miller himself came to see the play at the Performing Garage and, not happy with the production, denied the Wooster Group the right to perform it. Ultimately, the play was rewritten and renamed* L.S.D. (. . . Just the High Points . . .).*]* Then back to rest and last performance of "Personal History." A good house but very sober. After everyone left I stood in the theatre and just felt all the HISTORY of that place came down around me. But I thought how lucky we have all been to have had the Garage and how I have so often just taken it for granted.

DECEMBER 6, 1982

Liz asked me to take Jack *[now six months old]* out for a walk while they painted the upstairs for the benefit. Taking Jack for a walk was both exciting and frightening. He was like this vulnerable innocent expression of something in me and yet more. Something OTHER that I could fight to protect as I walked over to a more violent neighborhood to visit Kim, Pam, and Michael. Jack started to cry when he got in that strange place and only I was able to stop him and he fell asleep on my chest which was incredible to see that little open mouth. That little sucker and then his face. The panic when I put him down. Then back out on the street walking him. We were out about two hours.

JANUARY 8, 1983

Got a call from Bob Carroll who wanted me to meet Susie Figgis, a casting director from London. *[Figgis had heard of Gray through the screenwriter and director Peter Wollen, who was a fan of Gray's monologues.]* I wondered what was up. Most of the day was spent in rehearsal for The Crucible and then I fixed dinner for Renée. I made up my mind to dress up and go off to the Algonquin where I met Susie for drinks and a second dinner and found out that she was in fact the casting director for this film [The Killing Fields, *directed by Roland Joffé]* which is about this New York Times correspondent who had been stationed in Cambodia so it's all about the Pol Pot regime and I immediately felt that I had no feelings for it. I wasn't sure whether she was trying to seduce me but I didn't take the bait even after we ate when she said, "Now it's time for bed." I left at midnight and wandered around the porn district for an hour looking at some porn books and hanging out by more deadly games.

JANUARY 11, 1983

These rushing days. Very little time for sex or love. Up late and rush off to Warner's to meet Roland Joffé. Spring-like weather. I rode up with Arlene K. on the E. Train and talked about her property, then met Willem in the waiting room and talked briefly about Jack Frank. And then I had a long session with Jaffe in which he filled my ears with confusing stories about Cambodia and Kissinger's theories of "Spheres of Influence" in which there are no longer independent countries—just pieces on his Machiavellian chess board. I came out feeling quite exhilarated and thought that even if I didn't get in the film I would surely go to Washington to gather material for my next monologue.

JANUARY 12, 1983

Pavel says, "In what book is it written that you must be monogamous?" It's the old question of me not taking responsibility for my life (each day). It has to be done each day. He points out that I long for some ten commandments written on the wall that I must follow. He said, what kind of relationship do you have when you feel you have to cover up what you do? Then he told me about his coal mining days and how he and a friend ended up in a hospital and got initiated to sex by being sucked off by a nun.

JANUARY 21, 1983

The Crucible did not seem as good or the audience didn't seem to like it as much. I almost fell asleep during the opening. Long record. I'm drinking and eating too much at night and I'm getting fat. That's all there is to it. I'm getting soft and fat and bald.

FEBRUARY 6, 1983

Feeling depressed all day from no sleep, too much drink and marijuana. Got back in time to write in my diary and get ready to receive Renée's call. She called from school and we didn't have much to talk about. I told her I would be willing to go see Frank with her if it would help resolve something. He said he didn't know what to make of the two of us. With most couples he could offer some help but with us he was confused.

MARCH 2, 1983

I had another frantic day. [The casting director] Juliet Taylor called to tell me Roland Joffé was interested in me for his film and wondered what my schedule was like. This and too much coffee put me into one of my old panics about how the plane was going to crash or I was going to get appendicitis. But luckily I was able to get The Mass. Arts proposal written up. I ran into Pavel at West 4th Street and I had a rather manic exchange with him telling him that I was up now but was afraid of crashing once my tour ended. I told him that things were going alright with Renée.

MARCH 3, 1983

Juliet Taylor's office called again to say that Roland Joffé really wants to make sure that he gets in touch with me so I'm still excited about that but I find myself more excited about going to THAILAND than doing the movie. Renée fixed a nice calf's liver dinner for me and we went out to bed early.

MARCH 7, 1983

[Los Angeles]

Got to Warner Brothers early. Nice place. I was a little excited but not as much as I thought I'd be. Roland put me at ease because he didn't audition me. Said I'd be good for the role ____ who is the soft embassy man who turns to drink in the end. He said I'd be good for that and I agreed then we just went on to talk. He talked a lot and is really obsessing on the film. Told me all the artists, intellectuals and actors were shot in Cambodia so that he was unable to find any Cambodian actor and is thinking of casting a Cambodian doctor in the role. Also is thinking of Alan Arkin for the lead. We had a good talk. I told him of some of my work and how I was going to hitch to SAN FRAN California. Also we talked of therapy and Pavel and his therapist. I think it went well but I still doubt that anything will come of it.

MARCH 25, 1983

I find that I have a real hard time keeping up with my diary. I think it was a whole mixture of things. Much of it has to do with the fact that I have to write down all I say anyway and the other part is that I know Renée will want to know who and what I've been doing here and at one point I know she'll try to read this and so I feel very inhibited about writing.

MARCH 29, 1983

Beautiful drive to the Airport. I've never seen LA look so good. Clean bright city of crazy nonsense architecture. Money, Money. Big sad face, well and nice empty plane. Window and great view. No one next to me. Two Bloody Marys and bad Movie. A little sleep and we were in New York in no time. R. was all upset when I got in. Had typed me a long letter about how Laurie who I had slept with once was about to be programmer at the Collective. Oh boy, what a lot of stuff to come home to. It never ends. Am I bringing this all down on myself as some ongoing punishment? R. keeps saying get serious for a moment. Willem got the role in the movie and will make big bucks. We went to sleep early.

MARCH 31, 1983

I'm a little nervous about the Joffé movie. Juliet Taylor called Jeff to say it was between me and one other but that Joffé was leaning towards me so I'm just trying not to think about it. Rested at home and then fixed big feed after spending much of the afternoon shopping for it. Renée came over to my place and we ate and then took a cab up to see *[Martin Scorsese's]* The King of Comedy. A so-so film. De Niro was good but that was about all. We walked down to an Irish bar and had some Guinness and listened to some Irish music and talked.

APRIL 1, 1983

Being driven a little nuts by the feeling that Juliet Taylor called Jeff again and said "they" were still leaning toward me and would try to let me know by the end of the day but it didn't come. This led to all kinds of magical thinking—if I turn off this light will it mean etc . . . and I had a vision of Roland somewhere thinking and fluctuating with each blink of the lights. So I just walked around trying to forget it all. Did buy a Turkey to fix. R. got all excited and said she wanted to invite Halle and Harvey over for Turkey sandwiches on Sat. after three-hour movie.

APRIL 5, 1983

Jeff called and said I got the movie! Sudden fear of fame! Would I still be able to interview audience after I do movie? Coupled with great feeling of power and relief. I tried to call R. but her line was busy so I went over to the Garage and Jeff told me that the film was only paying $1,500 a week and $350 expenses so I was a little let down having had all these high money expectations but we made a call to Joanna Ross and R. called around and we found out that it was a good standard offer and to go with it so we called and said yes. Went out for a walk to air my head and buy two books. Rollo May book on anxiety and [*Walter J. Ong's*] "Orality and Literacy." Ate alone. R. all upset that I'm going away. She wants to come.

MAY 4, 1983

[On location in Bangkok, Thailand]

Oh no! I'm all mixed up one day has crossed into another. All of this day happened yesterday. My Rama Tower Hotel is big and weird. Have a back room with a giant bed up on 9th floor away from crazy streets sounds. Roland took us all out for dinner. Wonderful food and good conversation. I sat next to LENG who had been a member of the KHMER Rouge but seemed very pleasant. When I think of it I'm a little overwhelmed that I was sitting with killers and the Cambodians from Long Beach are so happy and smiling all the time. We went to three B GIRL houses, the first was the craziest. Really mad bumping and grinding and grabbing on crotches was overwhelmed by the fact that some of the girls looked twelve or thirteen. John Malkovich and his wife Glenne who I like a lot left after a brief visit and Julian [*Sands*] and Tom [*Bird*] and I headed over to another place and after a while there I headed out to be alone and ran into this youngster on the street and she was working in one of the clubs but she didn't seem to want to talk to me and got up to dance another one with pretty eyes came on to me and said she was going home with me and did giggling all the way. I can't say no. Sex had been no good for me. I couldn't let go. Somehow she got the radio to go off at six. Up with Frank Sinatra I think it was. Her singing along and asking for her 500 baht. I couldn't talk her down and didn't feel like it. Also I could not get back to sleep and had a sore throat which put me in a panic. So I got up and opened the windows because I thought the air-conditioner was doing me in, God was it hot and I started my day with a big breakfast. Tom, Ira [*Wheeler*] and I had our first rehearsal with Roland, which was weird. A lot of talking. Lunch and to bed for more sleep then off with Ira and Judy [*Moorcroft, the costume designer]* to buy shoes then back to bed for two hours and then my massage lady came and that was a full relaxing hour for 200 baht. A quick drink of whisky and met Ira for a fancy dinner in the Rotisserie and we talked about our life and how he had been married three times and was a grandfather and a retired businessman. To bed at eleven. Slept right out.

MAY 6, 1983

Rushed breakfast in order to get out to the pool at eight for group shot then back to my room and rehearsal with Roland, Sam *[Waterston]*, Ira and Julian where we did an improv and I know so little about the subject and all these political words that all I could come up with was "How can they get by on all that white rice and no greens?" And I really don't know how people took that. Roland is so serious. After the first rehearsal Ira and I went down to see videotapes for about two hours. They were very heavy particularly that Front Line reporting and the school that was hit by a Khmer Rouge rocket and all the horrid mixed up jumble of it all. Ira and I had lunch together and then I went to sleep and back at five to work with Roland and Ira and I went off with Judy again to be fitted.

MAY 7, 1983

I got a good night sleep and was up at 6:30 and out to the pool. Off to a good start. At breakfast found out that Ira had been in the Navy with Tinky *[Gray's mother's brother]* and they had also trained in New London together. Ira and I went with Susie to have lunch with Tim. Very pleasant but in some way disturbing. I think it was because he went to MIT and could speak Cambodian. Reminded me how I used to be threatened by Rocky's college friends and I think I twisted it by wondering how he could work for such a corrupt government and be so together—me still the outsider. We had a long session with him and it was hard for me to follow all the facts because my history is so vague. After Ira and I went to see the Emerald Temple. Very garish very hot I couldn't understand our guide. It was over 110°. Took a cab back and met with Roland, after talking with us awhile, he gave us a strange pep talk about how we had to give up our personal lives and dedicate ourselves to the making of this film. A bunch of us went out for dinner at the Indian place. I found out that Sam was the same age as me and had spent his summers in Matunuck, R.I. Nell *[Campbell]* the new girl from Australia drives me nuts. It's her legs.

MAY 9, 1983

Took my Malaria pill and a ROMP of a day. The set was the hospital and all these—what looked like <u>real</u> sick and <u>real</u> poor people were all lying around in these fake bloody bandages but the Khmer Rouge Army really looked savage. Particularly the little ones with their guns. I didn't stay on the set—I don't know why—but fled back to the hotel to spend time by the pool.

MAY 10, 1983

UP at 6 with a small hangover and off to the pool for a swim, then talk with Ira, John and Nell in coffee shop. Nell got wild that we were going to see the Ambassador and wanted to come along. Heavy rain on the way. Ambassador talked as though Cambodia were a SHIP he was trying to guide to the port with dignity and told a very moving story about how he cut the two flags down and carried them out over his arm. It was very hypnotic. Like a piece of theater. Still wants to convince us that all America wants is self-determination. Cambodia like a great ship he was trying to sail into port with DIGNITY. How he tried to get everyone out. Then down to visit Tim. A man into the world politic as a structure. No fear of nuclear disaster. All of them believe in Political compromise.

MAY 11, 1983

Up at 5:30 to be ready for 6:45 trip to the American Embassy set which is a school that has been converted to look just like Phnom Penh which it does. The heat was outrageous. I'm sure well over 100° all day. At last there was some shade and a little breeze but I found it impossible to even think. Just sit in the impossible heat and wait. The idea of preparing for any kind of acting was lost to me. A talk with Tom about "Search and Destroy." He told me that it was just recently that he found out that he was a decoy to bring the enemy out so that the planes could come in and destroy. Once a month they had a "mad minute" or "minute of madness" where they emptied all their M–16's into the bush. We waited all day without working and then the long drive back. Some sad homesick feeling. A lovely sunset out the rear window. Small chat with John and Sam. A bath and drink at last. Glenne called me to go out with John and her to the FRENCH PLACE.

MAY 12, 1983

Woke about 4:30 and got up at 5. I couldn't take my mornings like this. I don't know how Sam does it. (Driven?) An interesting drive out to the set but makes me want to see the countryside less and less. It's all very poor. At last I got to shoot. Doing the same small actions over and over which I liked but could not tell what my face was showing and felt a little self conscious like I could see the close-up already.

MAY 13, 1983

I just missed a call from Renée and I felt sick about that and called her back to the tune of 1,000 Baht and really nothing to say. Just panic at spending the money. I walked down to the tailors but the pants were not ready. Spent the rest of the afternoon out by the pool with two of the Cambodians Suon and Nay. Also Ira. I was happy to be around some of the Cambodians at last because I was curious. This all led to Ira and I going out with NEEVY who is very cute, Nay the ex–N.Y.C. cab driver, and the star of the movie, Haing S. Ngor who is a Cambodian gynecologist who lives in L.A. and had been tortured by the Khmer Rouge. We had a good time together laughing at the restaurant and when we asked the woman to turn off the musack she turned off the air-conditioner. We went back to the hotel bar and Sam was there. His wife had a new baby while he was here. Ira bought us drinks.

MAY 14, 1983

I found that I was very intimidated by the command of facts that Sam has. Also the fact that he went to Yale. All of that made me feel all those old inferior feeling of the past. I felt stupid and ill informed. We talked about America as a traditionally isolated country and about how El Salvador was different from Vietnam. Then we went out for a big meal with the Cambodians. It was a nice big Chinese family place and we all sat at a round table with a Lazy Susan and shared a big expensive meal. I walked back with Nell and some of the Cambodians and went to bed early. I feel like I'm getting fatter and fatter.

MAY 15, 1983

Right after breakfast I rode out to the location for the invasion of Phnom Penh. It all looked very real. There were about 3,000 Thai extras all waving white flags as the Khmer Rouge tanks rolled in through billows of the black and white smoke. The heat gets unbearable. It must have been 120° in the sun and yet Roland appeared to be calm, his ADs have to do all the yelling. The Cambodians were saddened by watching this reenactment of the invasion. Some of them had been there for it and others had just escaped four hours before. It was in fact a fearful night as I watched them run it over and over.

MAY 17, 1983

Very long and hard day. The worst yet. From 7 to 7. The Embassy in outrageous heat, I ran my scene in the office with Sam. At first I was in a real panic and Roland had to sort of calm me down. So I was a sweaty mess then _____ told us it would be another hour before set-up. It seems as much energy goes into the technical aspect as it does paying attention to what the actors are doing. I felt very shallow. Like a soap opera actor. That feeling I often have before I settle into a role. So I spent much of my time thinking about how I could have or should have said my line. Very Frustrating. In fact I hated hearing myself and seeing myself on the video. I was completely exhausted when we finished at seven but made the mistake of having too much to drink up in Patrick [Malahide]'s room (a kind of "good old boys" men's club has begun) by the time David [Henry], Patrick and I made it to Solemn Village for great fish dinner I was seeing double.

MAY 18, 1983

Up very early with a hangover. Should have replaced my water with water not booze. Could hardly get started. Wandering around the sun in a fog. Hour long drive out to new location. Used to be a garbage dump. They cleaned it up and built a bombed out house on it. A thunderstorm came up and it clouded over which made it a little cooler. I ate chicken soup which made me a lot better and the sweat just poured out. There were about five helicopters on location and we were told that we'd only be taken up about ten feet but we had a real ride with the doors open and I was amazed to find I had no fear. It was such a relief to get up there off that ground and to feel above it all. The power of it. Craig *[T. Nelson]* was sitting by the door and went into a real panic and was grabbing my leg without even realizing it. I think because he was so afraid it made me not afraid. We went through it all two or three more times. Craig asked the NURSE for Valium but she didn't have any. The third time up he was yelling like a cowboy. I pitied the poor Thais playing wounded Cambodians in the sun. Supposed to be a village that was wiped out by a bombing error. Long day. Dust and dirt and black inhaled smoke from burning rubber tires. My bathtub was like a swamp.

MAY 19, 1983

This was a long day of doing nothing but sitting on the bus and reading Tom's book about the destruction of Cambodia which I found very depressing. One horror story after the other which I found hard to believe or hard to take and didn't want to believe because published by Reader's Digest Press. It was very hot so I really didn't emerge from the bus until late afternoon to watch the children swing on ropes and drop into the dirty river. Craig was a little depressed because he got a call that a friend of his had committed suicide by OD'ing. Thoughts of Renée and I swimming in the Esopus *[the river near their rented house in Krumville]*. Thoughts of me going to Bali alone for the whole summer. I keep alternating like crazy. Was a little upset or felt left out because not used. Cocktails in Julian's room. Very crowded. Judy and Susie showed up to crash. I ended up going out with Sam, John and Glenne but wondered what fun everyone else was having. Ended up in

John's room with Nell. Walked her to her door but didn't POP THE QUESTION. DID NOT SLEEP WELL.

MAY 20, 1983

Disorientation. Woke up all night often not knowing where I was. (As if it mattered.) Obsessive thoughts that I should have slept with Nell. Was glad to be in my room and awoke early because Renée called at 6:15. We had a long talk. She upset because I sound like Hal the computer. Says she wants to marry me. She told me that Pavel had a massive heart attack and had asked Amy about me. R. seems to think he is alright but resting. New location: A soccer field in what felt like 110° heat and the Cadillac limo was falling apart as hundreds of Thai looked on. First my window wouldn't open then the car over-heated and then the air-conditioner broke down so it was like being in this hot box. I kept talking to our new "bodyguard" who claimed to be an elephant expert and Ira dripping wet with sweat kept saying please stop, I'm trying to get into character. Roland told him he was supposed to be close to tears. It was a long hot day with some funny moments. At last the muffler and tail pipe dropped off which had me laughing out.

MAY 23, 1983

Still not sleeping well. Very "on edge" Tom showed us his video of return to Vietnam. Very emotional, gets your heart. I cried to myself with all the complexity that went with aware of the sentiment and the kind of American stupidity that allowed all those "boys" to go in there and fight. Ira broke down in tears. Very Naïve (American again) and couldn't understand why the tape wasn't popular in U.S. We all sat around and talked after. It was good. A kind of "MALE CLUB" I thought I've been longing for. Went to fancy travel agent with Ira and bought ticket and hotel for Chiang Mai [city in northern Thailand]. Rested in the afternoon and read book on Buddhism interested to find that [Alexandra] David-Néel refers to it as psychoanalysis. Also spurred by the old idea of paying attention to it all and emphasis on memory as tool.

MAY 26, 1983

Off to the grandstand location at nine and did my scene with Sam where we went through the crowd talking about Military Defense Department. It was not easy to concentrate on my lines with two horrible 888 troops and a military marching band all coming up at me for my cue. I think we did about five or six takes which was not bad. Nell entertained the Thai troops after lunch. It was a short day. We all got off around 4:00. On the way home Sam told me I had done well. When I asked him why, he said I simply "did it." What do you get off on? I guess the simple execution. When I got home I gave up thinking about Nell and went for swim in the British Club pool. I saw two beautiful Thai women there with two English men. They were outstanding. Walk up home from the club I was suddenly overwhelmed by the beauty of the faces coming at me out of the crowd. At times I can't tell the men from the women. Too many drinks and out for late dinner with Ira.

MAY 28, 1983

[On location in Chiang Mai, Thailand]

Woke at 7 after a good sleep. After breakfast we were picked up by our guide and driver and head out for the all day trip. First the elephant farm where they went through their routine shows for the US tourists. The bath in the river was nice. It was good to be out in the country. Ira and I even took the ride. I was a little down on the whole thing because we were with all these other tourists and I figured they'd be at the hill station but it turned out we were the only ones up there and there was a funeral or wake going on and they had a little two year old baby laid out and the men were playing these bamboo pipes and beating a drum. Lee, our guide told us that the funeral procession would go into the jungle and the witch doctor would throw eggs on the ground until one didn't break and that would be the spot to bury her. If none of the eggs broke they would come back and kill more animals and drink the blood and go again after two tries they leave the body for the wild animals. We went to a house that had their wives and 22 people living in it. All three wives live in one room.

MAY 29, 1983

Woke at 8:45. Felt a little out of it. The excitement of being in a new place was already beginning to wear off. Long trip to another hill tribe. More advanced (TVs). Ended up with Witch doctor reading our palms at little homemade altar with flashlight and batteries. Said if I have children I will die early but no have children, will live long. Also said I had my lucky lottery number on me and at last found laundry tag ending in 275 could win 3 million B. Back in town to buy silver cup and then to lunch. Ira admired that I could stay friends with Liz through it all. Went back for swim in the rain then got very dark about 3:15 and I went across the way to get #63 again and have my massage under pink fluorescents as the rain came down. At last for 400 I got her to take her clothes off. She was very beautiful with long glossy black pubic hair. Fantastic legs and ass but would not roll over so I finished off fast in missionary position then watched her take a shower. Very beautiful. Made me sad. Beauty like that makes me sad.

MAY 30, 1983

Renée called at 7:45. She keeps asking me if I'm alright. I get frightened about her coming makes me think of marriage and long-term commitment which always and still freaks me out. Do I prefer to live in fantasy world of shadows and dream?

JUNE 1, 1983

Woke at 1:30 in the afternoon and went down for a swim. A banana. Some milk and peanuts and we were off again for the location and by now it felt like an endless dream. Dark skies and it cleared a little and a breeze came up and it became a very beautiful night. The man rolling through here and there. The extras were in a party mood and we were all a little up to begin with. It got very weird that the singer was singing Danny Boy phonetically. I had a "full house" Turkey dinner around midnight and then we went back for the New Year's Eve countdown scene. Then fell asleep under the stars while they set up for another shot of the dance and I had to get myself up out of that to sing Auld Lang Syne with the phonetics woman. The last shot of the day as the sun was coming up was very difficult for me. I was not sure what Roland wanted from me so after Billy *[Paterson]* ran away I just stood there and stared out over the empty dance floor. Six bombs went off that must have woke everyone in the neighborhood.

JUNE 2, 1983

I got back at seven. Had breakfast took a sleeping pill and went to bed. I woke up off and on not really knowing where I was and at last got up at one to find a bright sunny day and went swimming with Ira, Billy and Tom. Lunch at about 3:30 and back to bed at four. Up at 6:30 and to avoid depression, charged down to take another swimming in the pool. It was very beautiful. I was the only one in the pool and I swam on my back looking up at the clouds thinking in the third person "He did this." Back in my room at 7 and not heard from anyone about cocktails. Ira called to read a sad cute letter from Neevy and said he and Craig were off to farewell dinner with Roland. It's hard to believe they're both going. Ira gave me my pictures of the trip to Chiang Mai. I had drinks alone but it gave me a headache like I'd lost my taste for booze. Tom and I went to a nice Szechuan place at 8:30. Billy and Patrick came too late. Tom and I walked to King's Castle and sat it out until one. I took Joy home. A sweet little girl and was tempted not to use the safety but did. She seemed so clean and kept saying she was not a BUTTERFLY = SURPRISE AT ELEVATOR.

JUNE 3, 1983

I couldn't wake Joy. She was like a little animal. Went for my swim and came back and fucked from the sweet brown rear then down to breakfast and I still couldn't get her up. Offered her banana and she was insulted. At last got her out about 11.

I went off to the pool and spent most of the day there only coming into the hotel for lunch and a nap then out to the pool again to socialize and back for a very painful massage from Sy at 5:30 then off to the Foreign Correspondents Club for some a farewell party and also to begin the farewell party and combined birthday for Ira and Billy. Sat with Craig and Sammy whose real name is Sam Pol and wants to be called that. Big downpour. Flooded streets and over to ChaCha then five of us got a tuk tuk and went down to Pot Pong singing all the way. We took over King's Castle in the worst way. I got up on table to dance. Joy was very upset with me and kept telling me to get out. We all ended up dancing at Rififi. Got to bed about 2 after long bath.

Gray later mentioned Joy in the published version of Swimming to Cambodia: *"At first Joy seemed happy to see me and we could ride on that novelty. The softness of her skin was like a kind of heaven on earth and I wanted to keep it that way and not think. But when I sat long enough with Joy I could see the joy drain out and a kind of melancholy despondency creep into her face. . . . When we got back to the hotel I realized something was wrong—because two basic intentions in making love are pleasurable relief through sex, and some recognizable change in 'the other.' I could never really see the change in this particular other. And why should I expect change? After all, I was paying her. . . . Also I think it had a lot to do with language. Eighty percent of erotic love for me is the language in and around the event. But she spoke very little English. All she could (or would) say, over and over, was 'Joy like you.' I figured she said that to all the guys, but she was so convincing. I really wanted to believe her."*

JUNE 5, 1983

I got up five and took a cab out to meet Renée. I was very nervous got there early. Her bags were the last to come through so we didn't get out of there until seven. Came back and made love and went down for the breakfast then briefly over to the location in a very hot sun and Renée suffering from jet lag to watch them roll around in an APC. We walked back to the hotel so Renée could get her SPAULDING hat to protect her from the sun then walked over to the other location to have lunch. Renée was not hungry but I ate a lot of Turkey and walked back to the hotel for another round of fucking and she went to sleep and I walked back over to the location to watch them blow up the shoe store which took about two very hot hours to do. Had an interesting talk with Neil the Australian journalist about the difference between Thai Laos Com. Viet. people. Told me a story about how he had offered a Laotian a year's pay to take him somewhere at nap time and he wouldn't go. Back to the hotel and dressed in my all white farmer's clothes and we all went off to Ambassador *[John Gunther]* Dean's for drinks. I got quite drunk on scotch and some of us ended up at the open seafood place.

JUNE 7, 1983

We woke up around 8:45. Went out to swim and before that had quick sex. It's the old story. Now that my sexual drive has been somewhat satisfied I'm beginning to scrutinize Renée and think of her as not the perfect woman for me but what is most maddening is that I like her as a person but just don't think I want to settle down and have a family. After all how would I make a living? Sometimes I feel hope for a new monologue but I feel that I have to do a lot of research first. We spent a day in the city. Shopped for silk and went to a tailor and then the pool. Went to eat lunch at the little place but it was closed so we took a cab to see the reclining Buddha which was ridiculously big! Back to the hotel to swim and then down to the bar to drink with Phil Achs of the London Times. Craig and Tom and a bunch of us went off to a little Indian place in an alley which was very cheap and Craig ended up paying for all of us and giving 100 Baht tip. It began to rain and everyone left but John and Renée. John and I sat around and talked shop. John tries to make me believe that he doesn't like doing movies but at the same time get the feeling that he is bragging and really wants it.

JUNE 12, 1983

DREAM: I was diagnosed as having an incurable disease (referred to as a cancer) that was killing me slowly. I was taking care of some pet fish and put them in the oven with some "wild" fish. Went in a panic to open the oven and all the fish looked at me with intelligent eyes—like dog eyes. I managed to get one out of the oven and it turned into John Malkovich who seemed indifferent to being saved.

JUNE 13, 1983

Made love. Renée was in one of those funny aggressive moods and wanted to wrestle and beat me up. I lay there like a big lump and let her. Panic to pack. Not enough room so went to buy a new suitcase. After packing we had time for a last swim. Renée and I sat separate on the bus. I was feeling upset that I missed Craig all night, back to same old problem being around a group. I'm curious and want to be everywhere at once. Slow trip on narrow road. A strange landscape that reminded me of nothing then Cha-am beach hotel at Phetch Base [near Hua Hin, Thailand]. Outrageous huge swimming pool. Gulf of Siam like Far Rockaway in August. Fear of what? Police guards with revels. Barb wire and stray pack of dogs. Swimming pool. Giant barbecue. We sat with Roland and Cherie. Nell by my side taking over: "Don't let Renée tell you what to think." Knows how and where to get me. Sliver of a new moon and evening star. Walk down to the beach after dinner. I slip in the pool late, alone. Black water. Fear stray dogs wander by the pool. Bats. The sky of stars. Open outdoor feeling at last. Back in room I get into a horrid scene with Renée. Tell her I can't be in a relationship. Make her cry. Why didn't I tell NELL to shut up? Why can't I fight with Renée? Yell and scream instead of telling her it's all over? Late suffering NIGHT HOW WILL I EVER GET BACK?

JUNE 14, 1983

I climbed into bed with R. to make up quietly. Make love without too much feeling. Going through the motions I really couldn't stand her crying last night and felt that I had been stuck with the worst part of the child in her . . . We watched a scene be shot around the pool that was filled with trash. A wandering kind of Bergman Antonioni look. We ate lunch at location and went back to the hotel to swim rest and prepare for cocktail hour out by the sea in the wind.

JUNE 18, 1983

Renée and I made love twice. Once before the swim and once after. We got out on the beach about noon. R. helped me with my lines and then we walked down the beach and I watched her go in swimming. I

still don't feel like going in this water here. We went back to the pool.
It all looked like a National Lampoon Comic book. Everyone drinking and ordering food. The people watering the lawn with masks on
and the waiters taking running short cuts through the flower: drop two
bottles of Kloster: "Sorry sir, no more Kloster." Renée and I drank beer
and ate chicken on Square. The day went fast. I ended up talking with
Ivan [*Strasburg, the second unit director of photography*] about my
work . . . Renée and I walked on the beach. It was very beautiful. She
tried to get me to commit to living with her and when I wouldn't we
talked of breaking up then the whole evening got crazy. She went for
a walk with _____ while I unloaded all my problems on Ivan. R. cried
in Julian's arms. Julian swam out in the night sea. Fireworks went off.
Ivan, R. and I went down by the sea to get stoned. Renée wandered
off. I began to see way into a golden kaleidoscope scope going so fast
it made me dizzy. I ended throwing up like dog. Covering my vomit
with sand I saw my body as a Skeleton made of sand. Somehow they
got me home. [*This too is revisited in* Swimming to Cambodia, *with
Gray describing the scene in more vivid detail:* "Each time the vomit
hit the ground I covered it over with sand, and the sand I covered it
with turned into a black gauze death mask that flew up and covered
my face. And so it went; vomit-cover-mask, vomit-cover-mask, until I
looked down to see that I had built an entire corpse in the sand and it
was my corpse."]

JUNE 19, 1983

Woke feeling quite out of it. Not much sleep. R. was ashamed to go out
and be seen. Went for a swim. Ate breakfast with Sam Pol and Umber
too. Feeling quite depressed from the grass. Went to the pool and then
rested and had lunch on the balcony. Off for the night shoot at 5. Nice
at the Hotel. Sunset and then a big wind and it was suddenly cool. My
scene came quicker than I thought it would but took a long time to
shoot. Me trying with all my might to focus on the technician's words.
Came up with "a homing device in the middle of town" and "LONG
NECK." Roland giving me a lot of direction then at 2 we were done
and everyone applauded. I felt real good to have it over and done with.
Got a private driver home. A fan letter under the door from Italy. I tore

it up in front of R. at last she made me flush it down the toilet. Two beers, a sleeping pill and to sleep at three.

JUNE 20, 1983

Woke in a little panic. Renée's last day here. I'm so glad she's traveling with Cherie. I was off at 5 for a photo call and they were due to leave at 5:30 in David Puttnam's *[producer on* The Killing Fields*]* car. We had a nice photo call with everyone laughing and cheering then I went to sit on the porch with Tom and this incredible fatigue came over me. I was so tired that I felt dizzy and I had to lie down on the floor. Shortly after I got up David Puttnam came over and told me that I was very good in my last scene and I thanked him and credited Roland and said he was a good director.

JUNE 23, 1983

I slept well and late. Got up to do all my healthy stuff and then met with *[the publicist]* Minty Clinch who gave me an hour autobiographic interview to which my only regret was that I told her I was in a porn film. Then I had a wonderful meal with the Cambodians at a beautiful teak summer house on the beach. Julian, Nell and I were walking along talking about suicide and guilt and all of a sudden we looked over at this house and like a dream the woman was waving to us by a table that was covered with a wonderful food repast and we all walked in, sat down and ate. A wonderful relaxed meal. Some talk about Buddhism and heaven and hell then down to the sea to watch a man cast his net. Walked back to say goodbye to Nell and David Henry whom I felt I hardly knew. "Goodbye mate" was his last line. Had a swim and a walk down the beach at "magic hour" ran into Ron *[Cogan]* the hairdresser who was coming back from a long walk. Had some drinks and went out for dinner with Tom, John, Penny, Ivan and Judy Freeman and got to hear Roland run down for the first/last time. They talked about him in a way I never could have. Talked about his glories. Everybody was kind of letting out their frustrations. Had a swim alone at the hotel and went to bed early in nervous preparation for the long trip.

JUNE 25, 1983

Went to the set location to try to catch Tom's scene but they had big battle scene instead. In the middle of all that black smoke I suddenly saw the sun and left for the hotel to try and find Billy and H. for the beach. Big party: Athol *[Fugard, the South African playwright and actor; he played Dr. Sundesval in* The Killing Fields*]*, Rose, Patrick, Bill and H. Karon beach. We swam then went for a big feed. Lots of beer and at last talk about salary. Billy makes $3,000 a week. I felt lied to and lost my faith. I figured it was going on anyway. Why am I always the one that is underpaid? Must get an agent. Swim after lunch and walk on the beach. Kept thinking of getting back and getting an agent. Perhaps more envious of Jon Swain *[a British journalist portrayed by Julian Sands in* The Killing Fields*]* than anyone else here. . . . Sat next to *[the producer]* David P. He talks, you listen. Hard to get a word in. . . . David does not like process of film because prefers the original perfect vision. Penny *[Eyles, who worked on continuity in the film]* tried to talk with him about this. David said it was between Roland and Louie Malle. Fun ride back. Made people laugh under full moon. As I began to distrust David's perceptions I got paranoid about his praise. After all—66 TAKES? NO WONDER THE CREW CLAPPED.

JUNE 26, 1983

Wonderful day! Blew it all out on the beach. Ivan, who is courting me, invited me to the beach with a group and so much happened, or seemed to happen. I thought Ivan had drowned in the rough surf and called everyone from lunch (Ivan wanted to know if Judy Freeman came). After a nice lunch and a talk with the half Scot half Thai woman who was fasting for thirty days in one of those lovely cabins, Ivan got me to swim far out and I was not terrified and I think it was the first time I've ever done it and enjoyed it. I was just in the arms of an overwhelming sea. Then I began to hear Jon Swain and get him to swim out and all this time I was worried about my money which was hidden in the truck and I kept having to check in on it. Everyone wants me to let it all go. At last Penny got me to leave it on the beach and take a walk with her. She told me that I was a strange one and could not believe it. I told her I was stoned. We saw water Buffalo and I walked with the herd boys.

I ran from group to group. I cried in front of Penny when she asked me about Liz. Penny told me that I said things that people thought but didn't say.

JUNE 28, 1983

It was not easy to say goodbye to everyone. I went over to the location and gave it a try. Athol was very supportive and said: "Carry on from here man. Go back to Renée." I was able to make my exit with Tom.

JUNE 29, 1983

Tom and I sat up in the upstairs of the plane and had a good time popping Valiums, eating, sleeping a lot. In fact, we slept most of the trip away. Landed and took off in Karachi without even knowing it. Flying up top you don't even hear the engines. We went right on through $3 cup of coffee in Frankfurt Airport then short stop in Heathrow and then across the Atlantic in no time. Sleeping, eating good food. Fresh Salmon. I got Tom to tell me some war stories about following VC blood and shooting a man in half. On we went in a kind of travel coma. Tom giving me this rap bout how he now wished he'd not hurried back. It was all a fast long blurry trip. Clouds, sun, drink, sleep. Watch stupid movie of missing child with happy ending. Last words of child blurred by Thai airplane captain overhead to say we were to land in Frankfurt and we landed in bright clear day. We took the bus in. I called Renée from the airport. She was surprised to hear that I was home so early. Go to it, Athol said. Carry on from here and don't look back.

Immediately following his time on The Killing Fields, *Gray went back to his novel. Shortly thereafter, he began writing the story of his almost three-month stay in Thailand, what would eventually become* Swimming to Cambodia. *Gray premiered the play, originally presented in two parts, at the Performing Garage. He debuted Part One in December 1983 and Part Two in February 1984. Later, he combined the two pieces, edited it down, and delivered it as a single monologue from October 27, 1984, to January 5, 1985. Gray won an Obie Award for this show. He then wrote and rewrote as he traveled around the country, performing* Swimming to Cambodia *more than two hundred times over the course of two years. The monologue "was constructed by recalling the first image in my memory of each previous performance, so it evolved almost like a children's 'Round Robin' game in which a phrase is whispered around and around a circle until the new phrase is stated aloud and compared with the original," Gray wrote in the author's note to the published version of the monologue. "The finished product is a result of a series of organic, creative mistakes—perception itself becoming the editor of the final report."*

AUGUST 5, 1983

[Back in New York]

Oh hellish hot city! Made love and went to the bank. Went over to the Garage to sort things out. Ron came in and we had a short visit. He said he spent the thousand he owed me on vacation in Europe. Ron called Liz in L.A. and I listened in. She seems to be having a nice vacation and likes it out there because it's DRY and Jack is all of a sudden walking and plays with the neighbor kids. She made "loving" fun of Willem and the movie. Said it was like college stuff and that she was absolutely unthreatened. A little strong competition there? I did some more busy work . . . Obsessed on Thailand . . . Still feel I have at least two novels in me. India and early R.I. My autobiography up to College? Don't write to be published but keep on writing everyday! The only way to maintain mental health.

AUGUST 11, 1983

A long interview with Maggie the Harvard student in which I thought I made the discovery that the reason I didn't "act out" in my work was that I had decided to reverse the theatre with life. That I would begin to test my reality in the world and then use the theatre as the place in which I told about it.

AUGUST 15, 1983

DREAM ⟶ I was in a dance class and came on to a black woman. We made out in class. We took all parts of each other's bodies as a promise or recognition that we would make love at some point. I went to Pavel and looking away from him I told him that I felt my problems to be insignificant compared to his heart attack. He said something to the effect of "That's what they all say." I then told him about the black woman and then started in on what I felt to be the most important story. SOME OF THE STORY WAS TOLD IN THE JUNGLE. Ivan and Phuket and he got up in the middle of it to go feed his cat. I waited on the couch and began to get angry. Renée's voice came to me and said now you are angry with him. Express it. I started yelling at him from the couch and he came back into the room as two people. One Pavel was like a fiendish bag lady or Froggy the Gremlin who kept interrupting my story and make fun of it. Whenever I expressed my anger it sounded like distinct performed rage. The other Pavel was the new thinner man who had shaved and was sitting across from the bag lady Pavel and he watched it all. Before I finished my story he said my time was up and this was a surprise to me because he had never done that before.

AUGUST 25, 1983

I wrote close to three and a half hours just grinding it out and trying to get through the whole story. Also making up new names for people and starting to fictionalize. Liz has become Cal and Sarah, Leslie but I don't know about these name changes and wonder if I shouldn't go autobiographic. I find that all the sex scenes are exciting for me to write and I get into the most vivid detail with them only to finish and read an interview with Iris Murdoch about how she hates pornography and then pass heavy judgment on myself. We had a late lunch and got over to the river about three. It was cloudy. I almost fell asleep except for the flies, had a half waking vision of my loss of innocence and fears that I was hopelessly sexually obsessed and that that was how I first looked at people now—to see first if they were sexually attractive to me.

SEPTEMBER 17, 1983

I fell into reading from my 1977 diary. A lot of it was sad and hard to take but I was amazed to see how my handwriting had changed since then. In fact you can watch the evolution of it. Liz and Jack come over for a visit. It rained and I went down to Renée's for a late steak dinner and then we watched TV. "How Green Was My Valley" while Renée typed. She's all excited about this possible producing job. Then I drank some dark beers and started to read Francine [Prose]'s story but no sooner did I get into it that I got the idea to write up the Hassid story [later included in his 1993 monologue, Gray's Anatomy] and started in on that before bed. I was so influenced by Francine that I could feel her voice in it. I think we went to bed late about 1:30. Well, it's the weekend and I'm trying to relax but there feels like so much to be done.

SEPTEMBER 26, 1983

Up at my place and Renée got off to an early start to drive Mr. Birdseye around. [Shafransky's first paid film job was as a production assistant in charge of minding actor Stacy Keach Sr., who played Clarence Birdseye in the commercials for Birdseye frozen foods.] I spent most of the day over at The Garage writing letters and making real estate calls and finding out that there is no property I can afford in Conn. and from all reports—none along the Hudson. Some co-op in Pleasantville for $33,000 and even then I would have to pay over two hundred maintenance. So, I guess I'll have to give in to my claustrophobia and try to deal with it. It was a nice day but I felt hungover so did not really go out. Renée came over after her exhausting day and told me how she had to stand around while 30 people worked very seriously making the frozen Broccoli look perfect. She was not in a very good mood. We drove to her place and I called Roland who just got in. Same old Roland. He gave me his talk about morality not being a "moving feast" and then I asked—or Renée slipped me a note about having a drink with him and he said to call him at eight tomorrow. We went to bed while watching "All About Eve."

JANUARY 2, 1984

Renée said that I never mooned over her and looked deep into her eyes. I thought about it and realized that I only did that with people I was obsessed with. All those secret illicit loves I've had and suffered through. That will never lead to having children of my own.

APRIL 1985

HISTORY IS THE ELONGATION OF MEMORY IS THE ELONGATION OF HISTORY

The monologue /Swimming to Cambodia/ has grown and changed as I've toured it throughout the United States. In the course of performing it I've had a great variance of responses: applause, laughter, hissing, booing and one balled up program hurled at me. Things could be worse I knew. In El Salvador I'd be shot before I even started talking just for the length of my cock.

One of the events I have held on to is that such surrealist stories have emerged but how depressing it is for me to think that a positive story can only emerge from shock, a vast negative ground.

In Part Two, I make a joke that all actors are no one and I later call them saints. I see myself as a conduit to those stories.

This was the first monologue in which I spoke of events not directly experienced in my own life. Some of it was made up from stories and reports from other lives and therefore open to vast opinion and interpretation.

The thing that frightens me most comes from my own internal landscape and that fear is that I tend to reinforce my basic cynical fatalistic and pessimistic stance toward the world. BY SEEKING OUT ITS DARK SPOTS. The one thing that prevails is mankind's inhumanity to mankind. As I believe STILL, as long as there is individuation there will be conflict and as long as there is conflict there will be war but individuation seems to be a necessary ground for being.

Freudian speaks in me that there is always a constant precarious balance between dark and light. The yin and yang. Civilization and its discontents.

Looking back on it after the fact, I realize that Swimming to Cambodia is an attempt to balance those poles. Like any work of art it is an attempt to become God out of a loss of contact.

An attempt to create a tiny, balanced universe. An attempt to play at being God out of a lack of contact with the real or imagined source.

And like life it is a fixed and imperfect text.

In hindsight, the only sight that I'm aware of, I realized part of why I called the piece Swimming to Cambodia is because to realize the Cambodia Genocide would be like swimming there for a person like me.

After having searched on and off for two years, in 1985, Gray bought a second home in Phoenicia, New York, in the Catskills. He described first encountering the house in Terrors of Pleasure: *"I noticed this little red Adirondack-style cabin up the hill. It had rough-cut siding, a nice porch with screens that were rusted and ripped, and a pine tree nearby. It was up on a small embankment and looked over a pretty rolling mountain." The following winter, Gray bought the house for thirty-one thousand dollars (with four thousand dollars in escrow until the owner fixed the foundation)—with both money he'd saved and an inheritance from his grandmother—imagining it would be "a cozy place to write the Great American Novel." The entries that follow were written while he was first living in his new house. Almost immediately after he bought the house, it became a ceaseless and demanding money pit.*

JULY 5, 1985

Just before returning to the house, I have a dream that someone has torn it down without my permission and left a perfect grass plot. A new beginning. Like a graveyard. Like a putting green.

As we drive up to the House I say "Oh damn it hasn't burned down yet."

ONE POSITIVE THING = The house this time took me away from the FEAR OF AIDS.

Alright! Alright My biggest fear is that when I at last get to the Hamptons.

WHEN I
AT LAST GET TO
THE HAMPTONS

I will find that the ocean is just the Ocean.

JULY 6, 1985

THE HOUSE
I remember that the real big shock after I bought the house and moved in was that I didn't feel anything special about ownership. I mean I realized that it didn't make me any more secure. It just made me realize that I was passing through. It would have to be left to someone.

JULY 9, 1985

When I took Renée over to the bus we had to wait for a half hour so we listened to this rabble rousing _____ religious show and they were praying for all homosexuals to stop their filthy habits before the AIDS spreads. Then there was a man talking about the new Homosexual Blood terrorism $\longrightarrow$ salad dressing sperm terrorism $\longrightarrow$ about how they were consciously polluting the blood and also sending AIDS victims to prostitutes to help spread it into the straight population.

And all the time, there's this crazy guy out in the parking lot, walking around talking to himself, adjusting No Parking signs, then going into the door marked "no admittance."

Renée said, "The world out there has gone mad."

JULY 9, 1985

Was getting ready to go over for the cleansing on the land and I found the well open and I thought Oh my God why didn't I look sooner. Indeed some animal has fallen in and rotted of rabies and now I'm going to catch it. So I freaked and drove as fast as I could to the water plant and the only point that kept me calm was to think of telling this all to an audience → I alone have escaped to tell you. *[In fact, Gray did include this detail in his monologue* Terrors of Pleasure, *as he did several of the quotes from visitors and workmen in the following entries.]*

JULY 10, 1985

First visitors. Jehovah's Witness

"Isn't that a lovely thought that we are going to live forever? And it's just around the corner. Adam and Eve didn't have children before they sinned. Until you understand this all your prayers will be like putting paint on a house that is falling down."

Oh when they jack up that house the windows are going to pop and the doors are going to blow. You'll never get nothing closed or open again. Hey, you didn't just buy this house did you?

Well, I hope you have good fire insurance and from the way you give directions you'll probably collect.

OH OH OH
JEASUM CROW It's all built on clay! HA HA. He had one of these wrap around
blinds like it was stuck on

JULY 12, 1985

Having screens just at the far end of the porch has created a diabolical situation. Like some sort of giant lobster trap all the moths and flies have flown in and stuck. When the chimney sweep was here, a beautiful bird flew in and I guided it out with a broom.

The chimney sweep told me to watch out for first leaves and be careful to cap my chimney to keep the rain out and animals because they could get stuck and eat their way to the house. I know for a fact that there is something eating the house now. It's chewing right above me while I write.

JULY 19, 1985

Read a review about "Memory Babe" *[Gerald Nicosia's biography of Jack Kerouac]*—His hero worship was more an evasion of an insupportable self than a strong identification with other people . . . Kerouac had myth to him all right . . . but it only came through his remarkable ability to become his own "true" self on paper. Without paper and words he was a loser. His relationships with men as well as women were painful and unresolved; he was a bleeding ball of contradictions and private hells. He was in the flesh infantile, insecure, paranoid, and desperate. (He) was afraid of driving, terrified of flying, fearful of falling under wheels of trains. He ruthlessly sought out new experiences, then tried to redeem in words what he had botched in life. Well, I thought so much of it applied to me.

JULY 20, 1985

I walked up to Fred Fraudt to see if he was in to talk about the foundation. No one was in but as I was leaving I heard what sounded like a young woman being sexually penetrated on the other side of the stream and I got very turned on and as I walked over to hear it better the stream mixed in with it then it turned into a baby crying.

AUGUST 13, 1985

INFIDELITY

The mystery of a child exploring with the full response of a man's body behind it. The new female body like a foreign country and I do mean country matters, every experience was completely different. And almost every time I fell in love. Could I please be faithful in my infidelity?

SEPTEMBER 12, 1985

Renée and I walk back through the craziest architecture I've ever seen TO WRITE MARRIAGE VOWS

SEPTEMBER 26, 1985

Had this dream that I was arrested for holding a mirror up to people on a beach in England. I was taken to a very fancy English Prison where they had carpet on the floor and I got angry with the head guard and said I was going to file suit. There was an invalid in a wheelchair who was getting all the attention and I made fun of her warden to make the other inmates laugh and to draw some of the attention she was getting, to myself. Somehow, I escaped from prison and found that I was on the beach yelling out to all the people who were fully dressed and very ugly. "Hey I was put in prison for holding a mirror up to people on the beach"—and as I was saying this I saw a reenactment of myself holding this long body length mirror. I was standing in the surf. Some people seemed to listen but no one did anything, I could feel that the police were about to arrive but it didn't matter to me because I had all intentions of going back to jail. I had just stepped out to protest and be heard, not to try to escape or run away.

After I did my protest, I started back to jail and suddenly I realized I was free and that I didn't have to go back if I didn't want to. This was such a surprise to suddenly realize this and I stepped out on the highway to hitch and I get a cab and as I was riding I realized I was now in a movie that I was making up myself. It was an instant film that I was the center of.

SEPTEMBER 27, 1985

I have been thinking that a lot of this passion may come from drinking and that I should make every effort to stop for a while. I have these enormous fears that I am some portion of Christ. Something about the mirror dream perhaps.

If I continue being who I am now, I see disaster written on the walls

OCTOBER 16, 1985

We had to make up death—not the threat of death or the fear of it—but it was hardly seen any more. Or was easily avoided. Then I started to see AIDS, the new plague, everywhere. Well not everywhere. If it were put in a road side bulletin board it would somehow have made it—yes maybe less fearful. But now it was leaking out in small portions like the way sometimes in certain rural, say non-urban situations, you might see a mother lose her tit. AIDS was like the nipple and I would fly to it and stick. How or why did it happen that the life giving creative act had reversed itself? How could something that feels so good be so bad. . . . In the face of it all, I can't believe we're still so polite to one another. Somehow I think all that politeness comes out of the illusion that we—you, I—that we will not be the ones. That we will not die. And when I really look at it I see myself tumbling toward it . . . the very realization of or meditation on eternity leads me to almost despair because once you can just begin to get the slightest inkling of the fact that you won't be here forever, it begins to make you not be here now.

Mid-80's AUSTRALIA

[Touring Swimming to Cambodia *and traveling with Shafransky; this entry is likely from 1986 as Gray performed twice in Australia that year]*

Edward said they are not laughing because they are slow and also you have an ironic sense of Jewish humor and I realized I had no sense of humor before I moved to New York to some extent New York City saved me.

He had come to the show and I had made eye contact with his girl turned out she was Jewish. I'm automatic charm to Jews.

Hazards of the trade. Keeping *Swimming to Cambodia* fresh and the realization that I'm incanting the same neurotic fears each night.

I don't want to do another monologue. I want to do a book. A book is meditative and private. The reader can go back over it again. It goes deeper or has the potential to go deeper because it is private. The performance is written on the mind.

I was beginning to see how the New York audience had put the stamp of humor on Swimming to Cambodia. To some extent they made it what it is. Perhaps that's why it doesn't play as well or fall out in other places. Melbourne WAS a PIE IN THE EYE sort of place.

Strange dreams:

1. Liz waking the spirit of a cat off a death mask. I could see the spirit disappear like smoke and turn into something like a hologram of a kitten. A ghost. The spirit of the cat was headed toward me and I rejected it. (Liz working witchcraft?)

    I rejected it by yelling "Mom no, mom, no!"

2. Strange long dream in which I know I was guilty for a murder.

    I had the full sense that I was guilty and then Annette from Jones group book. Why Annette? She took the rap and went to prison. The evidence was a big package of blood like the wine pack here. Somehow I knew there was one piece of evidence left under a hospital bed. It was an L. L. Bean shoe with cobwebs around it. A red headed idiot boy who could read my mind would not leave the room and the more I tried to get him to carry stuff downstairs . . .

In my sleep, I thought enough of this dream. I'm tired of feeling guilty, time to wake up.

FLIGHT TO PERTH

The flight was turning into a bore and I began to wonder if my self-generated fear of flying all these years was not just a cover for boredom and that I would choose fear over boredom any day.

I order a third beer triple X Castel Marie. Anything but Fosters. With the beer she, the stewardess, hands me a little card that says have a fantastic holiday and it occurred to me or at least I had time to think about it that in Australia general leisure time is referred to as Holiday without any definite article. In America, it's vacation. A holiday would be Christmas or Thanksgiving or V. J. DAY (Victory in Japan). But there is something I like about Holiday. It comes I guess from Holly day but it rings of festivity and open celebration. Vacation is sort of vacuum. To empty out. To vacate.

PERTH

We had a big fight over fiction in THE FISHY AFFAIR [seafood restaurant] we waited in line for a long time and Renée said she only could wait because of the name of the place.

    We had a local (NAME) Gulled fish and fell into a fight about my novel. I said I wanted to do a book about "the male" or THIS MALE'S experience of infidelity and why it was such a deep or maybe not so deep part of my life. I wanted to mention names. She said write a fiction. I said I wasn't interested in becoming a good writer as much as I was becoming a good person. All fiction was a continuance for me. How to make a good ending? I wanted to be a journalist reporting on my life.

To trace the motion of my life as Spalding Gray, a reporter on myself.

We had a wild fight. The only time Renée came out of it was to laugh at two old men who were looking over at us. She couldn't finish her dinner and I knew I should at least pretend I had lost my appetite as well.

And suddenly I was back in L.A. and all the streets were buzzing and breathing have you heard the news about the new Seidelman movie? *[Referring to the film* Making Mr. Right, *directed by Susan Seidelman.]* It's being shot in Miami and its starring John Malkovich and Ann Magnuson and I could feel it all coming back—competition and what did I miss and I could smell that METALIC smell of ANGST in my pots and the muscles ball up in my calves and all of a sudden I felt my sex drive come back.

KEEP YOUR SENSE OF HUMOR

I'M NOT HOPEFUL

THERE WAS A MISTAKE!!

MY MOM DIDN'T LEAVE A NOTE.

<u>TRYING HARD TO UNDERSTAND MY WAY TO DEATH</u>

Don't you recognize me? I was in *The Killing Fields*

AMERICA = THE COUNTRY THAT DARES TO BE HAPPY WITH A BIG TOUCH OF SADNESS WITH A BIG BIG BIG TOUCH OF SADNESS.

In 1986, Gray signed a contract with Alfred A. Knopf, thus beginning his five-year struggle to write Impossible Vacation. *Before its publica-*

tion, he managed to wrest some humor from this experience by creat-
ing a narrative that became his 1990 monologue, Monster in a Box—*a*
story, as he put it, "about a man who can't write a book about a man
who can't take a vacation." He performed this monologue with a large
box containing his manuscript—the "monster" of the title—sitting on
his wooden desk.

JANUARY 7, 1986

[Los Angeles]

The press here seems to think that my neurotic self-absorption is particular only to New York City but I say, "Just scratch the surface of any
place."

During the writing of this book I began to think my vision, my way of
thinking had in some way been polluted and that I should go back into
a meditation retreat.

SELF INDULGENT
THAT I WILL DIE OF AIDS because I'm not among those that are
helping. Do nuns die of cancer? Yes and that is because they _____ not.

GOD I love you RENÉE but I am not YOURS.

I have to leave Renée. Dear Renée I have this awful feeling. I kind of
know I can't be in a relationship.

Dear Liz,
I don't know where to begin . . .

I don't.

Idon'tknowwheretobegin I have two of the grey notebooks you held in
India. The Irish drug is alcohol. I have an awful feeling you should be
checked for cancer.

I would rather write this book than have a child.

APRIL 1986

Dear Renée,

I can't and won't make any more promises. I'm in love with change. I can't say when I want a house or if and when I want children.

In October 1986, True Stories, a film directed by the musician David Byrne, opened in New York. Gray had a role in the movie—which centered on the 150th anniversary celebration of a fictional town in Texas—alongside an ensemble cast including Byrne and John Goodman.

1986 REFLECTING ON SHOOTING "TRUE STORIES"

About an hour outside of Dallas, we could see the location glowing under lowering skies like some sort of Barnum and Bailey Space City. It was transcendent. Besides the location for the American Embassy party in *The Killing Fields*, this was the best location I'd ever been. There in the middle of these flat Texas plains was a huge yellow and green striped circus tent. All the Honey wagons *[film industry term for an actor's trailer on location]* were lined up. Then beyond that was the most spectacular structure. It was the stage for the talent show. It was made of translucent corroded green plastic. There it sat giving off rays of green light into that pitch black Texas night. It was a thing of rare beauty like a great square spaceship (THE KIND DAVID MIGHT DRIVE). Beyond that endless Texas plains spread like a sea of land and I walked further out and could see the suburban TRACK HOUSES' lights glistening at the edge of civilization like a town at the edge of THE SEA or me walking on the bottom of a dried-up sea. Up until then I had felt landlocked in Texas but now my head and mind opened up to the same feelings of freedom produced so often in me by the Atlantic and Pacific.

The fantasy that I had been chosen as the first straight articulate sufferer of AIDS was beginning to take over. I had begun to fantasize that the AIDS cause needed me to speak out and I had even developed this elaborate theory as to who had transmitted the virus to me. It was a woman I HAD SLEPT WITH YEARS AGO whose father worked for the Department of Defense. I saw the INCREASING breakdown of immune and internal defense systems as a reaction to so much external defense spending. It was a sign from God to tell us to stop spending money on star wars and start spending money on education and food (other than cheese) for the poor.

AND I AT THAT MOMENT I SAW I had been chosen as the spokesman to bring this information to the people. Well, you may laugh and say perhaps I had had too much leisure time on my hands and I should really be working in a hospital and you're right that was the other idea that was taking me over. The more fun I had on the film set the more guilt I felt. It seemed to go hand and hand. Each morning I woke up I'd promise myself to send away for a Peace Corps Application. But mostly the issue was AIDS.

Just as I thought I'd come to something about the nature and construct of my paranoia, the door of my honey wagon flew open and Bill Edwards from wardrobe hurled in a copy of New York Magazine which fluttered like a great insane paper bird and then landed on the floor. This was followed by him shouting, "There's the article on AIDS you were asking me about." And he slammed the door.

Terrified I jumped back from the magazine as though it were the giant virus itself and the whole bottom of my mind dropped out. There was no paranoid puzzle left, there was just plain BIG FEAR. There was no outside eye left to examine the fear. Everything suddenly had become FEAR. That was the new reality and there seemed no way out of it. I was totally convinced that I was dying of AIDS and I began to freak. Who could I run to I wondered and then I realized two things. One was that I didn't know anyone well enough to drop this craziness ON which at the same time gave me the distance to realize that it was craziness. The other thought was about how I liked all the people on the film so much that I didn't want to bring anyone down into my fear. In other words I had to wrestle with it myself.

It was then that I realized the inside of this claustrophobic honey wagon was GOING TO DRIVE ME NUTS. I opened the door and stepped out again into that supremely transcendent night. Now everything was a carnival glow of lights. The circus tent was light and the great green corrugated plastic stage sent off its great green rays into the BLACK night. I headed straight out into the plains. I was trying to walk fear off. Faster and faster I'd walk and as the fear hit me with the stars in and around my heart I would let out with little shrieks and groans. Not wanting to get too far away from the location I began to circle it in a great arch keeping within earshot in case the A.D. called me. And as I walked the fear took over until I couldn't stand it and just stopped and said, "Alright Spalding just stop and accept it. So you're going to die," and at that point I had a vision. I had never had anything happen to me like this before. It was not a hallucination but rather like an image laid over the image of reality. It was like the pictorial scrim DROPPED over that Texas landscape. I could clearly see BOTH THE LANDSCAPE AND THE IMAGE and clearly be in both places at once. And what I saw besides that Texas night was my old therapist dressed only in a diaper and kneeling in the sky surrounded by thunder clouds and a frozen lightning bolt. It all looked like A STRONG CONTEMPORARY Blake engraving only it was my therapist and he was reaching down to pull me up. OUT OF MY fear. He was not pulling my body up, he was pulling my spirit up and he brought me into a blissful condition of the moment. I was suddenly present in life and death. I was there. I was here. I felt delivered to an extreme state of calm elation. For a moment I was in WHAT I COULD ONLY CALL a state of grace and as I stood there I now saw that this cloud-caped image of my therapist was surrounded by long brown tubes that were made of some organic woven STRAW-LIKE substance. Those tubes in the DU CHAMP PAINTING OF THE NUDE descending the stairs except these tubes extended horizontally RATHER THAN VERTICALLY into the night. And I could see that some seemed to go on forever and others were truncated and STOPPED at various distance over the plains. Seeing these tubes I thought I almost understood something. It was like the ambulation of an idea and a feeling. I thought I understood that there was clearly a constant swirling incomprehensible mix of good and evil in the world. It was not at all clear like the EASTERN YIN and YANG pattern in which the dark and the light CLEARLY balance off each other. It was instead a great untranslatable swirl of cosmic weather which no earthly weatherman COULD EVER GET A HAND ON.

I realized that there was a no speaking line into that swirl. It was the line of acceptance. A quality of grace in the middle of that turbulence. The eye of the hurricane and that there are very few people on earth that can go to that place without HELP and that help came through a relationship to a helper, to a guide. Some people go for the big ones. Buddha, MOHAMMED or JESUS. OTHERS GO FOR THE LITTLE, LESS POPULAR ONES. Other small thinkers and ones like me of little faith go for small ones still on earth but SOMETIMES it takes a relationship with some other—a lover, a therapist, a lesser God TO LIFT YOU OUT OF GUILT and sin. THE only sin of not being where you are. And standing there elated and in the present, I realized I'd just experienced some sort of classical transference.

From 1986 to 1987, Gray was an artist in residence at the Mark Taper Forum in Los Angeles. He set out to find interesting people on the streets that he could interview onstage at the Taper. The challenge: none of them could be affiliated with the film industry. Like Interviewing the Audience, *this project relied on Gray's creating an immediately genuine relationship with the people he found. The theater hired an assistant, a young woman who went by the nickname K.O., to drive Gray around the city seeking out entertaining interviewees. "We're going to senior citizens centers, golden-age drop-in centers, high schools. We're driving down to Long Beach to look for Cambodian refugees. We're driving over to Venice Beach to talk with homeless living in lean-tos," Gray recounted in* Monster in a Box. *"Nothing, nothing, nothing. No one." Gray finally managed to find forty people to interview—three Valley Girls, a woman who believed she'd been picked up by a spaceship on the Ventura Freeway, and a waitress who handed her film script to Gray while they were onstage, among them. The show was called* L.A.: The Other.

JANUARY 8, 1987

Well I'm back at it. One of these uneventful trips out *[to Los Angeles]*. I talked too much to the woman next to me. That old assertion of age. Also drank too much and fell asleep as I was not in the greatest of moods for K.O., I drove my rented car back to the tacky old Highland Gardens and then K.O. and I went right off to that Mexican place down on Sunset which I like. Nice people. K.O. seems to be doing her job well. I think she is kind of intuitive as a stage manager. Also I like the way she talked. She's like a Sam Shepard character when she talked about going water skiing she said the day was better than a June Bride. Then she told me stories about how she would drive the speedboat around at the amusement park to sink all the trash from the fireworks. She likes to set off fire works. I went to bed early after a call to Renée and was kept awake by this INFERNAL HELICOPTER!

JANUARY 9, 1987

I think it was a good start. We drove to Watts and made "contact" with this wonderful old Black woman named Maggie who went on about the history of Watts and soul food, the food throughout by the plantation owners. She talked about how black people talk with their eyes and at that point I wanted my eyes to be a video camera doing close-up because no audience could really see her dance and in that spontaneous mood talking about Caucasians and black history.

JANUARY 10, 1987

I pulled an all nighter. Went to Bill Talen's show, went out after, tried to be generous. Got out the coke and smoke, also Champagne. Went dancing. Did some more drinking and back for more coke. I think I was in my bathtub at 6:30 drinking beers. NO MEMORY OF WHAT WAS SAID.

JANUARY 20, 1987

Once Renée said I forgive you, your body. I was thinking, God how generous of her.

Now on this bed, I was not dissecting. Her body came together into one working whole when love was involved. There was no place for scrutiny. I knew later, it would come again perhaps on the beach when I tried to shape her and cut her with my eye again making her into the perfect woman.

In February 1987, Gray sold the house he'd bought in Phoenicia—the calamitous house he'd depicted in Terrors of Pleasure—*for forty-one thousand dollars. Soon thereafter, he bought a country house in Carmel, New York, on the other side of the Hudson River from Phoenicia. In the journals, Gray often refers to this house as Sedgewood because it is part of a larger, cooperative property named the Sedgewood Club.*

MARCH 18, 1987

[Los Angeles]

I'm having problems with Renée. I can't seem to bear her getting dependent on me. I saw a man on the street with a woman in a wheelchair and I got scared. Would I be able to do that with her? What I mean is that I don't seem to be very capable of "deep love" for another or for Renée. It seems to be that I go the deepest with self-love and this is a bit frightening but it still feels good to get close to Renée physically. The touch of her body is still a comfort.

Jonathan Demme's film of Swimming to Cambodia *opened in New York City in March 1987. "Before I'd seen Spalding perform, I was horrified at the idea of being trapped in a room with just one person speaking at a desk. I didn't want to see him, even though everyone kept telling me how much I'd love him. When I finally did go to one of his shows—I think I first saw him in* 47 Beds—*I was instantly won over," Jonathan Demme recalled. "With* Swimming to Cambodia, *I* knew the film would be remarkable because the piece was so remarkable. And any fear I'd had about one man at a desk onstage—I knew we'd have an advantage because we had the ability to do close-ups and cut-aways and sound." Demme shot two consecutive performances of Gray before a live audience at the Performing Garage in New York in November 1986. "Renee raised the money for the film—and she raised enough for us to be able to do it really really right," Demme said. "It was a very low budget film, but we were able to get John Bailey as our cinematographer, Carol Littleton as our editor, and Philip Stockton as our sound editor." For the most part, Demme preserved the look and feel of the stage show—with the addition of the camera work and lighting as well as the occasional sound effect (such as, at Stockton's suggestion, fluttering helicopter blades). In addition, Laurie Anderson, a friend of both Demme and Gray, wrote and recorded an original soundtrack for the film.

MARCH 19, 1987

This was one of those hysterical phone days. All these calls coming through and news about the good reviews [of the film of Swimming to Cambodia] in U.S.A. TODAY. Renée got so upset about not being in New York for the success of the film that she decided to fly back on Thursday. I made her go for a walk to try to calm her down . . .

The movie of Swimming to Cambodia was indeed well received critically. "Mr. Gray's feature-length monologue brings people, places and things so vibrantly to life," Janet Maslin wrote in The New York Times, "that they're very nearly visible on the screen." Roger Ebert praised him in the Chicago Sun-Times: "Like a good preacher, some of [Gray's] power comes from the sheer virtuosity of his speech." Rita Kempley of The Washington Post was also impressed (though may have offended Gray with her physical description of him): "Gray's characters are every bit as comically effective as Lily Tomlin's, but they're coming from this nondescript white guy who never gets out *of his chair. Armed with nothing but a glass of water, a couple of grade-school geography class maps and a pointer, he sits at a battered, wooden desk like a teacher. Even his hair is the color of an erased blackboard. With comic sugar and unforgettable imagery, he teaches us about 'the worst auto-homo-genocide in modern history,' the 'redneck' Khmer Rouge's slaughter of 2 million fellow Cambodians."*

And yet not all critics took to the film. Pauline Kael, in her review in The New Yorker, *wrote: "He's an actor who has discovered strong material, and he builds the tension—his words come faster, his voice gets louder. He thinks like an actor; he doesn't know that heating up his piddling stage act by an account of the Cambodian misery is about the most squalid thing anyone could do."*

JUNE 3, 1987

This was not a productive day for me. More obsession about AIDS and looking at the bites on all my fat (FAT PEOPLE HAVE MORE FEELING IN THEIR FLESH) I tried to write in the morning but it didn't work with this L.A. project hanging over me. This much I've learned. I am one of those creative people who can only do one thing at a time. As I read in the Jung book: "Ill-timed interpreting interferes with the spontaneity of the creative processes."

JUNE 12, 1987

As for "SWIMMING," what the studio people don't understand is that I am not acting. What I'm talking about was a real issue to me or for me at some real point in time.

JUNE 14, 1987

There is in me (like with mom) this horrid regret mechanism. I will make regrets up just to have them. Like this morning, after breakfast, I was regretting the fact that I didn't smoke more marijuana with Liz. After good sex and late breakfast, I did some writing. It's a bit confused going from the story to the analysis of the story. I like to think of it as post-modern. I like to think of it as Moby Dick.

JUNE 16, 1987

I'M WRITING "IMPOSSIBLE VACATION"
A CHRONICLE OF PERSONAL GUILT
I want to be the best at what I do.
I would like to do one thing well.
The monologues.

JUNE 19, 1987

Go to AFI *[American Film Institute]* to look at TERRORS tape and what a horror. It is neither interesting nor funny. *[Thomas Schlamme directed* Terrors of Pleasure *for an HBO comedy special.]* It's badly directed and depressing for me because this means now that I have one more thing to deal with. I mean that type needs a lot of work and Renée I know or I hope will help me out. Renée went off to a meeting and I walked back to the house to return phone calls and sort of hangout in that lazy limbo that I tend to fall into here.

Upon the success of the movie of Swimming to Cambodia, *Gray began to get more film offers as an actor. Soon after the movie was released, Robert Mulligan, the director of* To Kill a Mockingbird, *cast Gray as a new age Jewish grief counselor in his 1988 film,* Clara's Heart, *starring Whoopi Goldberg. Immediately after Gray finished shooting* Clara's Heart, *he was cast as a Jewish obstetrician in Garry Marshall's 1988 film,* Beaches, *starring Bette Midler and Barbara Hershey. In addition, Columbia Pictures commissioned Gray and Shafransky to go to Nicaragua with an American fact-finding team—a group investigating America's covert funding for the Contra war against the Sandinistas and helping Nicaraguans who had suffered as a result of U.S. involvement—as research for a film. "The script itself would be a fictional account about how once we got down there, did our thing and gave away all of our personal belongings to the Nicaraguans, our bus doesn't show up to take us to the airport," Gray explained in* Monster in a Box. *"And suddenly we, or our characters, are trapped there and become very much like the people we've come to observe."*

JULY 1, 1987

[Traveling from Los Angeles to New York]

Panic day. Head out for New York. Renée all upset because she may not be able to update her passport in time for Nic. *[Nicaragua].* Nice overcast fog day. Neighbor's full pink roses against that grey sky. We sat on the ground for over a half hour before take off. A long cramped flight. Me trying very slowly to read about Nic. Where is Nic? I'm so bad with historical fact books. We landed in stormy dirty rainy N.Y.C. We got back to piles of mail and a stuffy loft and all the memories about the good old days came surging back.

JULY 3, 1987

It's taking me forever to get used to this humid air. Very scattered in the loft. Jack *[LeCompte and Dafoe's now five-year-old son]* came in to tell me a great and vivid story about Thailand. The length of the fingernails, the hand positions, the Elephant and the man hawking fans. It was all very vivid and he seems to have a great sense of himself as storyteller. I mean he told me to sit down and then he went at it only to stop when Willem came in who strange to say is not as good at telling a story as Jack is. Liz is still obsessed with her identity as artist prophet. Says that she already had a vision of Willem as Christ and now he's up for the role in the Scorsese film *[Martin Scorsese's* Last Temptation of Christ, *which Dafoe starred in as Jesus].* She wants to go on location to shoot it. Also she got sick in Thailand. It took Renée and I forever to get out of the city. We didn't pick Halle up until 3:30 and got out about 4:00. I was afraid to swim alone but it was very peaceful and beautiful down by the pond. I took a little dip then we had a big feed meat cookout and went down to the deck for a sunset swim. I took a nice quiet lazy walk.

JULY 5, 1987

Item: SEX   Received: ME   Paid: RENÉE
Balance: HOPE
When Renée would not get into it with me, I sort of slept. In the morning we did it. She wanted me to make her have a baby. I had a feeling I

would have shoved it in and made it happen. KNOCKED HER UP . . . I long for the audience.

JULY 6, 1987

I HAVE LOST TRACK OF WHAT IS IMPORTANT (FOR ME?) TRYING TO KEEP A GRASP ON THINGS. I ran-walked and after breakfast I went into a full writing mode. Deep into vivid sex fantasies of Elisa. It is like going into a trance and when I come out of it I go into a panic. Like writing the book is a sort of dam that holds back present reality. Then it all pours in and I begin to obsess on Renée's body as (perhaps a metaphor) for imperfection.

JULY 7, 1987

Rainy stinky day. Made love. Walked. I ran. After breakfast I got hooked on the hearings *[the National Security Council member Oliver North's televised testimony before the joint congressional committee created to investigate the Iran-Contra affair]* and wanted to go all the more. I just sat there and listened. Whenever Renée is in the room she figures it all out (the human logic of it) faster than I do. (Like Liz used to) I have to pay attention to what I pay attention to. I fixed a big lamb stew pea soup for lunch. It kept raining and we were both getting cabin fever. Renée seems to be running away from her writing which of course makes me insecure. Me not even sure if she can write a film script. We headed off to buy a TV in that horror mall in Mahopac. On a rainy day that place can really put you out. We were almost falling asleep. We bought a Magnavox and headed for food. Ended up at the Carmel Diner. Roasted chicken. Me two scotches under the table *[as described in comic detail in* Monster in a Box, *Gray often brought his own liquor—small airplane bottles he'd saved from his frequent traveling—to restaurants and would pour from them into his glass under the table]* and then the not-so-bad train ride down . . . Talked with Renée and I put on this in-control mature voice about how we should split up. REMINDS ME OF WHAT I DID TO LIZ IN INDIA.

JULY 21, 1987

I'm embarrassed by the depth of confession my book requires. I sat and
looked out the window and just strained for structure but nothing came
but I did have good hot sex with Renée which is almost always a relief.
Perhaps I'm thinking too much about the book when I should be writing it and just turning out the pages because even as I sit here now that
story of going to India came back on me. I took the 1:15 down and got
to Pavel early so I sat in the park and read. It was very hot. Pavel went
for two hours which meant I got to tell my story of Bali and his eyes lit
up also I told him about the vision of transference. Life is not the craziest mystery to me now, its death. I'm not sure how helpful Pavel can
be for me. Renée says it's too late in my life to be taken apart and put
together. I'm too formed. 1984 [the year he began touring Swimming
to Cambodia] was a bit of a change and it really made me appreciate
Liz's work.

JULY 24, 1987

I guess I'm about two days without a drink and I'm pretty on edge in
the evening so we took these wasteland drives. We went to Danbury
[Connecticut] which was real depressing. Renée said this is America
and I want to use it as a study. It all reminded me of [Don DeLillo's]
White Noise. We ended up eating dinner in this huge Mall on the way
home. It had skylights and a merry-go-round and I really wanted a
drink and I thought I was in purgatory. Renée says PURGATORY is the
place where you can't tell differences. Renée started in on me about the
issue of the baby. She seems to think that she is the only one with a will
to get things done. She says the bathroom would never have been built
if not for her. I wonder what it is I want under all this OTHER WILL.
I wonder what would happen if I was left alone. I told Renée I was the
uncle type. Late night swim under heat lightning and cherries. AND
CLUB SODA TO BED EARLY.

JULY 25, 1987

Rocky called and scared me by saying that years of excessive drinking
may create irreversible negative personality traits. Another humid day.
Just as we are about to leave I begin to work on the book. I am going

over what I wrote and some of it is not bad. At worst, it is a little defensive and preachy but it is the kind of modern male stance in the face of mortality—mine and how my LINEAGE got broken when the family got broken. I am still off the booze. It's the cocktail hour that's hard to get through.

JULY 26, 1987

Woke to another heavy humid day. The storm didn't seem to help. ARI the Dutch Greek photographer called early and I put him off until I could talk to Annie. *[The photographer Annie Leibovitz shot Gray for* Vanity Fair's *Hall of Fame page].* She *[Leibovitz]* arrived early with all her generators and assistants and went right down to the water right down that private road. Then she had to go out to buy another table in Cold Spring. Then the rain came. Then it cleared and the generator started up and people started to come down to check it out. I realized we didn't have a leg to stand on with complaints to the Bemans about their Jacuzzi because for some reason they were home for the weekend. In the middle of the shoot, I began talking to Annie about Nici *[a woman Gray met in Australia]* and began to have the fantasy of falling in love all over again.

JULY 28, 1987

[Traveling back to Los Angeles, where Gray and Shafransky were to do research for their upcoming Nicaragua trip as well as shoot "Bedtime Story," a half-hour show that they co-wrote for a PBS TV series called Trying Times. *The episode is about a woman whose biological clock is ticking—literally—as she demands her husband take note of the clock protruding from her stomach. The show starred Gray, Jessica Harper, and Louie Anderson and was directed by Michael Lindsay-Hogg.]*

We were up at about 5 AM for that early plane. The big rush for the plane where I didn't resist THE DRINKS and had two Bloody Marys and two glasses of champagne which put me in a real tailspin. But first-class was nice and people gave us the eye. We were the only ones to look the way we did. When I cut in front of a guy in line he said, "You got some nerve. You didn't even book first-class." The movie was good. *[David Anspaugh's]* "Hoosiers" was well-directed. The trip seems shorter in first-class. At last we got onto our Bungalow at about 2:15 . . . I sneaked out for vodka and discovered a yoga place next to the liquor store. What a contrast. Pavel says I'd have to give up drinking for a year to feel the positive effects. I took R. out for $35.- worth of sushi and sake and back for a swim and fruit and to bed early. I was wiped out.

AUGUST 3, 1987

Up for the walk and then first day of shooting which I think went well. All that focused attention and getting a chance to act out and be in that dreamlike, the kind of LIVING DREAM OF LOCATION. There I was, barefoot in my PJs walking down this LA Street at 92°. It was all like a strange fever dream along with their intense dry light. But a very long 12 hour day which ended with me TIED to a Weber Grill saying, "father I amend my soul to the deep" under a beautiful ½ moon just up between those two buildings and it all occurred to me that I was still working out my water themes what with the water dripping through the ceiling and me jumping in the pool.

AUGUST 6, 1987

I have nothing more to report today except that I seem to be in better mental health when I'm working. When I'm not I begin to question everything. The point of life now seems not so much to leave the earth a better place but to just do something to make it keep going. A big point of my book could be that the person who seemed most positive in my life, i.e. mom, in the end opted to take her own life. Part of why I don't trust the positivists.

AUGUST 12, 1987

These days in the screening room have been good. We watched *[Luis Buñuel's]* The Exterminating Angel which I still do not like then the documentaries which are good but hard to take. In El Salvador and then Vietnam there were some gruesome shots. The leaders were the worst—the face of Duch *[Kaing Guek Eav, a leader in the Khmer Rouge movement]*—a rather nightmare face and the military leader.

The repression there is incredible. I think Renée and I were both very depressed after the day trying to figure out how we were not going to make fun of these events. Americans who go down to Nic to try to help out. So we will try to write the script from my point of view.

AUGUST 13, 1987

I can't think right. I'm hung over and we are rushing off for Nicaragua with the harmonic convergence coming on. I spent a boring day on floor 41 of HBO doing these ridiculous pick-up shots for HBO special [of Terrors of Pleasure]. Also making long distance calls. We went out for a late Italian feed and that's where I overdid it trying to keep up with Michael with three scotches and three beers and I hardly felt drunk at all. We went right to bed when we got home. I had tried to pack the night before but was in such a panic. I kept losing stuff and it all feels so crazy. I guess I'm more afraid of the flight than anything else.

AUGUST 14, 1987

[Leaving for Nicaragua]

We go to the airport real early. Had too much coffee. Had a crazy full Mexican flight which landed real fast because of the fact that we are up 8,000 feet. No time to get through customs but a long time to get a cab to the MAJESTIC hotel where Renée and I had taken new roommates. John who went to the Atomic test site to PROTEST and gambled with god at craps and won $15. which he is going to donate to a NIC hospital. He said he was shaking all over because he was actually asking for a sign from god yet he says he's not a spiritual person. I had a flash in the hotel that you could never do a Hollywood film about these people because none of them look the look.

While in Nicaragua, Gray and Shafransky stayed in a house that was divided into two with men living on one side and women on the other. Gray's roommates included a born-again Christian, a social worker, and a college student from Berkeley named Daniel, who suffered a psychotic break while there.

AUGUST 17, 1987

First the children's hospital. I liked the doctor there but all these sick children were very depressing. We took up a collection of $425. just after we left. Then all the Nic money was passed out from the bus which was a ludicrous sight. Then we went off to the marketplace to spend our money. Bought a painting and a box then back for lunch. Real hot. A little sleep after lunch and then a boring lecture on what I don't remember. Renée and I were passing notes back and forth like school kids. Oh these long hot days. Dinner was late and then we got blasted by this very intense American man who is not a citizen of Nic and an economic adviser. He talked for 2½ hours and really lay it on. I tried to record it but my tape recorder kept stopping. To bed early.

AUGUST 18, 1987

Dripping with sweat we heard all the testimonies from children being chopped in pieces to six kids being pushed out of a helicopter. I have this picture of these innocent children falling in horror. Daniel blasted me with his paranoia after. "Are you a reporter or are you here to help me?" I felt like I was tried as a counter revolutionary.

AUGUST 1987

NOTES FROM NICARAGUA
There are two faces in all the faces that my memory keeps going back to and I write this only to figure out why

There was this boy who didn't break the bubbles in the encampment of the deodorant. I call it that because that was the main item they wanted—DEODORANT and I thought it was NOT because they smelled but because it was an EMBLEM of America—IT WAS LIKE A GET WELL GIFT = DEODORANT

But the face I remember was of the boy that didn't break the bubbles and of the perhaps PARAPLEGIC BOY OVER EL SALVADOR

There was an untouched innocence ~~that was like all any one has longed for in the idea of Christ~~

AUGUST 22, 1987

Time for a brief drink with some of the group and then rush for our flight which was on time. The report at the airport was that they were not going to let Daniel on the plane. What a schlep. After a long day of flying, we got back to find Liz and Willem's stuff in our loft. I was so angry I could not get to sleep. Even took a sleeping pill and that didn't seem to help. At last I got to sleep and dreamt I was in the middle of Liz and Willem's redone loft just yelling at her and letting all of my rage out.

Among Gray's journals, there were also recordings he made throughout life—audio letters for friends and girlfriends, interviews with family members, recorded therapy sessions, snippets of his favorite NPR shows. On October 5, 1987, Gray recorded a letter for Pavel, his therapist, while sitting on Santa Monica Beach. In it, he told of going on a hike with Shafransky. During their walk, Shafransky tripped and fell down "wailing on the ground," and to Gray's own surprise this allowed him to feel closer to Shafransky rather than critical, as he so often felt—of her, of himself, of their not being "the super beautiful people, super rich, beautiful, power people of the world." Below, he refers to this experience again in his journals.

OCTOBER 10, 1987

When Renée fell down in that hot sun and brayed like a donkey it was at last refreshing to me because it was extreme enough to go beyond the bounds of a travel poster. It broke the frame. It was a possible tragedy doubled by the fact that it was in the land of the beautiful. The land of the perfect bodies and two images came back: Jack, when as a baby I took him to that strange place and he cried. It was as though he was crying for me. He was my vulnerability that I was carrying outside myself. The other memory was of the way I hurt Liz in Kashmir and then was able to love her again.

It was as though a bright searchlight had been blasted into all that flat beauty to make a single act of ugliness beautiful.

The following is a letter from Pavel from January 1988 discussing Gray's obsessive fear that he might have AIDS.

Dear Spaulding

As your letters keep coming it becomes clearer to me that this crisis that you are being beset by, is that proverbial crisis of middle age and that your reactions to it are deeply driven by the need to stop postponing life anymore. You are using Aids and remorse about past fucks to create the illusion that adulthood is not their yet.
I think it has caught up with you and you may as well accept it as being much less painfull then aids or any other horrible disease. It is not going to kill you.
Well I am not so sure about it. Of course adulthood in some way will kill you, but merrily and very slowly. One also gains a lot new insights and new creative powers, once you can accept that inevitable fate. This second life only begins at fifty.
You do not need aids just because you do not want to grow up.
One day maybe, hopefully they will conquer aids, probably in our lifetime and then the land of fuck will open again. Who knows. I always thought that the nineties will be a replica of the sixties. Middle nineties I guess. Don't hold me to dates.

Best regards:

1. 26.88

[Gray and Shafransky were invited to an American film festival in St. Petersburg, Russia, where The Killing Fields *and* Swimming to Cambodia *were screened]*

LENINGRAD

I had this dream just before I woke up. I was riding on the back of a bike with this BOY/MAN. He had the body of a boy and I was somehow aware that he had the psyche of a man. Mature. His shoulders under a white T shirt were beautiful and I held on to them to keep my balance and I found that I was holding more and more to his beautiful undulating shoulders that were going up and like a dancer's. Soon we were on the edge of a great cliff by the ocean, and then there were three of us. Myself, he and another man. And I was overwhelmed by the view. It was like one of those breathtaking California Ocean views. But then I realized that all three of us were on the edge of a cliff that was slanted down and I had the feeling that I might fall at any moment and I remember saying, "I shouldn't have smoked that marijuana last night." Then I had a sense that if I could get rid of my fear that I was going to fall that I wouldn't. That is if I could only relax. Now just to go back a bit I also was aware that I was in love with this man-boy and that I only had three days before I had to go so I knew I should not hesitate to express my love. Because I had promised someone (maybe Renée) that I'd be back in three days. So we were on the edge of this cliff and the boy-man said to me "you are so filled up with fame."

Then I went to bed without him and he crawled in to bed with me and he was dressed in camouflage and I began to make love to him. To pass my hand over his chest and down over his hips and was giggling and his skin was soft and warm and brown and just as I was about to pass my hand through the back of his thighs to feel his balls, Renée woke me up or I woke up on my own I'm not sure which.

MAY 1, 1988

THE FIRST OF MAY

I couldn't stop examining my skin for signs of cancer and old age. My arm had turned into a Milky Way of freckles and yet I couldn't stay out of the sun.

> Mom wanted—she needed to be ARTISTIC.
> I'm now in the presence of Mom.
>> That's right dear.
>> The message is—try to be artistic.

Is it important for me to know why Mom killed herself?

OPEN WITH THIS because she couldn't paint. That's what "TO THE LIGHTHOUSE" was about.

But "Swimming" was my CROSS.

Why does madness feel like insight?

MAY 7, 1988

[Gray spent part of the month of May at MacDowell, an artists' colony in New Hampshire, writing Impossible Vacation*]*

I remembered to take the little man for a walk today for our first walk and we stepped out the door. I saw all the birds and I thought maybe if I'm still, one will come and land on me and they all got closer and closer until one did twice on my shoulder and once on my head; almost on my head like my pet bird used to do. The only aspect that kept this event balanced were the constant annoying May Flies.

Today I have been included in magic.

["The little man" was an eight-by-ten drawing of a Balinese icon, a man with four legs, a grass skirt, and no head; his eyes in his chest. Gray was given this picture by a healer in Bali who infused it with power to help make Gray feel more present. As he told it later in his monologue Gray's Anatomy, *one day when he was leaving his MacDowell cabin to hike in the woods, he heard the little man say in a small voice, "What about the walk? What about the walk?"*

Gray went to the little man, cradled him in his arms, and then went outside. "There, about seventy-five feet from the cabin, is a huge maple tree with red buds on it. It's about fifty feet tall," Gray recalled. "As I'm aiming the little man's eyes up at it, the thought occurs to me that if I call a sparrow, it will come and land on me . . . All I do is have the thought come to me and a sparrow swoops down and begins to circle my head, so close in that I can feel the wings in my ears. I have chills. I am very high at this moment, and I feel very, very superb. This bird lands on my left shoulder and simply sits there, breathing . . . So I knew there was magic in the world."]

JUNE 11, 1988

Renée talks about her dream of a small wedding up at the Duchesse Anne. I drag my feet and look at other women on the street.

JUNE 1988

Renée caught the flowers at Peter's wedding. She caught Anthemia's bouquet and it was as though in a movie. It was as though Renée had magnets in her hands and all the other women were so catty and jealous.

Ron said, it's no big deal to get married. It's when you have children that you are cemented.

JUNE 22, 1988

Renée woke from all these strange dreams, me with two cocks, front and back, one for affairs.

AUGUST 4, 1988

I get stoned to meet the other me. The other side of everyday me. But I can't imagine marijuana replacing booze. I want to drink to relieve the MANIC MIND it all sets off.

AUGUST 5, 1988

We had Ron and Donna over for a nice cook out and I was saying how I sat with DOORS keyboard player and how I said to Ron I was never really a fan of the DOORS.

Then when I went to buy coals LIGHT MY FIRE came on full blast. SYNCHRONICITY is more exciting for me than any circus or fireworks, etc.

DON DELILLO [*From his novel* Libra] on secrets page 26.

"You're here because there's something vitalizing in a secret. My little girl is generous with secrets. I wish she weren't, frankly. Don't secrets sustain her, keep her separate, make her self-aware? How can she know who she is if she gives away her secrets?"

AUGUST 31, 1988

[*Gray and Shafransky rented a house in Sag Harbor, New York, for a month while Gray was working on* Impossible Vacation]

Here we go; we are out at Sag Harbor and the whole place wants to make me feel like we are in love and I kept thinking we should have been through this already. After all how long have we been together and why do I hold back?

Every real sight and event has a fantasy with it of how it could be otherwise. It's like I'm here but not here. I am here and I am somewhere else too much.

SEPTEMBER 22, 1988

Living is like dying and telling the story is like coming back from the dead to be reborn.

NOVEMBER 6, 1988

One of the fears about death is that there will be no rebellion—that "I" will be like an ant and just belong to it all—no individualization just all this overwhelming ONENESS. No individual VOICE left.

JANUARY 20, 1989

I needed to choose the book to make it important. It was interesting that Renée set up what I should ask for and when I did and got it, I chose the book. TO WRITE without an audience is to be alone in the worst way. It is to be without a super ego that I answer to each night. And the nights are so lonely.

Walk away from temptation.

I know it's sort of crazy and competitive but I can't help WANTING TO REENACT Christ in the desert from LAST TEMPTATIONS. But I liked that scene the most and I kept wanting to go to an American desert and do a BIG FAST as in: "books on a desert island . . ."

We as Americans need to win our spiritual identity back from India.

I was hoping my book would be a creation and not merely a report.

JANUARY 20, 1989

I made up my mind because I ran into an anonymous fan on the street who said I was the best part of *Beaches* for her and then when she said, "Is that really where you want to be?" The answer inside was "NO." I need to stay on the EAST COAST of AMERICA and try to come from a quiet mind and see what comes next.

JANUARY 23, 1989

[In December 1988, Gray debuted as the Stage Manager in Thornton Wilder's Our Town, *directed by Gregory Mosher and starring Penelope Ann Miller, Frances Conroy, and Eric Stoltz at the Lyceum Theatre on Broadway]*

Maybe I've made a big mistake with the book. Maybe it's the telling of the story that cures me and not the writing of it. That I am straying from what I do best.

Being in OUR TOWN is like being STUCK back there again = some kind of smothering SECURITY like it's a metaphor for all that is always going on.

Renée said, "Maybe you just had a fantasy of yourself as a writer and you're working that (hollow) fantasy out."

JANUARY 1989

Yes, the synchronicity comes in when I'm searching for an answer.

After a visit to Renée while walking down West Broadway and thinking about India—(just after Renée told me I should finish my book) I was thinking to myself that the devils were at work in me again and I saw a newspaper that was wrapped around a pile of shit and it said "DEVILS REKINDLE A MEMORY." Then a man stopped me to tell me how wrong Frank Rich was and how good I was as the Stage Manager. *[In reviewing* Our Town *for* The New York Times, *Rich called Gray the "one major casting miscalculation"; Gray later reflected on this bad review in his 1990 monologue,* Monster in a Box, *which, in turn, Rich reviewed favorably.]* Then I thought, who shall I call next and I looked down and saw RON written in the cement.

APRIL 4, 1989

After working on the book and out for a walk with THE LITTLE MAN I began thinking again about the problems of fiction and how Liz and I made something transcendent in our relationship by transcending through work and our work was our love and unless that is somehow built into the novel as a working metaphor that is to say an image that turns you on as much as an actual incident in your "real" life does then if you can't find that your—my—writing is hollow.

I want to say that my life represented in the written or spoken word is already one step away from the unspeakable heart of the matter—to translate that into a fictional metaphor is to get even further away from the heart of it.

Could Meg *[the character Gray seemingly based on LeCompte in* Impossible Vacation*]* see that I needed to be an actor and direct me in a one man show of THE SEA GULL? But the truth is that we were held together by the glue of the performance group and it took us a long time to accept and understand that and that's where the heart of it lies, not in the fiction of going looking for Kashmir rugs *[Meg buys and sells these rugs in the novel]*; it also gives my character some mobility and deals more with issues of the times.

In short I can't seem to solve the problem of THE LIE THAT TELLS THE TRUTH.

JUNE 9, 1989

The worst fear is that I'll learn to be happy AT LAST and then get real sad when I see what I've missed.

JUNE 17, 1989

I was coming up my driveway and I saw an unexplainable light in the woods and I tried to pretend I hadn't seen it.

I have the feeling often that something is waiting to reveal itself to me the more open I get.

SEPTEMBER 19, 1989

I have been having the strangest dreams lately and because I've been working on my book I've not had time or patience to write them down but I will make a brief note here:

(1) Dream of Pavel and how we were in this room and he was surrounded by narcotic women and I challenged him by saying that he was trying to escape from the real pain of his life by overworking. I was accusing him of being a workaholic and when I did this, his head disappeared and turned white—a white fuzzy light the way ORIAH's did for me at Omega. *[Here Gray is referring to a storytelling workshop he taught at the Omega Institute in upstate New York where he asked everyone to look into each other's eyes as an exercise. When Gray looked into the blue eyes of a thirty-six-year-old woman, "her entire face began to slide off her skull. It was pouring down; it was drooling off like in a horror movie, like a bad LSD trip; and then her face turned in to an oval ball of pulsing light," as he told it in* Gray's Anatomy, *"all of a sudden the ball of white light came into a point and went Pfff! Whoom! and vanished out the window behind her head, and her face recomposed and smiled back at me."]* Then Pavel told me that that was my projection.

(2) Dream in which Renée, Liz and I and BETTY, Liz's mother, were all in one house, that the water came right up to—came right up to the front steps and Renée was running around real happy in the house like a little kid and Liz took my head in her hands and held it and said, You're wonderful. You are a genius but you are too self-indulgent.

(3) A real horrid dream of a woman seducing me and she lay on the floor, all beautiful and naked and I just lay my head on her belly and looked down to see an uncircumcised cock just like mine and she was a woman with a cock and then when she spread her legs it was like her vagina was an asshole just under her balls and flecks of fresh blood were all over her and her balls and the flecks of blood were sticking to my hands and I went to wash my hands and cut them on the faucet which was also like an uncircumcised cock.

And when I went out of the room to the toilet, I came back to find that I'd been robbed and she said, look in your wallet, and I found my money was gone but I found new money in an old spot in my wallet. New money I'd forgotten that I'd put there and I realized that I would never have found that money if I'd not been robbed of the original money—all these $50 bills.

Could be a dream about creativity and SACRIFICE and how new and positive grows out of the old negative.

I went out drinking with Sam. He told me that he and Susan were having a separation. We talked a lot about Pavel—a good common point between us. He told me that he did not discuss what went on between himself and Pavel with Susan. He kept it to himself. A private thing.

And I realized I have no private thing.

the nineties

THAT IS WHEN suicide comes. It comes when the shadow
part or let's say the part of you that you hate starts to take
over and fill up or push out all the other parts until you are
all the part that you hate and there is this one little part left
that is the killer and the killer is closely related to the self
hate and at last it does its dirty little deed.

APRIL 1, 1995

In 1991, Gray had a dream that he was standing on top of "a very tall tower or slender geological formation." A boy holding a drum— possibly a younger version of Gray himself—stands so close Gray can feel his breath. The boy kisses him on the mouth. Gray doesn't want to stop kissing but is afraid that if he doesn't, he'll lose his balance and fall.

"Being love is my last big public secret that I dance around?" Gray asked after describing the dream in his journal. It's a meaningful question, particularly in this decade, which ushered in years of romantic destruction and, subsequently, forced Gray to reconsider himself, privately and publicly.

On January 13, 1990, Gray met Kathleen Russo ("Kathie") in Rochester, New York. He was forty-eight years old at the time; Russo was twenty-nine. He'd traveled there to perform his new monologue, Monster in a Box, *at the Pyramid Arts Center, where Russo was the publicity director. They began an affair that weekend. In February 1990, Russo was offered a job as an agent at SoHo Booking, a Manhattan booking agency that primarily worked with dancers. She took the job and moved to the city the next month with Marissa [Maier], her three-year-old daughter from a previous relationship. Once Russo was living in Manhattan, especially after she moved to Tribeca, a neighborhood within walking distance of Gray's SoHo loft, in August 1991, the two became more involved. This violated a quiet understanding between Gray and Shafransky—or at least an understanding Gray felt they had—that he would sleep with other women only while he was out of town.*

"Having an affair was not uncommon for me, but I had them only out on the road," Gray explained in his monologue It's a Slippery Slope. *"They were the most powerful means of nonverbal communication I've ever known, as well as being fun. I always felt that it was safe to have them if they were kept out there and never brought home."*

For over a year, however, Gray did not mention Russo in his journal for fear of Shafransky reading it. When he finally did start writing about Russo in his diaries, he referred to her variously as "the other woman" and "H."—for Hester Prynne, the so-called adulteress from Nathaniel Hawthorne's Scarlet Letter.

Despite his ongoing affair with Russo, Gray went forward with plans to marry Shafransky in August 1991, two months after his fiftieth birthday. "I thought that once I married her, it would put an end to the affair with Kathie," Gray told his Slippery Slope audiences. "When I got married it was like a cork going into a glass bottle, and I started feeling, Oh, help, I can't breathe, let me out. The affair with Kathie heated up."

As with all of his monologues, this story is relayed with the distancing calm of hindsight. In life, Gray was in raw, torturous agony for the first half of this decade as he divided himself between two women— Shafransky and Russo. He did, indeed, go forward with marrying Shafransky, as described above, but the doubt he felt leading up to their wedding and throughout the subsequent breakup of their relationship ultimately precipitated another severe breakdown.

In the midst of this emotional collapse, Russo told Gray that she was pregnant. Soon after, Gray wrote her a letter asking her to get an abortion. Shafransky found this unmailed note stuck in The Philosophy of Sex, a book that Gray was reading at the time. Gray then confessed to Shafransky everything about his relationship with Russo. Despite subsequent requests that Russo not have the baby, she went forward with the pregnancy on her own. Gray tried, at the same time, to keep his relationship with Shafransky together. But a month after Russo gave birth to a son in September 1992—and the two women had an accidental run-in on the street in Manhattan while Russo was walking with the baby—Shafransky finally left him.

"Renée was the delight. Renée was always the delight behind the stories," Gray wrote in his journal in January 1993. "She was the heart of the story and I have cut the heart out. Now I'm afraid to go anywhere that the story can't be tied to an AUDIENCE."

Gray retreated to his former self, the one who had not yet driven Shafransky away, in his performances. This was the person he presented in his monologues that he debuted in 1990 and 1993, respectively: Monster in a Box, the story of his struggle to finish his novel; and Gray's Anatomy, about his quest to find an alternative cure for his macular pucker, "scrunched saran wrap" on his retina, a condition that caused blurred vision in his left eye.

In May 1993, not long after Shafransky had left him, Gray met his eight-month-old son, Forrest, for the first time. "Bending over him,

I looked down into his eyes, and fell in," Gray said of this meeting in It's a Slippery Slope. "I did not expect the gaze that came back, it was absolutely forever. Long, pure, empty, not innocent, because way beyond innocence, mere being, pure consciousness, the observing self that I'd always been trying to catch was staring back at me; they were no-agenda eyes."

This was a dramatic—and authentic—turning point for Gray: he became a father. The journals in the period that follow express doubts about Russo, sadness at the loss of Shafransky, fears about his work, and yet a clear, committed love for his son, Forrest. Gray was not miraculously relinquished of his weaknesses—he still thought about himself too much, drank too much, relied on the attention of his audiences too much—but he was powerfully changed by becoming a parent.

"I saw him as transformed. The passage in Slippery Slope in which he first meets Forrest is one of the most beautiful passages," Francine Prose recalled. "I was in tears hearing it, because it was just so beautiful and because I knew what he'd gone through around it. He was incredibly happy, once he resolved all of that, or apparently resolved it. That was the happiest I'd ever seen him—and the least tormented."

Gray was aware and grateful as a father—two things he seemingly hadn't been able to achieve as a lover or husband. Parenthood offered him a path out of himself, a reprieve from narcissism; he let go a little and was able to relax his racing mind. "The thing that was great about being with Forrest was that he slowed me down and I loved him because he was not needy in the park. He was not after anyone else's toys and he was satisfied with that little stick," Gray wrote in his journal in May 1995. "Then every so often I would look up and see that perfect blue spring sky with three or four puffy white clouds suspended and I would feel, this is good . . . this is alright. My heart filled by the simple presence of this boy. This day with this boy."

Gray also appreciated the wisdom and mysticism of a small child, as well as the reflection of the childish impulses he'd long observed— and been fascinated by—in himself. He wrote often about the child within him and within Shafransky in his journals, and also spoke of this in It's a Slippery Slope. "We had a strong case of arrested development going on just under the surface of our adult appearance, where there were two children who had never been seen or, rather, had been seen by their respective parents—and then gobbled up," he explained.

Gray felt caring for Forrest allowed him to move out of this emotional limbo.

Gray and Russo's second son, Theo, was born on January 16, 1997. Gray relaxed further into family life. He settled into his relationship to the baby, to Forrest, to Marissa—and found that in doing so, as he tells it in his journals, he'd come to love Russo as well.

Meanwhile, Gray came clean about his adultery in public. In 1996, he performed It's a Slippery Slope, *a story about both his learning to ski—the feeling that he'd found "balance" on top of a mountain—and his affair with Russo and the end of his relationship with Shafransky. He worried that this confession would push the audience away—particularly because many among them had come to know and love Shafransky as a character in his monologues—and that they would finally see him as unworthy.*

"Bravura stand-up unreeled with grand minimalism—his acting honed to a Beckettian simplicity that ripples out levels of meaning," wrote Laurie Stone in The Nation *before changing course. "Faced with the consequences of his impact on others, Gray loses his thread. He stops spinning tales of fear and loathing—and psychobabbles."*

"A clear-eyed and life-affirming performance piece," wrote Peter Marks in a positive review in The New York Times, *but only after a description of Gray as "that fellow at the party who convulses half the guests and leaves the other half muttering, 'Why are that man's neuroses any more interesting than mine?'"*

At the end of the decade, debuting at the Vivian Beaumont Theater at Lincoln Center on October 31, 1999, Gray presented Morning, Noon, and Night, *a paean to family life and to his new hometown of Sag Harbor, Long Island, where he and Russo and their children moved in 1996. In this piece, Gray described his life in Sag Harbor as presenting "a complicated present." By this he meant that Sag Harbor so reminded him of his childhood hometown of Barrington, Rhode Island, that it felt he had returned to his starting place and, for good or ill, was seeing it for the first time.*

FEBRUARY 24, 1990

What is it I don't want to see? Am I real tired of just LOOKING at life and describing what I ~~saw~~ saw?

Is writing my book making me blind?

So alright what if I do trust first thought best thought, so what when Oriah says the New Age people would ask me, "What am I sick of looking at" and the answer came in my mind . . . first thought, Renée maybe.

MARCH 16, 1990

The work should not SHOW EVERY THING. It should have some mystery to it—like LIFE!

MARCH 21, 1990

[Performing Monster in a Box *before premiering it later in the year at Lincoln Center in New York City*]

WASH. D.C.

THE PARODOX IS THAT WHEN I TALK ABOUT MYSELF I FORGET MYSELF

Here then is another reason why I like the monolog form. When I was writing about our summers in Jerusalem *[there is a scene set in Jerusalem, Rhode Island, in* Impossible Vacation*]* the order of the memory seemed random as I'm sure it is. The memories would appear to me as if on a wheel and to set them in print would be to stop the wheel but to speak them in different order each night would be to be free to spin the wheel until the right combination came up and what is the right combination? Finding the right combination is finally some intuitive combination of psychological insight and aesthetic form.

The monolog form is more open.

It is not set in print. It is a wheel that spins in a new way each night. It is more true to how reality is.

APRIL 1990

A longing for the acceptance of mystery in my life. My resentment at Pavel and all analysis for destroying mystery and real magic.

MAY 16, 1990

Today is rainy and a relief. I am at the point now where I find it difficult to be out in the spring day streets because the beauty of all the women drives me wild. I can't stop looking and wanting until the wanting HURTS so much that I get angry with them.

JULY 4, 1990

Riding home last night under almost full 4th of July moon I had a very clear vision of at most 30 short years left. I am beyond midlife now and I saw these 30 short years—they go so fast—as a series of little lines
       / / / / / / /
       / / / / / / /
    which would take me up to a very old 79 and I could see myself crossing them off and I could see how fast they could go and how finally there was not even a guarantee of 30 and then there was endless nothing for the one that is me that I've slowly come to love and know.

JULY 15, 1990

I have been off drink now for three weeks. *[Gray once again tried to quit drinking, this time as part of his effort to heal the trouble he had begun to experience with his left eye—mainly blurred vision that was later diagnosed as a macular pucker.]*
    I hardly have sex anymore, but I don't dream of that. I dream of beer.

JULY 1990

Now I awake each morning with a focus for my ANXIETY. Before it was free-floating, now it's more focused on my eyes.

Why does it feel bad to feel good? Why does it make me feel so much like a goodie-goodie? Why is health so _____?

IDIOPATHIC
    "THE PATIENT MUST MAKE DECISION."

JULY 21, 1990

SATURDAY

I'm thinking that I understand why Virginia Woolf killed herself and it was that she could only write about living as in TO THE LIGHT HOUSE but was not living it. She was outside of it all the time.

JULY 26, 1990

I don't like the way I am after 6 when I don't drink. I get real shut down. No expansive spontaneous anything. Just a sober, somber man. The little bit of white wine changed me a little. I get just loose and more outspoken but it's that horrid TAPPING DOWN I feel.

SO PENT UP like I'm sitting on something. I seem only to overcome that in performance where I'm the center of focus for 90 minutes.

At this time, Gray became increasingly obsessed by the disintegrating vision in his left eye—both as a disorienting health problem and as the subject for his next monologue. He began to seek out alternative cures in a race against time with his eye. His ophthalmologist advised him that, yes, he could try any alternative therapy he'd like—diet, acupuncture, prayer—but if the condition worsened, he would have to have surgery. In an attempt to cure his eye problem using alternative practices, Gray went to a sweat lodge prayer in Minneapolis, visited a nutritional ophthalmologist in Poughkeepsie, and traveled to see a so-called psychic surgeon—who claimed to be able to reach into the body to remove pathological matter using only his hands—in the Philippines. In Gray's Anatomy, Gray calls his psychic surgeon "Pini Lopa" and describes him as a fifty-seven-year-old man who looks like "a performer from Vegas," with "a powder-blue suit" and white leisure shoes. In his journals, however, Gray refers to the psychic surgeon as "Alex." When Gray saw Pini Lopa work on a Japanese woman, his "fingers seem to go right into her stomach," and he pulls out "a meatball the size of a cantaloupe." Gray witnessed many more of these operations—yellow and green pus came out of a woman's neck; "big bloody grapes" are pulled from a man's stomach—and then went through the surgery himself. Lopa pushed his fingers into Gray's eyes, and blood gushed out. "Blood!" Gray cried out in his monologue. "It's pouring down and someone is sopping it off my face." And yet there was no blood when Gray rushed to look at his eye in a mirror. Lopa recommended that Gray do this surgery for seven days, twice a day, for a fee of fifty dollars each time. Gray fled the Philippines before doing so. He could never resolve whether there was a trick played or if it was truly a miracle. Shortly thereafter, he underwent the traditional treatment—a microsurgery involving scraping the macula—that had been recommended to him from the beginning. In his journals, Gray drops into the story midway through, without entries leading up to his decision to pursue alternative cures.

JULY 30, 1990

Now, once again I'm turning inland from the sea. The sea, the place of great pleasure and relaxation for me.

"In myths, when the hero fails a crucial test because he lacks faith; when . . . his old conditioning reasserts itself and he turns away from the one thing he must do. And it is problematic whether the opportunity will ever arise again."

[From Storming Heaven: LSD and the American Dream by Jay Stevens]

There are times when you have to go with the flow and trust the great god of SYNCHRONICITIES.

On my way to Niagara [where Gray traveled seeking another cure for his macular pucker], I began to really wonder what my intentions were. Was I a reporter or a patient? Was I going to report on this event or give myself to it. And I began to see the reporter as that part of me that always held out, that always did it . . . for an audience. That I would suffer for my audience, that I would suffer in order to make a good story. And as the plane landed in Syracuse, I thought I could be in the Atlantic Ocean tripping on mushrooms and making it with Renée in that backyard and I almost wanted that more than I wanted to be healed or perhaps thought that would be more healing in the end but I still haven't made up my mind about the operation and I head toward it now not as though I have willed it and am not PLUNGING into it but rather dragging my heels, always dragging me heals. No, I'm not diving into it. I've not yet turned my fall into a DIVE!

The operation has the inevitable feeling of death. All my days are getting squeezed, all my days are getting squeezed in around it and it hangs like a black cloud blotting out the sun.

I wonder now if maybe I'm running away from Renée.

You see, I'm not used to functioning this way. I tend to adjust to what happens to me, ADJUST to events rather than attack and try to fix them. THE OPERATION feels like an attack on my eye. THE OPERATION FEELS like a major attack.

But I had to follow out this PSYCHIC SURGEON IDEA because of how much it has appeared in my life.

Do I dare ask the question: WHO AM I MAKING THIS DRAMA FOR?

Alex [the psychic surgeon]: "You've come here because you believe in God" as he pressed his hand over my eye. I want to operate he said. Is there blood? There's always blood, he said smiling.

> He seems too nice to be a charlatan.
> It seems like I keep failing the healer test.

It's not that they are all fakes. It's that they long to walk on the water and do their best not to fall through so much. They don't drown.

At dinner I get depressed. They said the healer's energy had gone down since the 70's. I felt the same for myself. (Rather than see a person, I tend to fill them up with myself to see me coming back at myself.)

I knew that if I started believing in this stuff, I'd stop my depression but I also knew I could only live in doubt.

RENÉE

IT WASN'T HATE. IT WAS THE REVERSAL OF LOVE—something going backward. I love you in reverse I kiss you going out the door.

Next to the pool is a large stage where a Filipina woman singing Tracy Chapman songs to no one and it goes on and on with full commitment. THE SAD PART WAS WHEN SHE SAID THANK YOU TO NO ONE.

PERFORMANCE ARTIST KILLED BY PSYCHIC SURGEON.

Performance artist dies from AIDS spread by hands of Filipino psychic Surgeon.

THE STORY WILL BE MY ONLY HEALING. I ALONE HAVE ESCAPED TO TELL YOU.

AUGUST 7, 1990

[Back in New York for the surgery originally recommended by his ophthalmologist]

I am in the hospital in the waiting room and am amazed how profane it is. I'm sitting under a TV that has a show TALK show about dominating mothers. A very difficult place to develop positive energy then again DAY'S INN was not much better.

AUGUST 9, 1990

Days of looking at the floor and sleeping alone. Renée on the floor. I have to sleep face down. It has all been very uncomfortable. *[After his eye surgery, Gray was required to keep his face down for fourteen days to prevent glaucoma.]*

DREAM: I am backstage waiting to go on in a Shakespeare play. Maybe King Lear and a blond boy maybe 14 or 15, who I take to be Jack all grown up, is lying on his back on a platform whistling and I scold him for it. I, to my surprise, am able to express direct anger without guilt or qualification. Jack sits up and stops. He looks at me all innocent and wide-eyed. He looks almost like a cartoon character in something like little ORPHAN Annie or the little prince. I go for a long bike ride and I find that I'm way out in the country somewhere, a countryside I don't know. I'm riding through green fields and the air is turbulent like it has just rained or is about to rain and I came to this rushing stream or more like a swollen river and it is all rushing down under the bridge. I see a speedboat being sucked under. I see it underwater and I think I'm going to have to go that route and I realize I'm naked and that I may have to kick myself to a fence board and go down stream and risk drowning.

And then I think oh no I can't do this because there are no witnesses (I don't realize that it's the dreamer who is the witness) so I don't risk it because there is no one to see me do it or realize that I am missing. Then I realize its time to get back to the theatre and in fact I feel it is too late to make it on time. I decide to ask this family who are in a strange sort of Camper for a ride. I can see they have room but they just fold everything up and the father drives off. The father of the family. At last, I realized that without a ride I will never make it back and my absence will have ruined the play which means they will most likely cancel my run of MONSTER at the MITZI in reaction. [*Gray performed* Monster in a Box *at the Mitzi E. Newhouse Theater at Lincoln Center from November 2, 1990, through May 27, 1991. On November 21, 1991, he moved the show to the Vivian Beaumont Theater, also at Lincoln Center.*]

AUGUST 19, 1990

SUNDAY

My eye is back to 20/60 like before when I was so upset. Now, after the 20/200, it feels better by contrast.

More dreams of drinking.

SEPTEMBER 22, 1990

BOOK

SOLIPSISTIC
NARCISSISTIC
SELF-INDULGENT
PIECE OF POOP

DECEMBER 3, 1990

Well we're back *[at Sedgewood]* after five weeks and on this gray December day I did reconnect with this place and love it for so many reasons.

When I walked down to see our little lake almost healed—with a few more inches to go, my heart filled up as I saw it there in our first light snow and I saw it both as it was then in the moment and also all the other ways in which I have experienced it in the past as well as future. Ice skating under the moon and cross-country skiing in the snow that day last winter. So there it was the wonderful use of memory and the way it came in beautiful layers around the present moment.

DECEMBER 17, 1990

Fears that here I am about to marry Renée and I don't even know if I like her scripts. I only know I like what she does for me. Is that bad? Look out.

DECEMBER 22, 1990

I was expecting Bill and Sally after the show *[Monster in a Box]* but Demo and his actor friend came instead which worked out for the best. I could tell they really liked the show and it was a great show one of the best. A lot of people stood at the end and it was three excellent curtain calls.

I rode down on the number one train with Demo and his friend who is trying to be an actor here in New York and says its so discouraging because it's all about selling sex. And he wanted advice and I learned that all I could do really—what I always do—is tell him my story and as I told it I had the incredible sense of how lucky I have been. That somehow by a series of wonderful chance events I've come into my own wonderful form of theatre and it could have so easily not happened as it did not for so many others and suddenly I had that sense that I was that one sperm that had reached the egg. And for the first time in a long time, I felt blessed.

DECEMBER 27, 1990

I got blasted on Christmas and still feel poisoned. How could I have slipped? I had one beer, one Bloody Mary, two and a half shots of peppered vodka, two glasses of wine, and two of champagne within two hours of that fine dinner Renée fixed. I had one of the worst headaches I've ever had.

DECEMBER 29, 1990

I can't seem to rid myself of this endless hypochondria.

There is a very hard lump or gland in the right side of my neck and I have this strange discomfort or odd sensitivity in maybe the muscles of my arms. I have very few good days where I make it through without all these fears even though I gave up on drink.

JANUARY 23, 1991

I went up to the Beaumont last night and I thought the show went well but it was something else very far from being intimate BUT after the show I was amazed when Renée told me that I left out the section: "How shall I do it dear . . . ?" *[In* Monster in a Box, *Gray talked of sitting with his mother when he was twenty-four years old; she was holding* The Christian Science Monitor *in front of her, and Gray, annoyed with her for putting a barrier between them, flicked the newspaper with his finger. "And she pulled the paper down," Gray remembered, "and looked me right in the eyes and said, 'How shall I do it, dear? How shall I do it? Shall I do it in the garage with the car?'"]*

And was at first depressed but the next day (today) while talking with Anne Rhoney I realized that there was something in me—perhaps some private aspect of myself that was not ready or able or did not want to give that story away and that realization was a sort of turn on that something so subconscious still existed in me.

FEBRUARY 9, 1991

Renée has gone to L.A. to look for work. Hard for me to work in the day because of many upsetting vitreous floaters in my right eye. Renée called me to say she's not pregnant and she only seemed "a little disappointed." She told me to read MIRABELLA MAGAZINE, an article about how everything gives you cancer even herbal tea. The report got me so upset that I went out to the Manhattan Brewery with Munz after we saw BRACE UP [the Wooster Group's version of Anton Chekhov's Three Sisters] at the Garage. I was split focus between the show and watching a young (maybe 23) Japanese girl to my left. What beautiful skin she had. I could not stop thinking about touching her naked white, white naked body. I had that old fantasy that just being around her would meet 97% of all my needs. Fears too of what will become of Renée and I now that we are officially childless. A relief and a sadness came over me. It's hard for me to live a meaningless life and enjoy it.

FEBRUARY 19, 1991

I think I want to live in a story of my own. I cast myself in my next story and then I tell about it. I need to cast myself again.

I go out and look for a story and then I cast myself in it and tell about what I saw happened or what happened to me. And I have to have something to support me other than despair which is what takes me over when I'm not performing.

$$\downarrow$$

I'm taking an hour here to be my own therapist.

FEBRUARY 27, 1991

My fear is that I will get so good at artifice that I will no longer lead an authentic life.

MAY 3, 1991

DREAM
I am on the top of a very tall tower or slender geological formation and a young boy—maybe a younger version of myself—has a smaller version of my new favorite drum placed straight on—and he is standing so close and I can feel his sweet breath (like slow dancing in 7th grade) and I'm afraid of being up so high and am barely able to keep my balance— then he begins to kiss me on the mouth and I love it but plead with him

to stop because I'm afraid that his kissing me will throw me off balance and I will fall.

(Being love is my last big public secret that I dance around?)

JUNE 6, 1991

I turned 50 years old yesterday and I never thought I would have made it. All I want to do now before I die is learn how to laugh. Last night I had a DREAM that I was watching some big Russian play or extravaganza LIKE CIRQUE DE SOLEIL (where I didn't laugh) but just as the last scene was being played out I ran between the two men who were playing it out and I started to laugh BUT I was still laughing onstage and then there was the blackout. Next I was in a small elevator going up and down and not able to get out.

Renée made a wonderful surprise party for me and I drank a lot of champagne. She also bought me a great suit. Renée really loves me! What a fool I'd be to throw all that away.

JULY 1, 1991

DREAM
This was a very disturbing dream. Someone had stepped on my face although I don't remember how—perhaps it happened while I was lying on the beach—and I had to have plastic surgery performed on ~~the~~ my eyebrows and TREVOR was my surgeon. The operation destroyed my innocent whimsical look. I ended up with dark thick ethnic eyebrows that made me look all heavy, stern and serious and I was very upset because I know that these eyebrows would never allow me to work in the same way again. Fear of HOLLYWOOD MAYBE?

JULY 17, 1991

Pavel said, go do it do what you have to do to learn from it see if it works. He also said GUILT is the mother of COMPASSION.

[This is an allusion to Gray's desire to see more of Russo. He had, according to Russo, just returned from a camping trip with her in the Adirondacks.]

JULY 21, 1991

SUNDAY

I'm on the train to R.I. and Block Island. I cannot believe that I'm still
in this paralyzing ring of sadness and depression. I find it almost impossible to read or see anything that doesn't threaten me. I look forward to
drinks at five. The drinks are about all that calms me down. Deadens the
pain. Something about east coast SUMMER maybe. I don't know what
triggered this one but I think it started—if not with that great sex—then
at least from the constant obsessive calling it back over and over until it
eats a hole in my head and there is no peace of mind. *[This is a reference
to his time spent with Russo.]* A certain amount of major masochism
operating here that makes it so difficult to stand seeing happy people.
I run from laughter and have fantasies of going with Pavel to see all
his patients dying of Aids. I make that child up in my mind and even
EVEN see her in the back of the car. Mel told me that John Malkovich
must be a masochist because he was happy with Michelle Pfeiffer and
then walked away from that. He had it all and walked away so he could
feel. . . . the PAIN. I am making life a mess for Renée. I can't look at my
book. It makes me sick I can hardly look at anything. It is like a skunk
beast SKUNK beast is in my ear lapping with his tongue saying ⟶
GOD IS DEAD ALL THINGS ARE PERMITTED

*Gray and Shafransky rented a house in Wainscott, in Long Island,
New York, for the months of July and August, in anticipation of holding their wedding there on August 24, 1991.*

JULY 22, 1991

This is the perfect location. Its like a HOPPER painting and I walk out
nervous and instead of the perfect house (BE HERE NOW) I see her
and her child *[Russo and her daughter, Marissa]* and my child with her
all living at Sedgewood waiting for me to come home then I think I
have to call Pavel and I remind myself of mom when she was crazy and
calling her PRACTITIONER and then repeating what he said over and

over. I don't have my voice of Pavel. I have no calming nurturing voice in me or do I? Sometimes I can calm myself and talk myself down but it takes constant work.

Now I am being filmed for CBS so I'm suddenly calm. It's as though the camera adds meaning to my life as a sort of witness. I feel less alone knowing that this event is somehow larger than me or going to be in more places than me.

JULY 23, 1991

Oh God! this is starting to get as bad as 1976.

The skunk mouth the skunk tongue is in my head saying all things are permitted God is dead therefore all things are permitted

AUGUST 1, 1991

I got sick at last and then I broke down and cried. Renée said that I hadn't cried like that since I broke up with Liz. I thought then that I must be breaking up with Renée but I had to marry her first. This is an insane twist if it is true. I've not been so unhappy and depressed for years. I had to get sick. It was the only way. Renée asked if the house was haunted. I thought I could see Marissa in the guest room. The empty beds make me crazy. I keep thinking of them as filled with children. I was too sad to ride to the ocean this morning. Sad and sick. Renée rode alone. She said it was nice. I lay sick in bed and told Renée that I felt I used her as a nurse to get famous. Just used her to keep me afloat.

Renée made me love her again when she told me that birds choke on rice so she is going to throw bird seed at the wedding. I keep saying lets call it off. Renée says we should do it now. Calling off the wedding would be BREAKING UP.

AUGUST 6, 1991

I started talking about how Pavel said maybe Renée should be prepared to be a single mother and to be in an open relationship. Renée flipped out and got angry but by the time we got to the beach she was crying and she told me to go back to New York. This made me cry. As soon as she started to cry, I cried and then comforted her and we were able to stay on the beach for an ~~our~~ hour. Renée said she didn't want to be a single mother. She'd rather talk to me than to a baby.

We went to Robby *[Stein, a child psychoanalyst and friend of Gray's]* and Freya's for dinner and before we went I told Renée that I could stop groaning if we could make an agreement that I would try being married for one year. She shook hands and said but don't tell anyone else.

I was able to enjoy the dinner party but I could not taste anything because of the cold. But we found some nice people to talk to and Renée seemed happy but she was smoking and drinking a lot of white wine. She was very upset because it looks now like the head of Columbia pictures, the man who wants her film is about to get sacked. I cannot believe it. With all else that is going on now this has to happen. It is too outrageous but Renée didn't get as upset as she might have and when she asked me to guess why I couldn't and she said it was because she had fun doing it.

H. *[Russo]* was saying that I was talking about leaving Renée after Jerusalem. How could I be? The eye operation was coming up. *[Gray and Shafransky participated in the Israel Festival–Jerusalem, a performing arts festival in the spring of 1990.]*

Maybe H. likes the way her life is. She said she did. Maybe she likes having the child *[Marissa]* all for herself. You never thought of that one did you? You have to look at all sides.

AUGUST 9, 1991

Afraid this is the beginning of THE TWO YEAR nervous breakdown that mom went through at 50. Ron thinks I should take Prozac and I'm afraid.

AUGUST 11, 1991

I got swept out to sea. I got caught in a TROUGH. I panicked and started swallowing water. Because I was in a panic I lost my strength so I cried for help. Renée thought I was calling for her to come in then she realized it was for help and she got Phil Hampton, a chiropractor from

PA to go out with a boogie board. I was able to swim toward him. He came with two other men. I felt comforted to be with them.

[Later, Gray confessed his reluctance to go through with the wedding in Gray's Anatomy—*though he did not mention his affair with Russo—and recounted the above experience as being one of almost drowning. "They're pulling me up like Christ between them, holding me, trying to take my photograph with them; they won't even give me a break. They recognize me," he added in his monologue. "They said they recognized me from the* Swimming to Cambodia *poster, the way my head was bobbing half out of the water! Art imitates life; life imitates art!"]*

At night I got drunk. I couldn't stand the loneliness. I kept seeing that imaginary child playing like some beautiful pet in the yard. She is always NOT my child but I have easy access to her and she loves me. This fantasy takes me over to the point of total painful groaning obsession. It becomes a giant pain and the only relief is vodka.

AUGUST 13, 1991

Today there was a review about Anne Sexton *[Diane Middlebrook's* Anne Sexton: A Biography*]* in the TIMES I get afraid of what it said:

"In the end, we are left not with a portrait of a ~~deeply disturbed~~ poet and her work, but with a portrait of a deeply disturbed highly unstable, selfish and self absorbed woman who happened to possess the talent to channel her neuroses into the therapeutic channels of art."

of this Renée said, "at least you're not cruel."

THIS IS A BIG ONE AND ITS STARTING TO COME DOWN AND IT FEELS LIKE IT'S GOING TO KILL ME—I keep thinking she's YOUNGER & SHE HAS A CHILD

AUGUST 15, 1991

I went for a walk on the beach. I thought I will phrase it this way, Renée if there was something going on in my life now that might cause us to break up in six months would you still want to marry me and she said yes. But give it a year. She'd rather be married for one year than not at all. I took her out to eat at the American Hotel *[in Sag Harbor]*. It was very beautiful with all the candles and lobster but I did it. I told her I was having an affair. She said it was like a cancer to her and I understood. She said I told her to relieve my guilt but it causes more pain in her now and that she thinks—and she is right—that I scrutinize her and judge her in relation to the other younger women. She also said that she wants to get married so she will be other than LIZ who still hangs over me like some shadow. Why get married only to get divorced in one year? Is there any transcendence? Any hope? Last night we had pretty good sex but then I woke up with that awful anxiety in the pit of my stomach.

The child is after me again. I go out to rake the lawn and the child is beside me with her little rake and I see now how and why people talk out loud to fantasies. They can't stand the pain anymore, the loneliness. And I do see the wedding as closing down a window on the head of THAT CHILD.

AUGUST 16, 1991

Yesterday was a very strange day. I started off bad and then Ron *[Feiner, Gray's lawyer, who joined the Universal Life Church in order to perform the wedding ceremony for Gray and Shafransky]* came out to work on the marriage ceremony and he gave me a Xanax which did calm me down make me more open and talkative $\longrightarrow$ more talk about me and my family etc. rather than about Renée and I and why "WE" are getting married. (God, I can't believe how self centered I am) Then we went to the beach to check out the spot. But most upsetting for Renée was going over the pre-nuptial agreement in front of Ron. She was embarrassed by it and also by how I talked about how getting married felt like a watershed for me and I—at this point—could not tell if it was a beginning of a new move toward the future or the beginning of the end $\longrightarrow$ again acting or maybe even pretending and tricking myself into the idea that I have no will or choice in it. I think I keep having the fantasy that I can live a life without consequences.

But at times when I look at Renée and I together I feel I've not really been able to be supportive of her. Over the years I've been like a big taking baby and maybe that is why I'm pushing so to give her the wedding. It makes her so happy but a lot of her happiness does not spread back and infect me. Instead I get anxious about the money and how I will never be able to do another monolog because what I'm going through now is both way too private and too scummy and duplicitous. I hate being divided like this and yet I keep inviting it. I hate not telling Renée every thing, all my endless fears and needs. I have to remember we are two different people.

ROCKY just called in the middle of all of this and I kind of broke down with him on the phone and told him how much I hated myself and how I felt like a performance machine. That Renée was winding me up like a crazy neurotic wind-up doll and pushing me out on stage and that when I wasn't doing that I was at home obsessing. And all I can feel is the time clock ticking and soon another crack of an opportunity to jump ship into another life will close. Rocky says Saul Bellow marries a new wife for each new book ⟶ then in the middle of this Renée came running to me with her heart all a flutter wanting help with some child that was attacked by yellow jackets. And she felt she needed to HELP trying to get the Arm and Hammer Baking soda out and reading the back of it. With her hands shaking.

Also, you have to understand how this house here, as beautiful as it is, keeps freaking me out because all the empty beds remind me of all the children we didn't have and will not have and how I'm headed toward becoming a dried up curmudgeon.

On August 20, Gray met Russo on Fire Island. Shafransky had gone to New York City for a few days. Gray and Russo were together for one night. At the end of their time together, according to Russo, she told him, "If you get married, we're through."

AUGUST 20, 1991

All private stuff. Went to National Seashore at Fire Island. WILD time—Hurricane BOB is on his way and I drive home with no windshield wipers. The storm seems to calm me because my head is such a Hurricane that its good just for a little bit to have ~~me~~ it outside of me. I'm in such conflict. I'm trying to be honest with myself but can't get to it. I don't want to live a life of regrets but no matter what I do I seem to set it up that way—that all action creates regret and I lose my center. It's like the regret mechanism. The other place offers less responsibility and that's why I resist having that child with Renée it would be 20 years worth. And I'm getting old and I don't feel like I'm living and that is making me insane.

I had to marry her to leave her?

AUGUST 21, 1991

Bob hit and when Ken the Caterer said, "Look what you've done. First you almost drown and now you cause this." I smiled and Renée said this is the first time you've smiled in a month.

Renée says she hates me but she is determined and so willful to go through with this wedding. She said, "We will get married and then we will get divorced in six months." But I knew she was just saying anything to put me at ease because it did. I thought by then I might be able to leave her.

Everything is falling apart.

AUGUST 22, 1991

Every time I look at the date on the calendar I feel like I'm going to the electric chair.

Is all of it really only grist for the mill? It feels like it now.

AUGUST 24, 1991

SAT.

It's the wedding morning and there are men here chopping up all the trees and two cleaning women upstairs vacuuming empty, never used rooms. Renée stepped on a bee and I began to think it was the power of mom. Last night we spent $800.- of dad's money on one dinner while Chan sat next to me talking about riding 100 miles in a day and nothing makes sense and the FEAR is still there. The fear is in me with the full moon and Rocky and I on the beach late at night talking about my sexual obsessions he doesn't seem to share in. My big hang up. Renée is so anxious about her script because no one called her to say they liked it. I had my regular morning erection but lost it when she told me this. But I got it back again and we had good but quick sex.

AUGUST 24, 1991

NOON—SAT.

Renée was standing over me helping me with THE BOOK and I'm looking up at her with totally insane eyes thinking this is how we will be in 10 years with no children—me at 60 hanging on Renée saying please please help me to write about MY life and it felt like Uncle Vanya again and Renée told me to go out and try to rake THE YARD not our yard but "THE" yard because this house is not real. I've not been here long enough. I have no center no real feeling for the place. All like theatre now and I do go out to rake the yard and Paula Court *[a photographer who had taken most of Gray's press shots for his monologues and was there to photograph the wedding]* comes and her body looks so great I want to jump on her and I think of H. and I think my god—I am marrying the wrong BODY and the lawn mower man comes and another motor starts up and its all making me crazy and I stutter when I try to speak to Paula I stutter like a little kid and this all has to be private because it would hurt Renée and Ron calls to say how are you doing and I see Renée's mother out the window like a great ghost and I say they are coming for me and Ron says—

"You are ~~bein~~ about to be witnessed by 50 people act in a role you never wanted to assume"

It is a performance. There are no private acts left.

AUGUST 25, 1991

Well, it's "OVER" . . . the event is over and how do I feel? Hungover and fearful of the future

The service on the beach was beautiful even though a few trucks came very close. Renée looked great in her dress and all that I feared DID begin to happen just from the event it all drew me further into love—that still fearful place for me. I both laughed and cried at Ron's ceremony and I did cry when I read Renée's inscription on the watch. It was a very strong moment.

I still feel a large and great sense of doom no matter how much people give me love and support. Witness my wedding toast. A sad one. That in spite of the fact that the sun will go out forever it's nice that people can still sit here and pretend to be in love. All getting back again to marriage and life as a performance and still and most of all now all I can think of is the most sad and melancholy of Shakespeare's lines.

"Our revels now have ended and these ~~as I~~ players etc. into air, into thin air.

"For we are such stuff as dreams are made on and our little life is rounded with a sleep"

These are the saddest most absurd and most true lines that I can come to after such an event. I know they come from the ego but where else?

AUGUST 29, 1991

I can no longer read my book. I smoke cigarettes and stare at it and it all breaks down in front of me. Does not hold together, does not make sense. Reads like some AA victim report. Some stupid confession. All literal and not poetic. The fantasy that I am a writer is broken and I sit here trying to figure out what I will do for a living.

I don't have time for a nervous breakdown. I have to get through this year. But how will I do it?

SEPTEMBER 3, 1991

I don't know how to WORK. I'm lazy I'm blasted with photos of Liz's perfect LAKE WORLD of groupness and it almost wipes me out, then our wedding photos. Who is that? "They LOOK like a happy couple." Can hardly bear to deal with anything. Skyy and dinner. Me two vodkas and wine. When Renée shows me the wedding dishes I explode. Me acting like a real asshole. "If you keep drinking and insulting me I will leave you." I drink to go to sleep. I wake early and depressed. Renée is in sexy underwear. I can hardly come because she doesn't come. I am thinking, what am I able to give to Renée besides (like dad) MONEY ——→ A HOUSE. Money is a substitute for LOVE and intimacy. "Your father always fed you well." —mom. I think I know what I can give to H. but maybe it's all fantasy and would require endless work on my part and I am really just a SLACKER. If I don't find my way into a community of people I can trust. . . . . I AM DRINKING NOW . . . I am now drinking my pre-flight Bloody Mary to calm me. I feel protected by ½ of a Bloody Mary and the plane feels safe—an escape—another escape from the real world waiting for me. *[Gray flew to Chicago to play a minor part in a Barnet Kellman film called* Straight Talk, *starring Dolly Parton.]*

But I want to try to talk about Pavel and what I feel is going on there. It was funny but he wanted to know why I told Renée I was having an affair. He tried to tell me that I am in an unnecessary panic over not being able to get enough sex. That I am in charge and I can get it when I want it but I tried to point out my fear of AIDS and he did not take it all that seriously. Renée is ready to go on without having a child. Pavel seems to feel there is something more complex going on in my work. He seems to think I have something like a number of personalities operating and Renée feels this is right.

Renée and Spalding got married—PASS THE SALT

It is Renée's open face that will HAUNT me forever. It is her happy face that I keep going back to and saying yes yes that's it. It is her face that radiates love and I love the way she loves me.

After Gray's trip to Chicago, he traveled to San Francisco to perform Monster in a Box *as well as* Interviewing the Audience. *Russo met him there—Gray had sent her a letter beforehand confessing that he'd gotten married but that he still wanted to see her. She stayed with him for a week.*

SEPTEMBER 8, 1991

Sunday

It occurred to me while in the bathtub this morning that I might end up in an asylum but Renée says all of what I'm going through is to avoid living and perhaps it has to do with feeling I have to make a choice between R & H.

SEPTEMBER 17, 1991

Renée came up from L.A. to visit. *[Shafransky was working on a film script in L.A. at the time.]* The first time we made love it was good. The other two times I couldn't feel it. Wasn't sure if I could come. Am split. Pavel is nuts if he doesn't see this.

Renée told someone. . . . I heard her say, that after going through the eye operation with me she knew she wanted to be with me the rest of her life. She wanted to marry me and grow old with me.

When I played the tape of the opening wedding monolog it reminded Renée a little of HENNY YOUNGMAN ⟶ my wife made me get married stuff. *[In San Francisco, according to Russo, Gray improvised a monologue about finally marrying Shafransky and played a recording of it to her.]* But listening back to the tape made me sad because I felt it was just another smokescreen. Another monolog that would allow me to escape from the real events.

THERE IS NOTHING
PRIVATE LEFT

SEPTEMBER 27, 1991

Renée says she's married to a misery. A black hole. She said she did not realize how messed up I was until she read the BOOK *[the manuscript of* Impossible Vacation*]* and then that was hard to take. When she had to read the details of the indecision. It made her want to scream "Will you make up your mind!" And I made her read that book right after we got married.

SEPTEMBER 30, 1991

Renée and I ate striped bass alone at the dining room table. She got me all hot and even crying on the idea of taking Peter and Ken *[two of the men who saved Gray from drowning before his wedding]* to Nepal for New Years. "That's what I'd do if I had your money."

Renée is so so loving and generous that she keeps blowing me away. That she would want to send me off with guys on a trip she really would like to take.

I wake up with an erection every morning and force sex on Renée. Then we work on MY BOOK. What a honeymoon!

OCTOBER 22, 1991

I'm back to the horrors of the book. I keep fantasizing that it is done and now it has just come back with all the flags on it *[with queries from the copy editor at Knopf]* and major chronology problems.

We went to the adoption class. I was angry with these people because of all their uncomplicated surety that they wanted a child. I was not sure. Neither was Renée.

JANUARY 20, 1992

I feel so lame working on the new monologue *[Gray's Anatomy]* because that subject is NOT the immediate issue.

The immediate issue is PRIVATE and will remain so.

It's HER motherhood that turns me on and its Renée, you and I against the world that does the other side for me.

FEBRUARY 15, 1992

I said I cannot stand Renée's body when it grows big and out of control and Pavel said, "Maybe it's you that is growing smaller." When I become like a little kid, Renée gets bigger. Pavel insists that it's me as a child remembering my mother's largeness. I can't believe how much all this seems to go back to Mom.

Why, I ask Pavel, can't I just shift to a new smaller woman? People do do it. I guess I'm afraid of the consequences.

FEBRUARY 17, 1992

But no matter how low I get I still seem to get some joy out of "PLAY-ING" it. I've become so good at playing my pain to save me from it.

I just called Rocky from the airport and performed the ultimate depression—Head cold, how did I get involved in this life, etc?

But after I left this little bomb on his phone machine I felt this little change of what? What was the feeling? It was a devilish glimmer; the projection perhaps into the future.

FEBRUARY 18, 1992

SPRINGFIELD, MISSOURI, HOLIDAY INN

Renée doesn't want to go back to the way we were but she did such a great job packing my bag that I almost cried.

During this period, Russo told Gray that she was pregnant with his child. "I met with Kathie only one more time and that was on the street to pass her money for an abortion, and I said, 'Get rid of it,'" Gray later publicly confessed in It's a Slippery Slope. *"And she said, 'I'm still thinking.'"*

FEBRUARY 27, 1992

KANSAS CITY MO.

So it's over, one way or another, IT IS OVER and yet my body missed her even though just yesterday my heart went out to Renée when she was working out on that stupid big wheeled bike and her hair was blowing and I wanted her to please stay young. The sadness I feel at Renée aging.

But when the possibilities go I feel trapped and OH HOW MY LONELY body longs for her and the way I used to TAKE HER ON A TABLE. H. was so wild with that stuff. How sad for it to be over. And now when I think ahead to September I have that meaningless dread again. I'm just worried about how I'm going to live in the same city with her there all the time in my mind. The horrid laughing. The gravitational pull of LUST.

MARCH 4, 1992

HOUSTON

I don't know if I will ever read over this. I think it would be too horrible to read over. But I can't remember the last time I felt good—did not feel like crying. Maybe it was in the swimming pool in Houston and I thought, just for a moment I thought—THINGS WILL BE ALRIGHT. And then I thought—no, not really, because I'm going to die forever and that makes me feel absurd. Stupid ANGRY—ANGUISH.

I'm sort of alright when I'm working but when I'm not working I fall through the cracks.

All I could think of before I went on last night was—what if she has that baby? I'm getting nuts.

I LAUGHED. (WHO GIVES A SHIT) But I did laugh when I was visiting Renée in L.A. I laughed at *Candid Camera*. Every time someone was going to hit golf ball at the TEE some guy would make a crazy squawking sound in a tree and I don't exactly know what I was laughing about.

MARCH 10, 1992

She *[Russo]* acts happy on the phone. That is what drives me wild. She doesn't act needy. Or like she has done anything wrong.

NO GUILT.

MARCH 14, 1992

Sat.

This is the hard part for me to write. I call H. to try to talk her into it. I think Pavel is all wrong—his emotional blackmail theory. But maybe I just get taken in. But I do and did get taken in by her and told her I still liked her. I also told her that I would stand by her in the abortion as well as put her in a good hospital. But here is the strange part. When she hung up I found myself "FEELING" that I was wishing she'd have the baby. Although I think it's the right thing—my heart is not in that goddamn abortion. Perhaps the most disturbing thing for me is when she reminded me that she had told me in Cambridge that she would not abort if she got pregnant.

MARCH 16, 1992

I have to write or call Pavel about this counter transference stuff. He's living through me and is confused about his feelings about the issue. He gives such mixed messages and will not admit to any mistakes because I will reject him.

The two previous entries offer glimmers of Gray's growing unhappiness with Pavel. In the months leading up to Russo giving birth, Gray felt that Pavel had misled and confused him. He complained to Russo that Pavel did not offer him boundaries—and Gray felt he, especially, needed a therapist who would offer him boundaries. Gray also was bothered by Pavel advising him to sleep with more women, rather than try to make sense of the mess he was already in. Shortly thereafter, Gray broke off his relationship with Pavel and did not see him again before Pavel's death the following July.

MARCH 19, 1992

ABOUT THIS HALL OF MIRRORS . . .

"A mock feeling and a true feeling are almost indistinguishable."

Gide

[From The Counterfeiters, *a 1925 novel by the French writer André Gide]*

BUDDHISM states that instead of seeing the real world the self creates a false universe of its own.

And in my case sells for top dollar

MARCH 23, 1992

The double bind hazard of my work is this ⎯⎯→ the audience applauds my assholeness which is transcended by my ability to tell it. So I only fly above it all when I'm performing.

MARCH 25, 1992

<u>SYNCHRONICITY</u> = When I get to the Vogue shoot I was telling the publicist about the class I wanted to do called WHAT'S GOING ON?

and there was music in the background and I suddenly realized it was the *[Marvin Gaye]* song *What's Going On* and my head just opened up. It made my day.

VOGUE SHOOT = THE DISTRACTION OF CELEBRITY

[Photographs were taken of Gray to run alongside a piece he contributed to Vogue *about writing fiction for the first time. The article ran in conjunction with the May publication of his novel,* Impossible Vacation.*]*

Every time I wake up, I think I'm in hell. I AM in hell. Renée tells me death would be easier and I agree. She is afraid that I will do something to myself. She doesn't trust me. A coward.

I seem to be only able to feel Renée's pain.

To save me from the pain of my life I began thinking about how to put it in my next monologue. Public pain.

On the flight to New York. What do I see from fear? When the plane goes bump. And I think we are going down. I blame it on our parents. Renée's father and my mother in some dark nether world plotting to torture us and bring us down.

I'M NOT AN ARTIST.
I'M A PUBLIC NEUROTIC.

I've cut Renée out of being the most powerful center of my work. I have KILLED HER. When I think this I think I'm going to go insane. How do I go on living with what I've done?

APRIL 8, 1992

I dreamt that Dad and I were taking a tour of the Barrington Harbor and we were very close in our memory and recollection. I remember that he put ~~my~~ HIS hand on my hand like a lover. And all of this was being taped. The tape was in a wooden box with a microphone mounted on top of it. I had the feeling that we could not go on talking or relating unless the tape was going. The tape had to be going.

APRIL 15, 1992

Phone therapy with Paul *[a therapist Gray began seeing in Los Angeles]* = "make peace with the beast." It all sounds like stories or a kind of mythology.

The beast wanted to have a baby with Kathie and the beast did it and now I'm split.

How can I talk with the beast when it has no words and is only in my body? It's the irrational part of me that I—or the rational part of me fears will eat the rest of me and put me in the hospital.

I only have my work. Nothing more.

Oh, I have DRINK.

APRIL 17, 1992

As long as I ACT insane I know I'm not. But there is no STORY; how can I write about another nervous breakdown. Who will care? They will only say "Pass the salt." And all life goes on around me. Without me as though I'm a dead man. Who cares about another Spalding Gray nervous breakdown and so the big fear comes again. What is left to say? And so I came to death again, Spalding Gray is a dead man.

UNDATED

Eugene, OR.

The fear is that people pay attention to me because I'm a celebrity. Without the film of "Swimming" I wouldn't be there.

Paul wanted to know where my RAGE was and I told him that all my rage and anguish is turned in on myself. But I think too it was in my

SEX drive. And the way that I make contact is through sex. Main way of body communication.

I see the sweet blue veins. How easy it would be to slice into them. With a sharp enough razor it wouldn't HURT.

APRIL 25, 1992

In the morning the realization of what I have done staggers me.

APRIL 27, 1992

This morning Renée cried on the phone, "That's my baby you gave her." My life feels over. Renée thinks I've never really seen her.

I can't see anything but my obsessions now. These feel like the John Cheever journals.

PHONE APRIL 27

Very difficult phone session with Paul. He refuses to give me advice because he says I get enraged with any parent figure and he wants me to accept him as just a person.

He thinks I have to do something for myself.

Paul says my rage is not conscious but it is doing a good job of destroying other people's lives.

My celebrity self is the only self I have now. What killed Marilyn Monroe? Not having self.

[An echo from Swimming to Cambodia; *Part One ends with these lines: "And just as I was dozing off . . . I had a flash. An inkling. I suddenly thought I knew what it was that killed Marilyn Monroe."]*

Gray's novel, Impossible Vacation, *was published on May 5, 1992. Despite his five-year struggle to write the book, Gray does not describe its publication, other than to mention his press tour, in the journals.*

The novel, a thinly veiled account of Gray's life, received mildly favorable reviews—particularly from critics unwilling to separate the indelible impression Gray had made as a performer from the more fleeting one he'd made as an author. "In the end, 'Impossible Vacation' is more a written monologue than a conventional novel: there's a narrowness of emotional focus to the volume, and Brewster, alone, emerges as a full-fledged character, while everyone else is relegated to a walk-on role," Michiko Kakutani wrote in The New York Times. *"At the same time, one finishes the book impressed by how readily Mr. Gray's narrative voice transfers to the page; how easily he's been able to translate a performance from the stage to the medium of print."*

MAY 19, 1992

The film of "Monster" is a failure in L.A. *[Nick Broomfield directed the film version of* Monster in a Box, *which premiered in Los Angeles on May 15, 1992.]* What next? The L.A. TIMES hates me and that always does me in.

[Peter Rainer's Los Angeles Times *review questioned whether Gray's self-referential storytelling should have been indulged yet again in the film and described Gray as "transfixed by his own limpid nuttiness."]*

AUGUST 10, 1992

What is this crazy love and money thing? Whenever Renée says K. is going to cost me a lot of money, I think ⟶ well, why not move in with her and get my money's worth? What an odd way to think.

AUGUST 14, 1992

Session with Michael *[a therapist Gray started seeing in New York after his falling-out with Pavel]* = "What stops you from moving in with Kathie?" Whenever he asks that question, I get confused and scared. The only answer is that I'm afraid it wouldn't work out, not that I'd lose Renée. And I wonder if maybe I feel that I've already lost Renée in some way and that was what I've been crying about.

　　*But he did say that I am having a hard time sorting out Renée's EGO POSITION from her WISDOM.

She's wise but not around Kathie. How could she be? That's where her wisdom has to stop.

At this time, Gray filmed King of the Hill, *directed by Steven Soderbergh, in which he played the supporting role of Mr. Mungo, a mysterious older man with dark sexual tendencies who eventually commits suicide. "We shot in the summer/early fall of '92," Soderbergh, who began his long friendship with Gray at this time, recalled, "so [the baby] was born and all that stuff was going on. But there was no indication of that. He didn't seem unduly distressed, or if he was, he surely wasn't showing us that. He came across as a version of the way he is when he performs. Bright and funny." (Soderbergh later released a documentary about Gray called* And Everything Is Going Fine—*a compassionate and well-received tribute—in 2010.)*

SEPTEMBER 4, 1992

Renée keeps asking me if there is something I am holding back from her. She wants to know why I'm so remote. I wonder if it has to do with how every time I tell someone else about K. (so far L. and S.), I somehow put K. and the memory of her back into my life. I give her life and end up missing her.

SEPTEMBER 11, 1992

THE DAY THE BABY WAS DUE.

I got up early to head off to IOWA. While I was doing yoga, Renée let out with one of her big groans and I, hoping it was about sex, went into the bed—run to see what was going on. She had had a bad dream—that she was giving birth to a freak lobster baby that was coming out of her stomach. It had claws but no head and upset as she was, she was still relieved that it was headless, so that it could be thrown in the garbage.

Then we did have sex. It was good and I left in a good mood. No tears today. Off to meet myself in IOWA but a bit of a bad feeling about how I am now making money for Kathie to spend on herself and Marissa.

SEPTEMBER 12, 1992

Surprised that I was greedy and envious of Frank Conroy [director of the Iowa Writers' Workshop at the time; presumably, Gray traveled there for an event related to Impossible Vacation] with his nice wife (they seem to get on well together), his five year old, his house in Nantucket, and how he loves it here, how he knows how much Marlon Brando weighs (320). But most of all, his enthusiasm that I lack so now. I seem to be feeling very bad about myself.

ABOUT FICTION—Frank said that he did not think it was the voice of God coming through you but rather it's ALL the books you have read that have created the voices and plots that sit in the back of your head.

SEPTEMBER 18, 1992

Renée got so disappointed when Peggy [Gray and Shafransky's couples therapist] said that therapy would most likely only make a 15% change in me. The next morning Renée came out of the bathroom and said, "Do you know what 15% is?" And when I said no she grabbed the upper part of my ankle and said from there down.

SEPTEMBER 25, 1992

I called K. and I ended up talking with her for an hour. And she said it would only cost 5,000 (ONLY) but what was strange and perhaps it had to do with a few drinks but I could not contact my rage for her. In fact, we were both very loose and open on the phone. She has not had the baby yet and is going to have induced labor if it doesn't come soon. She thinks it's a big boy. But she went on to say that I used to joke about moving in with her and kicking Blue Man out. [When Russo first moved to the city, two members of the Blue Man Group, the celebrated performance troupe, were her roommates.] When I said I didn't remember that she said, "I keep a diary too, you know." I called her selfish and she said so are you. Then a strange thing happened. She said I don't know how I'll ever be able to date with those two kids and I said I would be jealous. She said why and I just said I would. Because it's true. I can't imagine anyone else fucking her. Isn't that odd? What is that about?

A rowdy therapy session with Michael but before I mention that I do remember that K. brought up one thing that still hurts—the way I just walked away from her when she got pregnant and left her on her own to deal with it. I do think that was a big mistake that Pavel encouraged me to do.

As for therapy, Michael is very flip with me saying things like if you've told everything to Pavel what do we have to talk about? And I said nothing and he said let's get to know each other and I took a huge hit of Absolut and he said I looked like James Dean and I asked him if he had ever taken LSD and he said that was how he got into therapy. He said that the LSD always helped him see through the apparent ugliness and see a certain beauty at the center of things. I think he was saying it had made him an optimist.

Renée called this morning to ask about Ernie and got real upset that I didn't tell her that I talked to Kathie. She saw it as a betrayal. Aren't we in this together and how can you be friendly with her?

On September 27, 1992, Russo gave birth to a boy—Gray's son—and named him Forrest Dylan Gray. Russo's mother called Gray to let him know.

SEPTEMBER 28, 1992

It's been an unpleasant weekend. Humid warm rain and I'm still sick. Now into my second week. More talks with Renée in LA. She is now considering divorce. There is nothing happening out there for work.

Renée said that she can't trust me. That I'm like her father. All that she is reacting to is my compulsion, my storms. The way I can't hold on to them myself. I had to call her about how I flipped out over the blond who smiled at me on the street. Renée was very angry that I told her that. Renée said I had to learn how to suffer my own pain. Also Renée now thinks she's an artist because Florence told her so. In the middle of a long talk on Sunday, K.'s mother cut in to say it was a very healthy baby boy.

Renée says sadist in little boy's clothing.

Renée says why don't you just move in with K? Everything's in place.

OCTOBER 18, 1992

Sunday

Renée and I went to see the Dylan tribute concert. Renée got very upset when they booed. I got upset from her upset like old days with Liz. It was Renée's face that I loved then. It was filled with a deep sensitivity and concern. It took her a long time to get back into the concert.

I smoked some dope at the concert and got a little wild dancing in the aisle. Renée said she could not love me when I looked like that. A stupid, skinny, old man. Then lots of champagne at the Odeon. Very little sleep and all of that left me oh so nervous and sad all day.

This is the longest period in my adult life that I've gone without sex. That sexual self, that part of me that was that seems now like some distinct other.

OCTOBER 24, 1992

Saturday
San Francisco

I talked with Renée on the phone for an hour and twenty. She saw the baby all wrapped up and Kathie in her leather jacket and sunglasses surrounded by her entourage, her people. As soon as Renée told me this I split in my feelings. I felt her rage and upset and I wanted to be walking beside Kathie. I mean—and please read this over—I had an image of me standing with Renée and with Kathie.

And here I am running away and it's true. Renée said I have no right to cry anymore. I have to rise to the occasion. I don't know what else she said or we said because I am so confused. I told Renée that I was stuck in the middle and could not move. Can't get on the airplane and am impotent to boot. I find myself in HELL.

What is there to write?
What is there to read?

"Ramona called and said she'd seen Kathie on the street with the baby and it had destroyed her," Gray wrote, using a pseudonym for Shafransky for legal reasons, in the 1997 book version of It's a Slippery Slope. *"She'd gone to bed. Would I please come home? I went into another paralysis. I was paralyzed and divided. In my imagination I saw myself sitting on the bed comforting Ramona. And I also saw myself standing beside Kathie, meeting my son for the first time. For two days I was quite paralyzed. And for two days I was quite out of my mind, lying on the floor in a stupefied trance."*

OCTOBER 27, 1992

Yesterday I had a break down at the airport and they almost didn't let me on the plane. I got on because I thought Renée would leave me if I didn't come home. And when I got home she told me that she was going anyway. So it's over and I feel like a dead man. The only thing left is my work. "Our work." I feel dead and like I have killed myself.

The cab round trip to the airport is $80.- MONEY!

OCTOBER 30, 1992

The whole city seems ugly beyond belief; horrid and I can't go away to house in the country because I'd miss Renée too much.

Renée is sick of being the limit setter; she can't get what she needs.

I only see her for what I need from her. Please read this someday.

NOVEMBER 2, 1992

I'm up too early to take a train to Providence. Renée and I had a date last night. She looked sweet and even though she is out to take a great deal of my money, my heart went out to her when I saw where she was sleeping . . . on that day bed right by the window. *[Shafransky moved in with a friend for a few weeks and then to an apartment of her own in Tribeca in downtown Manhattan.]*

If Renée knew I was in touch with K. she would not be so pretty anymore, she'd be angry. She told me that every time she goes away I have to have an affair. And that is often true. What else is there to say besides Renée looked good and she was wearing blousy clothes to cover her big places, which she pointed out to me? Oh, one other thing, it was nice to hear her talk to Mary Beth's son. Renée would make a good mom ("the grounding reality of children" as Chan said) but also Renée is smart and I like to hear her talk politics. I had a long walk with Ken *[Kobland]* yesterday and Ken thinks I'm a DRAMA QUEEN.

NOVEMBER 9, 1992

After lunch I went out for a walk and was absolutely seized with a thought that I loved Amber *[an eighteen-year-old intern at the Wooster Group]* and that I could not live without her and now was my chance to find out and I had to get back and these "thoughts" these compulsions began to make me insane because I began to see all sides and I'm everywhere in my head and I was shouting out and even now as I write this I began to think about her. Is this what Renée calls ACTING OUT? Always have to have a perfect distant woman. A woman at a distance.

JANUARY 3, 1993

Having a real bad shaky day. Yesterday, Renée showed me her apartment and I don't think I could grasp it. Today, I have found that it is almost impossible to be alone. So I went and walked around and around Washington Sq. and on my way to the bookstore groaning all the way, I ran into a more extreme version of myself, the man was shouting at everyone. Far gone and for a while it shut me up.

Renée is going to Alanon meetings and I can tell she's depressed by the people and says all the alcoholics across the hall have more fun.

JANUARY 9, 1993

[In England, doing publicity for the Picador publication of Impossible Vacation*]*

The negative power of the mind. I thought of trying to get out of this press tour by pretending I was sick and now I am sick. I am very sick. My chest cold has blossomed into my head.

What am I doing in search of the miraculous? I can't begin to express how depressed I feel trapped in The Montcalm Hotel and it's raining out and I feel like I'm going to die. Myself keeps falling apart. There are these big gaps that I fall into.

I have nothing more to write except sad sad sad. I am working against myself to prevent pleasure. I'm only at peace when I'm on drugs or booze. I don't know how to go on without screaming. I feel such rage and pain. And I will never forget that chant I did on Jim's deck. I want to be in a group all chanting stoned on mushrooms. I'm going primitive and I can't bare civilization.

When Jim Barton said K. got good genes from me—"you're good looking and smart." It put me into a panic like when the sun bursts out and I feel so suddenly over-stimulated and I think what am I doing wasting my time. I've got to "use" my looks and "use" my smarts. I don't know what I'm doing here in England. It feels like such a waste of my body but I'm so sick.

WHAT WAS THE DATE MOM KILLED HERSELF?

But the image that constantly tears my heart, the image that rips at me is of Renée on her red bike with the fender rattling and her in her brown shorts and we are riding together down to the ocean to take our morning walk and I am there but not there. A kind of be here then sort of guy and she is looking back at me with love in her gaze and I respond. I let the love, her love, bathe all over me and we ride and we walk and her hand that I held is cold (cold sea/cold child). Then the moments all fall away and leave me thrashing. Leave me nowhere.

"You have to be a father or not a father. You can't just drop in."

APRIL 1, 1993

Back from skiing at Blake Street and already missing it. All the anxiety is coming back on me now. It's snowing again in Vermont and I can't get the picture of Renée out of my head. . . . . her lying on the couch saying, "You have broken my heart." So, here I sit. With all the old anxiety coming up. All the old sadness and indecision. Where to go next? Who to be with? Where to write? Should I fly back East? And the pure memory that pure head clearing memory of being out on those white slopes and how I didn't want it to stop or be over. Like when I get off six good turns in a row. Six good turns without thinking about them.

In May 1993, Gray called Russo and asked if he could meet their son for the first time. Gray and Russo had not seen each other for nearly a year; Forrest was eight months old. Gray visited them at their Tribeca apartment—Russo was still living with members of the Blue Man Group along with Marissa and now with Forrest too—on the same day that he called. He returned the following day, Russo recalled, to take Forrest to the park for a couple of hours. (In It's a Slippery Slope, *Gray told of taking Forrest on his own to Brewster just after he met him. In reality, this trip took place two weeks later.) Shortly thereafter, Gray learned that his father had passed away. "My father had died just three days after I saw Forrest for the first time, died not knowing he had his first grandson," Gray recollected in* It's a Slippery Slope. *"I didn't even know he was in the hospital dying, because my stepmother didn't call me due to the fact that she was so angry with me for the way I portrayed her in my novel." In the journals, however, Gray describes what seems to be a conscious decision not to be with his father when he was ill at the end—a decision he later mourns.*

"I found out that he was in a small hospital down by the ocean in Rhode Island and I went there and he was suffering from DTs and

completely incoherent," Gray's younger brother, Channing, remem-
bered of this time. "And the doctor said I should go out and buy him a
pint of bourbon. That's high-end medical care in South County, Rhode
Island. I remember, the next day, during my daughter's birthday party,
my stepmother called and said he had died. He did look like death
when I saw him; his face had changed, he looked like he had aged ten
years. But I didn't expect him to die that day. I don't think the staff
was aware that he was close to death. So nobody was with him. I think
he died in the night."

MAY 14, 1993

Dad's death. An absence of absence.
My next book, "An Absence of Presence."

[Gray's father died on May 22. In this entry, Gray may have been
anticipating the event that would soon take place.]

JUNE 8, 1993

In Montreal, I woke with a rare erection. And it made me feel more
lonely. Something about male anatomy, the way it stands out and
demands and reminds you like it has a mind or "head" of its own and
it must get in somewhere. It was so demanding.

3 FEELINGS about DAD'S spirit. When I was with Renée in Central
Park, we were sitting like we never sat before. . . . . quiet on a park
bench in the brambels and I felt a soft wind come and caress my bald
spot and at that moment it was as if it were the ubiquitous spirit of dad
passing over and touching me with some sort of graceful forgiving some
forgiving grace before he enter into the spiritual.

2 When I was saying a prayer for him at the little Balinese icon here in
the loft, I saw his spirit spiraling up and in some other world becoming
incarnate and making passionate love to mom.

3 When Chan drove me down to the grave sight, I picked three bego-
nias from a common bush and put them on his grave sight and I saw

his old face, old disapproving face up in the sky above me like Woody Allen's mother. "Don't pick flowers from these bushes."

JUNE 14, 1993

At the Sedgewood house, I see Renée (as she was) everywhere. I drink too much and I cry almost all the time. Like an indulgent child, I do the thing that feels good at the time and have no respect for the future.

I told K. that I had a secret wish that the plane would crash with all of them and she didn't even get real upset. She only said, "I'm sure a part of you would be sad."

Am I behaving like Henry the VIII? Ditch one great lady to get me a child? When I embraced her on the dock, it was not so much her but the both of them. That white sleeping moon face. That out of its head. The way he can sleep through anything and everything.

JUNE 20, 1993

Ron says that I have to resolve things with Renée. He thinks we are in limbo now. He says I would not have carried on with Kathie for as long as I did if I didn't like her. So its time to find a therapist.

Ron thinks a woman therapist would be good because women know how to make decisions and I am missing that ability. Women seem to have that quality.

To have gone to Rhode Island and sat by dad's bed—sad to say—would have been only an intellectual exercise.

Last night I called Renée to say good-bye. We talked about divorce for the first time. I brought it up. She said that it had been on her mind a lot but didn't want to bring it up (yet) because of dad's death and the opening of the monologue at the Goodman. [Gray's Anatomy *was set to open at Chicago's Goodman Theatre in September 1993.*] She also said that if I did go into therapy and found someone new to replace her that she would be very angry.

As for sex with Kathie, I worry that it is as charged as it is because it is all or was all being done "behind mom's back." It is not adult sex but juvenile and all hot because it's a secret. Not only is it behind Renée's back but also behind the backs of the kids. And I miss Renée's intellect and child like view of life and language like the way she laughed on the phone when she said Renaissance angels.

JULY 21, 1993

I went to see Martha *[a new therapist]* and I cried again when I told the story of Renée putting out her hand at the end of the great crossing and asking "Still Friends?" *[Gray relayed this story, from early in his relationship with Shafransky, in his 1980 monologue* Nobody Wanted to Sit Behind a Desk. *When Gray and Shafransky finally reached the West Coast after driving cross-country together, "Renée turned to me, extended her hand and asked, 'Still friends?' And we shook."]*

I did have a great time alone with Forrest but the fact that he won't select it out and remember it bothers me. That it is not yet a shared memory or a personal history between the two of us and the thought of how long that will take.

Today I feel such deep sadness. At times it is almost unbearable and I have to say Forrest sometimes takes me out of that sadness because perhaps takes me out of myself.

Kathie thought I loved her. That's what she said. And yes I did and still do make physical love to her but I'm so split.

At night alone down at the dock I thought how easy it would be to drop Forrest in the lake and watch him drown which reminded me of how mom told me that Chan was such a beautiful baby that she wanted to put a pillow over his face and smother him.

FORREST = MY MAP THAT I HAD THE POWER TO DO WHAT DAD NEVER DID FOR ME (MOM GAVE HIM NO EMOTIONAL ROOM BECAUSE HE WAS WOUNDED).

MY MAP THROUGH THE FORREST. I HAVE TO AND CAN CUT MY OWN WAY.

JULY 29, 1993

When I told Martha of the fantasy I had of dropping Forrest in China Lake and watching him drown, she said I could integrate these fantasies and mom could not, which Martha thinks drove mom mad.

AUGUST 4, 1993

It was the way Renée and I came together on that one LINE = "A HOUSE WILL BREAK YOUR HEART." Kathie would never be in tune with something like that. She is so proletarian. So materialistic but a good mother nonetheless. But I felt so connected to Renée at that moment. So in tune.

Renée asked me on the phone where it was that I felt most centered and I could not bring myself to tell her that its with Kathie and the kids. I only said it was with Forrest which I'm sure was hard for her to hear.

AUGUST 20, 1993

It bothers me that K. has the TV on in the morning and that she believes in an "after life."

FORREST = first he throws his head back and cries then he talks like a ventriloquist then he fights sleep. He goes up and looks for me last look and then it goes down on my chest and the delicious feeling comes. I am calm in his being. I think that I love him more than I've ever loved before/ his pale moon face glowing alabaster back at me. The sound of the Carousel and children crying.

K. knows things from just being a mother. That in itself gives her knowledge. We talked about how children create a balanced bond between the two parents. I see it with Chan I see it with K and I.

[Here, Gray is describing the first family vacation that he took with Russo and the children in Newport, Rhode Island, when Marissa was seven and Forrest was nearly eleven months old.] This clam house didn't serve clams. Drunken kids screamed dickhead out the window. Marissa gave up and turned out to sea and I turned to her and said "I love you" and the pain that I never heard it from dad and how I was a dad who could and wanted to.

SEPTEMBER 10, 1993

[Performing Gray's Anatomy*]*

GOODMAN/CHICAGO

Renée called about the dedication ("DEAD"ICATION) to the book and was afraid of being drawn in again to my perverse love. *[Gray dedicated the published version of* Gray's Anatomy *to Shafransky.]* Me manipulating her to stay around until I try to make up my mind.

The only joy in my life is Forrest and I'm now afraid that K will take him away from me. All I feel is fear. I'm a little more relaxed here in Chicago because I am in a forced situation. I am too afraid to fuck up my work so I work. Had I not got good reviews, I think I would have gone into a very deep depression.

SEPTEMBER 21, 1993

[Shooting Damian Harris's Bad Company, *starring Laurence Fishburne and Ellen Barkin; Gray played the minor role of Walter Curl, a crooked businessman.]*

Vancouver B.C.

Early to bed to get ready for horrid NIGHT SHOOT on this fucked up film.

Just after I cum the phone rings and it's Renée. She tells me Lincoln Center is almost sold out *[for the New York run of* Gray's Anatomy, *which premiered on November 7, 1993]*. I get up a little from that. I can't believe that many people want to see me before reviews.

When will I ever be able to enjoy reading a book again?

I began to think that anyone could play the role of CURL and I am unable to find my signature, my uniqueness. UNIQUENESS.

I'm sitting here in my trailer going over and over all the things I loved about Renée. 1) her eyes up at me when she was in the bathtub. It was her childlike trusting eyes. I had seen into them once so long ago on John Street when I was making love to her and I suddenly saw into her eyes. 2) It was the crazy kidlike way she rode her bike, her red bike so fast to the beach and how I'd be alongside of her groaning. What was that about? What was and still is wrong with me? Am I insane? To continually reject joy and want to beat it down? 3) The way she would visit me at Our Town and the lovely Christmas she made. 4) Her skin. Her neck, her breasts. The dinners she fixed. The sweaters she wore. The way she helped me with my dreams. All the things she did for me. What would cause me to do what I did and what is stopping me from trying to HEAL IT?

But I'm not supportive, that's the point. All I do is take. I only give to the audience.

Vancouver

Why am I working 12 hours on a film I don't even believe in for NO MONEY? Just because they wanted me.

Renée on the phone made me feel more sad but sad in a real and more connected way. But I asked her why she wanted the separation and she said that there was a long list. 1) I was not there for her (Renée's question comes to mind here. When she asked me and this is a big and important question—why was it that she spent so much time making a scum bag cad look so good on stage?)

OTHER REASONS for leaving me—BIG ONES I reconnected with K. and F. before I made an attempt to reconnect with her. But I do think it's interesting that Renée is still spending her time—some of it—making me appear to be Mr. Nice Guy on stage. I also think that I do that. I go out there in order to Charm.

SEPTEMBER 27, 1993

Coming home for Forrest's first birthday was like living in a sad strange dream in which my life was no longer my own. The kid is beautiful, no doubt. K was away. Marissa was there. She scares me. The indifference scares me. Pavel was right, I should have lived with them for a week before I got married. That was the one thing Pavel may have been right about.

I THINK I MAY BE CRAZY
I THINK I AM.

SEPTEMBER 28, 1993

THE SEA ALWAYS BRINGS ME BACK TO MOM. DID I EQUATE
THE LANDSCAPE WITH HER

Not sharing Forrest with all hurts. Not sharing Forrest with Renée
hurts. Not celebrating him hurts. Not holding him up to the world
hurts. He's so beautiful! It's almost like he is some sort of separate issue.
Like he came from outer space.

OCTOBER 8, 1993

[Performing Gray's Anatomy*]*

Cambridge Mass.

I feel very fuzzy about what I want to say. Because Renée and I have
been working so hard on the monolog, I've fallen behind with my journal so that things that once seemed important so very important days
ago have slipped away and I've just said goodbye to Renée and it felt
more OK perhaps because she stayed another day to work and we got
a lot of good work done.

In the Boston Phoenix Carolyn Clay calls Renée—"Spalding Gray's
Better Half." God, how right on.

OCTOBER 9, 1993

Cambridge

There was a brief moment I had sitting in Harvard Square listening to
street music and some guy leaned over to me and said, "You wrote a
great novel." And I thought, I should feel so very satisfied. So 25 odd
years later I realized I had done what I had fantasized or dreamed of so
long ago in Boston. And there I was . . . still unhappy. Or, still dissatisfied.

As for the show last night, it was not easy to do without Renée. The
audience was too abstract. I knew I'd have no contact with them after
and be very lonely.

There is nothing more to say except that I don't regret Forrest's being. I like sex with K. and I still love Renée.

Nothing else is new.

OCTOBER 17, 1993

I'm still afraid to write freely. I started the morning with coke and cigarette, this morning. Woke with a hang.

HONEST EYES = RENÉE

Those eyes in the photo on the wall and how I can't give over to any other human eyes. Kathie in particular. I can hardly look into her eyes and she made me do it last night at the busy Inn. And it was not easy. Her face is sort of twisted, weasely. Why am I writing this? But what is going on?

I did tell her that it was like a mail order bride and that Forrest was part dropped on my doorstep.

Then there was the constant farting and the laughter. I laughed with Kathie until I cried. Good lord! Think of that. I don't remember any woman I've done that with. That was a big one. I really laughed.

OCTOBER 1993

OCT.? SEDGEWOOD

At last I can sit down and write. FORREST has fallen down for his nap after hurling his bottle at me.

Being with him indoors is like taking some heavy disorientating drug. He is now NON STOP. I think just a month ago he would occupy himself more in one spot and I'm sure that has to do with his now walking. But I cannot think straight. Also all I do now is feel for Renée when she heard Forrest in the background.

OCTOBER 28, 1993

Renée called this morning to say she no longer felt sorry for me. She felt sorry for herself and she wants more money for what she calls collaboration. I don't know what to do. I do feel she is right and I also feel I've given her a lot of money.

Session with Martha yesterday at 3:00 and I brought Forrest. He slept in my arms for most of the session. She said he was a beautiful old soul whose eyes went on forever.

Martha's most important phrase to me was that MOM NEVER CON-NECTED ME TO MYSELF so what I have now is attachment to a woman and then the fearful abyss. She said, and I agree that it's just too hard for me to be alone. THERE is this terrifying abyss. After the session I took Forrest for a walk in the park. He was sleeping AT LAST. A long day for him. I picked him up in a stretch limo at 7:30 then after the radio station we were off to the doctors then back to my place while he helped me trash it.

Back to the ABYSS. I think that was what I experienced when I saw I was too far out in the ocean and I was measuring the distance from Renée on the beach and that the sea was the personification of the abyss and that I was not really dreaming but instead experiencing that cut off state from the mother.

OCTOBER 31, 1993

Renée said that she would "direct" me if I ever did a monologue about "the break up," our break up. Of course it would be a way of taking revenge. Forrest has to know his history someday. Renée pictures herself at 60 and Forrest a young man coming to her after reading my books and asking her, Who are you?

NOVEMBER 4, 1993

Martha seemed to have a breakthrough. I think she got excited about the fact that I could move away from the mother complex with Forrest. She got so excited and talked so fast that it was hard for me to follow. But I did see that the image of the perfect woman was in conflict with Forrest.

But then when I asked Martha what she meant when she said that mom never gave me to myself she also got very animated and she began to almost act. She frightened me with the intensity with which she re-enacted mom as the mom that instead of mirroring—that is giving myself back to me (MY GREAT NEED TO BE SEEN AT A PARTY ETC.)—she devoured me or swept me into her needy aura. That, according to

Martha, is when she became the devouring mother and said "me, me look at me!" So, if Martha is right I do have a big problem. But I don't feel I'm doing that with Forrest. In fact I do remember that last time I changed his big shitty diaper I was smiling back at him. What Martha said made sad sense to me. She keeps saying that I'm a victim of a Mother Complex and I will be somewhat saved by being both mother and father to Forrest. That is, I'm playing out both parts when I'm with him and that is why I related to Forrest exclusive of Renée. That is why she thinks I excluded Renée from him.

She also said that it is now an important time for me because in the same year that I outlived mom (and she said she did not think I would make it through the summer but did not want to inter"fear" because it would make her into another mother for me). And yes the same year I out lived mom I had a boy child and I am now trying to relive my childhood in a healing way through him.

Well it was a very loaded session. She also almost called me Forrest again.

On November 7, 1993, Gray opened Gray's Anatomy *at Lincoln Center; he performed the show until January 3, 1994.*

NOVEMBER 15, 1993

I didn't feel like doing the Monday night show. For me every show is one step toward the separation papers *[with Shafransky—this was the last time she would direct him]*. But the show went so well, the audience was outstanding. They blew me away. It was the best audience ever. If only we could have an audience like that when the press was there. I think I had a fever. I think I still do but I'm trying to ignore it. Also I think there is something wrong with my prostate because I keep having to pee.

NOVEMBER 16, 1993

The show did not go as well as the night before. Renée said the wonder went out of my voice and I started to get glib toward the end. Laurie

Stone from the Voice was there. Shit! After the show Renée gave me a talking to and said if I smoke grass and mess up my head she will kill me. Then we went to the board of directors dinner and I downed over a half pint of pepper vodka before then had a lot of white wine then went out to a local bar for champagne. I asked Renée to come but she said she had to pack up for Boulder. Then she called me about something and I called her back but I can't recall the conversation most likely because of drink. I know it was something about how she enjoys her independence, that much I remember. I am very depressed living alone and can do very little for myself. I'm too depressed to even unpack my laundry and put it in the drawer.

The loss of Renée makes me feel like someone has died.

I feel like I killed her.

I feel like I killed Renée.

NOVEMBER 17, 1993

I had Forrest over to the loft for dinner. I hope I did not give him the flu. There was one divine moment with him. He was in my arms on the couch and instead of fighting sleep he went into this blissful stare at the ceiling. It was as though he was hallucinating. His eyes were in a state of divine ecstasy. There are the times that he transcends being a child and becomes angelic. Then he passed into sleep and his face was all bliss.

NOVEMBER 30, 1993

Day after good reviews post partum depression. [*The* Los Angeles Times *described* Gray's Anatomy *as Gray's "funniest and most profound monologue since 'Swimming to Cambodia'"*; The Boston Globe *called it "graphic, funny, provocative and terrifying";* The New York Times *declared it "a rarefied exercise in levels of consciousness and perception that is more cogently of a piece and more emotionally moving than perhaps anything else Mr. Gray has done."*] What's next? As soon as I have something off limits in my life, I want to talk about it. Forrest! The way he was so good and then turned into a little wild thing teasing with his teeth at my wrist. Biting into my palm. I wondered why Renée was so up about the reviews when they didn't give her any credit as director and then I called her this morning to find her depressed and very angry. She even screamed on the phone. She says now she has to start all over to find her voice that had been buried for years in my voice. She said she never had any freedom. Never had a life of her own.

DECEMBER 5, 1993

The Good Morning America People arrived at 6 AM and I tried to sleep. The show was sad because they kept asking about my wife Renée. And I'm kind of at the end of the road with this surprise of ALCOHOLIC HEPATITIS *[one doctor diagnosed Gray with this, while another later told him he didn't have it]*. I never expected to get hit by it. I never heard of it. All I can say is that I'm glad I'm not dying from it YET but I feel like I've lost my two best friends, Renée and Alcohol. I'm now really alone although the visit from Forrest, Marissa, and Kathie did help me out. I mean made me feel a little better. Forrest slept for two hours which was a blessing. It is ridiculous that I'm performing Gray's Anatomy while I'm sick with a disease I most likely won't do a monologue about.

DECEMBER 8, 1993

I dragged myself to dinner at K's to bring her the bad news about skiing or NOT skiing. It was real hard to be there without drinking. Not easy to deal with Marissa's needs and the way she sometimes attacks Forrest, that makes me angry. But I had no protection. That bubble of alcohol. YES! GOD, how I missed that bubble of ALCOHOL that I would always wrap around me just to walk out on the night streets. Now to see the night streets without that protection for the first time in three years. Well, what a horror! And then I get to K and she does a good job cooking and then she tells me that if I really wanted Renée back I'd be down there now throwing myself upon her. Cooking for her—not taking "NO" for an answer. And this is coming from K. She at last gets me so upset that I go out to call Renée from a payphone but she's not in.

DECEMBER 21, 1993

K. thinks my madness is or was AN ACT. Case in point. She says I was flipped out in the car on the way to N.Y.C. from the beach and then I had that phone interview. And she said I was just fine on the phone.

I've gone back to drinking after two weeks.

Renée said I ate her. I did. She was my muse and shadow and I ate her up and spit her out as art.

Renée said, "Now I am on a journey that will let me die. That I will die fulfilled and without regret."

DECEMBER 1993

Martha turns out to be a Jungian!

Yipes! But she did cheer Ken for saying I was not manic-depressive.

DECEMBER 24, 1993

CHRISTMAS EVE

Lamb for Christmas dinner. A lot to drink. I'm back on it. My poor liver. I'm just not a controlled drinker. And how I love to drink! After I met K's family at COXSACKIE *[in upstate New York]* and what a warm place we met. God I almost had to pee next to K's father who is only three years older than I. After all of that we stopped at a store for beers and they tasted so good I couldn't stop. Then K said a cop was after us and that frightened me. But he never came. We went to New Paltz for dinner. I had four shots of Irish whiskey in a bar, while K waited with Forrest. 1234 right down and only felt mildly relaxed.

In the first week of January 1994, Russo, Forrest, and Marissa moved into Gray's half of the loft on Wooster Street. (LeCompte and Dafoe, along with their son, Jack, still lived on the other side.)

JANUARY 3, 1994

[Last show at Lincoln Center of Gray's Anatomy]

I was very nervous to see Renée. We both knew it, us, we were coming to an end because these were the last two shows.

JANUARY 10, 1994

I'm in the MAS office *[Gray's psychopharmacologist]* with a hangover. Could not keep my hands off the scotch last night while we were putting the house in order *[in Carmel; Gray kept this house after his relationship with Shafransky ended]* which was real chaotic but the drinking started early after I finished skiing at the Patterson. What a mess that was. Lines and short icy runs. So I started in on the beers Heineken draft at 3:30 and K. was in with the kids at 4:00. K. never seems to get impatient: "You can take another run if you want."

Dinner at the Carmel Diner was a riot. I could not stop laughing and now I can't remember what I was laughing about. I think much of it was regression. I was farting a lot real loud like mom used to do. Also the waitress was real beaten down. When I asked her the difference between lamb and duck. She went, "Bah" & "Quack Quack."

Woke at 8:00. My inner alarm. Hangover. Off to have the dreaded breakfast with Renée. I felt like I was going to the dentist. Sad ending but Renée was right—is right. Renée's story about our form of intimacy being a form of sparring, she saw how we made a little play when she played her HiFi for me and I said ?? What did I say? Because I don't remember it then it went to her telling me about how Steve Martin's wife left him because he was manic-depressive. But Renée told me she wanted the papers signed because I was about to go off on the road again and she did not want any legal responsibility for me. After we signed all the papers she said, "It's been an incredible journey." And I felt that.

JANUARY 11, 1994

DREAM: this was a very strong dream in the sense of the feeling that was in it.

I was traveling on a train with loose doors and somehow Forrest slipped out although I didn't see him go but I knew he had gone and I was desperate running up and down the train in hysterics. Then I was at the Performing Garage grabbing a woman's face screaming, My son is gone!

FEBRUARY 1, 1994

When I got out of the limo and looked back at Forrest, I was sure he knew I was leaving for a long trip or maybe forever. It was that face of great concern. It was that deep look. Those deep eyes. And as I sit here remembering it I'm sure (but I'll never know) that it was not a case of projection.

My session with Martha was odd. I wanted to leave after 45 minutes. I did talk about how worried I was that Kathie would have the next one if she was or did get pregnant. Also how I was not romantically in love with K. I also find it interesting that Martha is beginning to discuss her sex life with me.

We fly into Singapore [*to shoot John Boorman's film* Beyond Rangoon, *with Patricia Arquette and Frances McDormand; Gray played a supporting role as a tour guide in Burma*] at 825 mph at 37 thousand feet and as soon as I get excited about Phuket [*Gray planned to revisit Thailand during a break in filming*] I think of fearful things. Of Kathie being pregnant again and how she might not abort I think also of ROSEOLA and how that might hit me before Phuket. I think of the women I might meet on location and I try to think of skiing but not many memories come. It's like describing sex and so much of what I feel and think feel like old clichés.

FEBRUARY 7, 1994

In Phuket I dreamt of skiing. Every night over and over it was me rushing to catch the last lift up before 4:00.

It was incomprehensible that JB [*John Boorman*] could be paying me what I'm being paid and that I could also run off to Phuket

I WANT TO SKI!!!

ALRIGHT after lying
on the floor and crying
for a half hour I
came up with ——————⟶
                                  I THINK
                                  I'D LIKE

TO BE
A SKI
INSTRUCTOR

YES!

I've always wanted to teach something and this is it.
Why else did I have these dreams? I must learn to ski and teach it. I want to be out DOORS for the rest of my life.

I miss Forrest so much. SO MUCH I miss now the changing of his diaper and the way he lifts his legs for me. I miss his face I miss him

A PERSONAL HISTORY OF SKIING

I AM DRUNK
could I do a ski class in skiing and story telling

YES and you know what Kathie could put it together.

FEBRUARY 11, 1994

THE FIRST DAY OF SHOOTING This is the most boring unrewarding work! I feel like a stand in. A model. I spent the afternoon standing on the top steps to an airplane.

Kathie and I kept fucking waiting for FATE to come and change our lives. Forrest is the embodiment of that fate, that change. He—his whole birth has shaken my life to the bone. Now I worry for his life. I just had a thought now of Aspen and how Marissa cried out for me in the night and how quickly I ran to her and how good that felt. To at last be needed by her. Also I know I am "with" Kathie to some extent in order to get closer to Forrest.

I'D LIKE TO BE REINCARNATED AS A GOOD MOTHER

FORREST—Then in Aspen when I was at last alone with you and I lay you on your back on the bed about to become our bed you looked back at me with those eyes and you gave that look that pure look with no judgment or attempt at interpretation.

It was a look of mere being and what a long look it was
and that old cliché I'd so often heard did then come to mind. This
is an old soul. These eyes I am gazing into are not the eyes of a child
but old eyes. And I stayed with them until your eyelids began to flutter
and close.

I'm sitting in this trailer now remembering holding your pure moon
head in my hands as you slept that other summer night near Charleston
Beach. I had returned to Rhode Island and brought you back to no one
but the MOTHER SEA. And how I cried. Knowing that you would not
be the same come another summer. And now I am crying at the loss of
you, the loss of that pure child. Your head is starting to grow brown
hair and I can't even adjust to that. I understand for the first time why
people have children. I could never get that from dad. Or at least he
could never tell me.

FEBRUARY 11, 1994

I'm trying to think this one through ——→ I am afraid that Forrest will
reject me and I realized that this concept of rejection is not HISTORIC
for me or rather it is but I don't know with my own I want to say DAD
but I can't (SAD). My father SO FORMAL he was a very uptight man
at least with us only at the funeral did I hear from people how much
dad loved me (us) and that was the OLD story. Mom used to do it too.
She would tell me "your father is proud of you." I hope I'm always very
direct with Forrest. ALWAYS.

MARCH 3, 1994

Miami

It's cool clear and windy here. I have a hangover and that lost lonely
feeling again. I already miss Forrest. I did have too much to drink and
I overreacted to K., all after a very bad Cuban dinner that Forrest, at
least, had a good time at. White rice in his hair and even on his balls
which he reacted to later with laughter as he pulled the rice off them.
But I have had this guilt ever since I came back. It was this guilt that
I was more happy to see Forrest than I was Kathie. I would never be
with Kathie if it was not for Forrest. I am quite sure of that. I mean I
would never have left Renée for her. But really remember, Renée left

me because I could not be the man (I wanted) she wanted. But anyway, that presenter from Fort Lauderdale, I cant remember her name, told K. that I better get my priorities straight about loving Forrest more than I love her and then Kathie told me that her mother had said the same thing. So being a little drunk I started thinking that Kathie was bringing that up to let me know that that was a problem for her but during our walk on the beach she insisted that it wasn't and that she could clearly understand how my love for a child could be as big or larger than that for an adult.

MARCH 10, 1994

Burlington

Went to bed very early and had two DREAMS.

1) That I was invited to Bob Dylan's birthday party. It was a small gathering of people I really didn't know and I could not or would not look at him—the way they don't show God in the movies.

2) I dreamed that I had to cut out Forrest's (left) eye with a chainsaw (like Abraham and Isaac) and I couldn't. I'd keep crawling away with him on the floor and then have to come back and try again.

MARCH 28, 1994

O.K. I do like the way Kathie says, "Let it go." That one she has learned. "LET IT GO." That for me was a big one around that time with Marissa and Marissa is testing Kathie's love all the time LIKE me. Marissa and also Forrest are BIG MIRRORS TO ME.

SKIING. Why am I running after it? Why does it short out all the other reality around me and make me say BUT I could be skiing now!?

I have to say Kathie was really cool. This morning just before she left, I was spilling my shit out all over her and keeping her late from Garcelia [*Forrest's babysitter*] and WORK—SHE SAID, "I know I look good and you are not going to change that."

I WANT TO THINK OF NEW LAND and how big unfamiliar mountains change our consciousness. ON THE WAY OUT TO NEWARK

AIRPORT to go to ski in Burlington there was a front, a grey mountain of clouds and I flipped out. I thought, my God, how uplifting.

How fantastic! I never knew New Jersey had mountains and the longing for those clouds to be mountains cheated the feeling that there were and I sat there in the car thinking what in hell, what makes a mountain so important to me? And it came to me that it was simply HIGHER, a way of being alive, a way of getting high, both connected to the earth and above the earth.

BOTH ABOVE THE EARTH AND CONNECTED TO THE EARTH.

The combination of sea and mountains is overwhelming. I don't know what to do with it.

Vermont

Nothing is real for me suddenly. I had a view of Kathie as a SEX DOLL and Forrest as my play toy that just popped out of her. It all feels at times like a *Twilight Zone,* like Rip Van Winkle. I woke up one day and I had a family. But could I stand by them? Do I have the courage to live?

APRIL 11, 1994

Wanting to learn how to ski grew directly out of my fantasies about suicide. I want to directly test my levels of self-preservation and contact real fear.

APRIL 1994

Flight to S. F. from
Houston. April Something

After three beers, three Becks (one I had to beg for) on Continental, I watch the way my mood swings from BLISS memory to anger.

After 2 beers; bliss memory and how sweet it was. After my show in Austin I met Kathie and Forrest in the lobby of the DRISKILL HOTEL. I arrived with a group of people and the whole scene was rather confusing in the way that it often is after a show and then there he was MY SON FORREST cutting through everyone to get to me and I knew and know his motivations and intention was all pure because there is no language yet and therefore at least no linguistic manipulation. Kathie did or could not TELL him to do it. So for me there was all that trust of the non-verbal. That little guy cutting his way through all those others to get to me like the smell of DNA like a sweet little bird flying into a nest and nest is exactly what he did. He curled up in my arms almost in a fetal position and just HUNCHED in and I patted his back and just felt amazed and overwhelmed by his love. It almost outdid the love the audience gave me. Or rather, it was a nice balance.

Kate called this morning to say Ron died 30,000 feet up. *[The Wooster Group member Ron Vawter, who had AIDS, died of a heart attack, at forty-five years old, in an airplane en route to New York from Zurich, Switzerland.]* Renée cried on the phone when I told her. She said he was closer to heaven. And I cried when Renée cried.

If RON had a shadow SIDE it was THE ACT OF burning his candle at both ends (as it were). But for me and to me he was all heart. He was the closest man to a saint I've ever known. He was all heart so it did surprise when his heart burst 30,000 feet closer to the heaven he deserves. My heart is with him now and forever. AMEN.

JULY 5, 1994

> THEN AT LAST IT
> BECAME AN
> ACCUMULATION OF
> DEATH NOT IN THE
> ABSTRACT BUT THERE
> AT LAST AROUND
> ME AND CLOSING IN
> (1) PAVEL (2) DAD
> (3) RON & CYNTHIA *[Horner, the fiancée of
>   John Perry Barlow, a writer, former lyricist
>   for the Grateful Dead, and a friend of Gray's]*
> (4) Jackie O.

JULY 1994

[At Sedgewood in Carmel, New York]

JULY SOMETHING

I don't know how I am holding on to my sanity. Or is it that I've lost it? SYLVIA PLATH comes to mind. Also mom who didn't have the outlet of poetry. We have not had one sunny dry day in weeks. It feels like the whole house is ROTTING. It is all like a jungle outside. Then yesterday we—Chan, Amanda *[Channing Gray's daughter]*, Marissa, Forrest and I—were all trapped in the house as well as AGNES the 18 year old Polish baby sitter. And all the power went out for some time. Chan and I sat on the porch to watch the lightning strike in and around the trees. Forrest was in a cranky mood perhaps because of his cold. At last I got him to sleep by taking him upstairs and lying down on the bed with him so that he could gently kick me perhaps to feel his boundaries. Perhaps to feel that I was there but not too much . . . then one of those surprises happened, Forrest started to laugh just before he went to sleep. It was one of those delightful laughs that apparently came out of nowhere then he rolled over and went out. I too went out for a while. Then I get up and lay on the couch and talked with Chan in the humid POWER OUT. Chan expressed the same fears I always had about Renée and I, that without Bianca as his "KEEPER" he would fall apart and die. He was sure he would die of some major illness and I knew exactly what he was talking about because I had and still was going through that with Renée. I still feel that I will not survive this.

JULY 1994

Saturday Sunday

When I told Chan that I was afraid to speak my next monolog because of how it would alienate the audience he told me I could say anything and they would still laugh. He said that they had no idea of the real life pain that was at the bottom of it all. He told me that I was the "TEFLON of autobiographic monologists."

JULY 15, 1994

I sit here fearing Forrest's waking up. All that chaotic NEED coming at me. Forrest is like a sleeping volcano (SHADOW DANCING) LOVE at a distance. "He felt he could only experience the world through a woman's eyes." That Updike line came back on me when K. and I were driving over the swollen reservoir, the wind was blowing the backs of the leaves and I, at that moment, needed Renée to be there so I could feel it in its deepest way and that put me into a panic again. Renée would call that need for a perfect moment A FANTASY BUBBLE. I might call it a transcendent moment. A place I would like to be able to enter alone and without drugs.

JULY 28, 1994

There is so little that "works" in this world. SO if you are self destructive on top of that you will go down nice and FAST. THERE IS SO LITTLE THAT WORKS.

I CAN'T LIVE WITH BEING A BAD PARENT.

I do see how having children can and does make us appreciate our parents. Now mine are both dead. But I think of mom as the "chaotic mother" that Winnicott [the pediatrician and psychoanalyst D. W. Winnicott] wrote about. She certainly was that for the two years before she killed herself. So when I see that coming at me from Forrest I freak because I can't see an end to it. WHERE IS THERE AN END TO IT?

AUGUST 1994

[In 1994, Gray and Russo rented a house in Martha's Vineyard for the month of August while Gray performed at the Vineyard Playhouse. They returned every August—with Gray arranging to do a show at the playhouse—for the next eight years.]

MARTHA'S VINEYARD

I've been wanting to write in my journal for a long time now and could not focus because of Forrest and what I perceive as his constant NEED. It is odd that now life seems like a gigantic lesson from which we never learn or like Beckett, after we learn we die . . . so it seems to me to be very important to leave any wisdom behind, something so few people have the time or take the time to do. For instance Renée said that she sees the kind of therapy she is in as a great luxury.

PAGE 74 WINNICOTT

THE "CHAOTIC" MOTHER (As I write this I am aware of the guilt connected to my getting better. The big thing that stops me often is the question: How could I get better for Forrest and Kathie and not for Renée? And then as I write this I realize ONCE AGAIN: I am supposed to get better FOR MYSELF.)

AUGUST 9, 1994

I think I drank less last night. Also that crazy scramble to get dinner together was insane. I kept having to run out to the Weber grill then ZOE that dog would come hopping with deer ticks and Forrest would freak and I had to beat the dog off with my giant spatula. It was crazy and I could not center around my meal. I could not really taste or enjoy the wine. Not like last summer when Forrest would hang out in my lap. Now he has three bites and he's off into CHAOS again while I leave my meal and go after him. I feel like the house is burning down all the time and I'm the Fireman! Forrest needs 100% attention. JUST WHAT I NEEDED from Renée. When making dinner I turned my back on him for all of two minutes and he found my walkman, unplugged the earphones, put them on his head and went and plugged them into the bathroom wall socket and I caught him just before he connected with the JUICE. Getting him down on the beach made all the difference. We actually watched the sun go down together. I've not done that since I was with the kids on Block Island. I kept calling the sun "THE BALL." Watch the big ball go down!

I am now thinking about therapy and how we go in circles and how I need Martha to tell me over and over again that it could not work with Renée because she wanted me to be other than I was and that Kathie was a rare one and GOOD for me. Yet as I sit here now I think but Renée really wanted me to be a grown up responsible adult. And with Kathie because she doesn't police me, I drink, take drugs. In other words, with Kathie I keep falling into my shadow self and do not seem to know how to pull myself up and out for my own good.

I do see something remarkable in Kathie. Watching her plane take off framed in the fence I thought I saw another plane almost hit her plane. Then at the end of our phone conversation she told me almost in a matter of fact way that something did go wrong and their plane came within 100 feet of the other plane and all the businessmen groaned. It was the way in which she accepted this event that surprised me.

AUGUST 14, 1994

Opened by telling Martha about my dream. I called it an "incest dream" with Forrest. Of course Martha saw my desire to have union with the child within INNER CHILD <u>AND</u> here is the hard part for me to consider; when I asked her why I would always go after and try to kill the child in Renée (which Martha saw was there in her). She said that I was projecting my inner child on to Renée and then killing it in them as a way of killing that child in myself. She says that I have a beautiful whimsical inner child in myself that I am out to kill. (I am not so able to project that child on Kathie perhaps because she has already put her child outside of her self in the actual form of two children.) Martha said once again that Kathie was right for me "NOW" because she had so little judgment. I told Martha that I'd always seen Renée's judgments and strong (like LIZ) opinions as my necessary boundaries.

In regards to the dream about Forrest she asked me what Forrest was symbolic of. I told her that I was not aware of him as a symbol but that the one aspect that stood out for me about him was the way in which he was able to express his FEELINGS and then pass on like a thunderstorm passing.

AUGUST 21, 1994

WHAT I CAN'T STAND IN MARISSA, I CAN'T STAND IN MYSELF THAT IS: HOSTILE MANIPULATION OF THE MOTHER.

ALL I CAN SHOW AN AUDIENCE NOW IS MY SHADOW. MY SHADOW HAS COME IN TO RULE NOW.

SEPTEMBER 2, 1994

I'm flying to Denver and I can't stop crying that I didn't come to Dad's bedside. That I never did. That I could not give to him. That I am angry with him that, I was angry. That he paid me off. That for whatever reason, he could not bear paradox and confusion. I don't know who he was or what he wanted. And perhaps I'm crying for that. That I had to betray him.

In his death I betrayed him.

If only Dad had said something to me about some way he had perceived me as "GOLDEN." Why did I have to hear it at the memorial?

OCTOBER 7, 1994

NORMAN MAILER = it is not so much that sleeping with different women make us feel like different people. It is that some of US (ME) (ARE) different people.

I am understanding with my body why I want to live outside of N.Y.C. I don't want to go out anymore.

It is time for the ESCAPE FROM NEW YORK!

For the first time in such a long time these thoughts HAVE CREATED A FUTURE for me. I WANT TO LIVE!!!

As for Forrest—I can never leave him. I didn't know that in any way before I saw him. But as soon as I saw him I knew I could never leave him. It was the first permanent condition I'd known in my life.

NOVEMBER 30, 1994

Had a long lunch with Renée after therapy. Therapy—somewhat about MY SADISM toward others and toward myself. But we were with each other from 1:30 to 2:45. ("NARCISSUS HAS NO SHADOW") We, Renée said, were doing a "REALITY CHECK" and so we were but then at the end I could not let her go.

I had to tell her (and I am crying now) that I had felt that I could never go on and live a life without her and she said that that was a case of SADISTIC behavior of mine toward myself. Beating myself up again. I held on to that thought just long enough to get away from her and then it all came back again, THE GREAT FOG OF DOUBT.

Martha said, "Oh, you don't feel for Kathie because she won't show her vulnerable side." Kathie does not offer her NECK.

JANUARY 25, 1995

One of the things I don't think Martha understands when she says, "You are so much better." She does not understand that the way I center into being is through a well told narrative. So I come together in her office and then I come apart again.

In June 1995, Gray began to workshop a show about skiing and the dramatic changes in his romantic life; this would eventually become It's a Slippery Slope.

FEBRUARY 5, 1995

N.Y.C.

Perhaps all I know is cannibal love.

WILL YOU READ THIS?

MARCH 31, 1995

Vermont last day
of March STOWE

1) It's all about balance on the slope I have to find balance in my body which leads to my head. I have no head balance.
2) Uninhibited Bliss (perhaps my face looks this way when I perform).

I act from my unconscious then I do the monolog to process my actions. So it's a form of public processing and in that way it is a gift to the audience.

APRIL 1, 1995

April One April Fools
Day. I'm the fool

I talked with Kathie on the phone today. She called this morning and I
started in again on her and what Karen *[Russo's sister]* said about her
not thinking ahead and acting in the FUCK BUG heat of the moment.
Anyway Kathie said "Face it, we were both playing Russian roulette
with taking a chance on pregnancy." And I had to admit it. That is what
made it HOT (But why is it still hot now?)

But there is another thing I have to face here and that is that I did not
want to go through the hard part, the pregnancy, and used Renée as a
nurse to get me through it all. So Renée really got the battering. I really
beat her up and that part of me I hate. That is when suicide comes. It
comes when the shadow part or let's say the part of you that you hate
starts to take over and fill up or push out all the other parts until you
are all the part that you hate and there is this one little part left that is
the killer and the killer is closely related to the self hate and at last it
does its dirty little deed.

APRIL 30, 1995

SUNDAY

DREAM
I was in a "new version" of the house at 66 Rumstick. Liz LeCompte
was there taking a communal or CO-ED shower—DORM like shower.
Then I could hear from upstairs that she was with (another) a man
(I was about to write "another man") I had an overview now in which I
could see them . . . him guiding her in a posture of romantic love. I had
a cut off lower torso view of them through the door of Gram Gray's
bedroom which would mean I had an overview that was really outside
of or above the house.
    Then I was in the upstairs of the house and I began to hear their
sounds of love making and I heard Liz say, "Oh why does it feel so
good?" and I was starting to get so turned on that I had to leave the
house and I found that I was walking up West Broadway and ran into

Willem who was walking down from the park. He was pale and angry and I stopped him to CONFRONT him. We went and lay in the park together and he told me he was upset because he had been friends with me before he met Liz and he felt betrayed or that I had dumped him. All the time I was talking to him I knew I could just devastate him by telling him that Liz was with this other man but I didn't. I was able to keep it a secret all to myself. Willem and I were holding hands when we parted.

I think I remember Willem talking to me on the phone that summer I was in California and Liz was with him. And I think I remember him asking if it was OK and I said "YES."

MAY 5, 1995

N.Y.C.

Kathie, on the phone just now, suggested that I go back to Renée.

FORREST—I had a really good day with Forrest yesterday. That game of hide and seek I had with him and the way his face looked when he seemed to really think I was gone reminded me of how in a way I would play that game with Renée. I'd say "bye bye" and then disappear emotionally so I could see her face or feel through her. Maybe, I'm a little mixed up on this but I know I'm on to something.

MAY 5, 1995

[Staying at Sedgewood]

BACK HOME
TO MY LITTLE HOUSE
THE MOST IMPORTANT THING IS FOR A CHILD TO FEEL LOVE THEN HE OR SHE KNOWS IT and this happened when Kathie jumped down and put her arms around me after Forrest jumped right in and made more love! It was really a wonderful moment and then catching the train just on time. I can't believe it but I think I first realized I was in love with Kathie when I picked her up at the train.

I HOPE FORREST TURNS OUT TO BE CURIOUS AND CALM.

MAY 15, 1995

I am still laboring under the idea that the whole earth is a giant penal colony in which we are all doing time for crimes never to be remembered, that we committed elsewhere. The only events that save me from the continuous belief in that are my son, Forrest Dylan Gray, and the event of down hill skiing. Most of my life still seems to be dominated by coping with random CHAOS.

I felt sorry when I saw that Kathie had left her sandwich behind then later on the street I had the fantasy of her with M.S. *[multiple sclerosis]* and I felt sorry for her. Oh shit! I then think is love for me feeling sorry for . . . ? love = pity?

MAY 19, 1995

I said to Kathie, "This next monologue may be my last." And she agreed.

Then I went after her to try to make her cry. I told her that I told Bill Talen that I would not be with Kathie in 20 years. And . . . at last I did succeed in making Kathie cry. And this made me feel good? Made me feel . . . LOVE toward her . . .

We need two incomes to get by. 2 INCOMES undermine the MALE EGO.

MAY 23, 1995

One of my fears is being reduced by Dr. Mass to a set of pathological behaviors and that's part of why I didn't want to speak at Johns Hopkins. What if I am reduced to "Manic Depressive" or "Obsessive Compulsive."

Then my work is only an expression of a pathology and not that of THE HUMAN CONDITION—I want to be larger than a mere mental disorder.

MAY 26, 1995

Forrest still takes my breath away. The beauty of Forrest still keeps me alive. Garcelia's whole bedroom transformed by this sleeping beauty. That slum was transformed by Forrest in sleep. A slight breeze blowing the window curtain. The sound of the ice cream truck. What would have been desperate claustrophobia was transformed by his sleeping presence. His Barney Shoes. His belly. His peaches and cream moist ripe face. Please let this be somehow moved into tolerant waking.

JUNE 19, 1995

Will I ever read this back?

This is a history of the things that are happening to me. I have little more to offer. Maybe someone can live and learn from them. Honesty is the best policy.

Everyone else's life seems to be as bad or worse than mine, which is also depressing.

JULY 1, 1995

I had some hope while watching *[Wayne Wang's]* SMOKE that the ski monolog would be my next heartfelt and transcendent event. Heartfelt! As in "I gave her a locket and then I broke her heart. You're innocent when you dream."

THE PERSONAL CRISIS IS THIS and Martha is somewhat on to it. I cannot be analyzed and write about it for public consumption at the same time. The energy that goes into the writing is stolen from insight.

| DREAM | I need to record a dream I had a few nights ago. (We are innocent when we dream) ———→ This was an . . . a complicated dream and I could not recall the relationship of the people in the dream.
    There was a house for some reason I think of it as the Mason's house. Or, at least, the action was taking place in their dining room. And there was this "idiot" like a retard, like Benji in *Sound and the Fury*. And then there was this woman maybe a MOTHER type telling what I can only say were secrets the idiot never knew before. And I was thinking this is weird that this man is so old and he is hearing this for the first time you know like in the movies when you are the dramatic witness to a drama that has been unfolding for years but you are catching the dramatic or special time of the revelation. The man or innocent idiot (there is so much POWER in innocence as I said to

Suzanne Gluck about Forrest—Forrest is the only one with any almost A-MORAL power over Renée because he is innocent and no one can destroy innocence without producing enormous amounts of guilt) but this man was white and all faded as though someone had drained the blood from him. He was like a ghost of himself. After this all went on in the house I was then outside in a car and I was with a woman driver and the car was being blown sideways by a great wind and there was lightning in the distance.

JULY 3, 1995

It is as though I am rehearsing suicide. I keep killing myself in small ways.

Listening to the *[Jack Kerouac]* <u>ON</u> <u>THE</u> <u>ROAD</u> tape bothers me because it reminds me of what I hate about my writing. It has no INSIGHT in it. Its reflection is only memory and not memory with insight. It's like a little boy reporting all this NEWNESS to his Mom and as soon as the newness wears off he's gone.

JULY 7, 1995

This is the reality; I will either be old or I will not be. Age or nothing but no way out of here alive. This sadness and absurdity all rolled into one.

JULY 9, 1995

SUNDAY

But no . . . really . . . sitting on the stone wall of the pump house overlooking the reservoir eating my old tuna, jalapeno and "hot" hummus sandwich I had a peaceful sense of NOTHINGNESS and that was what I was going to come to. DEATH is NOTHING. It's not death that's sad, it's life. There is nothing sad about nothing. I had a very strong feeling that I am nothing visiting something. Yes, I am nothing visiting something and returning to nothing.

I am carrying most of MOM'S feelings with me most of the time. Could not be with Dad because not there for her. I'm carrying Mom's feelings and the only time I get rid of them is with Forrest.

AUGUST 26, 1995

[Martha's Vineyard]

Kathie and I took the long bike ride to Gay Head through Menemsha—the little "bike ferry." A long hard ride not unlike skiing exhausted feeling. What a ride and then just in time for a massage. Then I drove the kids to Oak Bluffs to get beer and treats. Drive back along East Chop to stop and watch the sun set. Moving into one of those absurd perfect moments where the day slipped into a kind of perfect harmony with the children. Forrest sitting in the front seat looking up at me while he licked his giant lollipop ring—BIZZARE CANDY JEWEL—and Marissa sat trying to decide which doll underwear she should ask for for Christmas.

Then off to the fireworks and all of us in the cold sand ROMPING. Deep Memories of my family together in one time harmony.

These little moments before they go soon again for no known reason. As in—Forrest hitting and going after Marissa on the way home. Her crying and Forrest's eyes looking like the flashing eyes of a mad man.

SEPTEMBER 14, 1995

No more morning erections. No more masturbation.

Well, I guess I know that I won't live another 54 years. I'm over on the other side of the years now.

UNDATED

MONDAY

Ran into Richard Schechner and Louise Kaplan. Richard—in response to my latest life story, told me I was like Walter Benjamin's view of history.

AN ANGEL BACKING INTO THE FUTURE.

OCTOBER 6, 1995

About a week ago Forrest and I went for an after dinner walk alone. The woods still has that PRIMORDIAL presence and I had to yell out loud to make myself known to feel myself there. The memory of Colorado and bears came back on me. Would I give my life to save Forrest? My flesh and blood. I wake up on the dock next to Forrest. Next to my son. My flesh and blood and thought even if I die, I will die a lucky guy.

OCTOBER 14, 1995

Telling Kathie that I was building the monolog as a vehicle to take off in and I really did see it as a little space ship out behind the house and I was going to fly off in it and I hoped that it was comfortable for me this time out.

In January 1996, Gray and Russo bought a house in Sag Harbor, Long Island. They first visited Sag Harbor together when they spent a weekend there the year before to celebrate Gray's birthday. Soon after, they began looking for a place to live there.

MAY 25, 1996

We went on a camping trip. One we will never forget—on an island in the Hudson. *[Gray and Russo and the two children went on a camping trip with Robert F. Kennedy Jr. and his family. Gray had met Kennedy when he'd hosted an event for the Natural Resources Defense Council—for which Kennedy serves as a senior attorney—the month before. Afterward, Kennedy invited Gray, Russo, and the children to join his family on their Memorial Day weekend camping trip.]* The highlight for me was Forrest's story and how fluid and committed his associations were. He just went from one image to the next. Kathie said that it took courage but I think more that he was in an innocent state of grace. That he had no doubt.

MARISSA and I are both DREAMERS. That is where the competition comes in. I saw the way she was able to play alone on the island and I felt for that. The men there were all filled up with the need for action. They preferred being busy where as I kept falling into a kind of contemplative reverie, with the view of the Catskills, all the time remembering how important my right eye is to me.

But what if something happens to Kathie? Am I ready or able to raise two children? NO! I have to be on the road to make a living.

MAY 27, 1996

I AM NOT JUST NEUROTIC (GOD DAMN IT!). I AM ALSO MISSING IN A BIG WAY THE PROCESS OF INTEGRATED RITUAL IN MY LIFE. SO, I HACK AWAY AT MAKING OR CREATING MY OWN MYTHOLOGY WHICH IF IT CAN BE APPRECIATED AT ALL IT WILL BE ONLY BY THOSE WHO SURVIVE ME.
　　AS FOR ME, THE REST IS SILENCE.

At this time, Russo told Gray she was nearly two months pregnant with his baby.

JUNE 1, 1996

I feel FAT. I feel trapped by Kathie's pregnancy. I am starting to buck and jolt again from the great feeling of indecision. How I cannot make up my mind.

I hate Kathie's stupid clarity.

JUNE 11, 1996

The humid weather has set in again. I think we are now going into the second week of this shit. I woke up with such a heavy feeling at night. And that combined with the TINNITUS in my ears [*Gray developed a ringing in his ears in 1994 that continued off and on throughout his life*] and the reality of my days of Kathie being pregnant. I feel trapped. I feel trapped and afraid. I am beginning to read [*Milan Kundera's*] THE UNBEARABLE LIGHTNESS OF BEING again. It's so well done.

JUNE 17, 1996

Kathie's 36th birthday

"For Sabina, living in truth, lying neither to ourselves nor to others, was possible only away from the public: the moment someone keeps an eye on what we do, we involuntarily make allowances for that eye, and nothing we do is truthful. Having a public, keeping a public in mind, means living in lies."

[From The Unbearable Lightness of Being]

I do not know whether to believe Kathie or not but she tells me she will get an abortion. Maybe I fear what I will owe her for this. I woke up at 4:00 AM from the sound of heavy rain.

JUNE 19, 1996

WEDNESDAY THERAPY WITH MARTHA
A great surge of positive energy when I said I was OPEN & AFRAID TEARS streamed down.

Afterwards I felt so light and sort of stunned and wondering. Even though it was raining I felt all this light and hope. I could at least see my way into it. And Abe was right! I continued to breathe all through it and the memory of when I saw our last fetus on the sonogram and how I saw it waving crying and I yelled.

LET ME IN
LET ME INTO THE WORLD.
Let me in! Let me into this world!

Kathie was ready to say that she would get the ABORTION she had come in prepared.

She had come into therapy ready to say, "if that's what you need."

JUNE 30, 1996

"Although the relationship between artist and muse can drive the creative process and enhance it, perhaps because of its very intensity the relationship is often fraught with danger.

The more intense the relationship, the more bitter the separation when it occurs. And when sex is a component of the relationship, as is so often the case, the ending can be catastrophic.

The artist-muse relationship seems to endure longest when there is personal distance between the two parties."

—SUNDAY TIMES

JUNE 30 (A RAINY SUNDAY)

JULY 26, 1996

THE LAST GOOD DAY OF SUMMER

It was clear dry bright and cool. We all went out in the canoe for dinner. The four of us. This odd strange family, drifting in the canoe. Me with a fever. Forrest feeling insecure because we were just drifting as we ate. And he's crying out paddle and the memory of us together in the hammock before the woods turned against me, me in the hammock reading SNOW WHITE to Forrest and looking up at the sun setting through the trees. I'm telling him that this is the forest.

Life keeps interrupting ART while father/mother death smiles over both SHOULDERS.

You see, around 50, I started to realize that I hadn't really lived. And that I had made a living on reporting on not living. I made a lively report on NOT LIVING.

Then I went out and tried to make up for all that lost time. I threw myself into every available experience and skiing saved me.

My love is so, so double edged. Double edged love and I see that same thing so alive in Forrest now.

This I love you, I hate you. All these PUNCH/KISS.

AUGUST 8, 1996

We drove, Forrest and I, to the airport in this FOG. Into the 8th DAY OF IT. Forrest was very upset when Kathie's plane had to turn back. I said, "Don't blame me, it was an act of god." And Forrest said, "GOD IS NOTHING" WHO TOLD YOU?/ NO ONE.

In September 1996, Gray and his family moved to their new house in Sag Harbor while also keeping the loft in Manhattan for trips to the city.

SEPTEMBER 8, 1996

ULTIMATELY, MY BOTTOM LINE RELATIONSHIP HAS ALWAYS BEEN WITH A FOXY MAGICAL THINKING GAME OF HOW CAN I SLIP THROUGH YOUR RANDOM ALWAYS PRESENT NET? TO LINK BODIES TO WORDS, LINK MY BODY TO MY WORDS.

Making love to Kathie looking out at THE TOWN and the white picket fence, I got lost. Where was I? What did all this mean?

SAG HARBOR IS ALSO A DISTANT MIRROR!
Looking at the town from the top of the little bridge I suddenly felt for better or worse I'd come home. I have been 40 years in EXILE. And now I've come back to THE HARBOR. Even my little sailboat is the same color and not named HALF-PINT but SMALL. So, in a funny sort of way I've come home. AND HOW?? HOW CAN I TALK about the place I live in?

SEPTEMBER 24, 1996

The way I am barraged. The way I am overwhelmed by memory here. When Forrest said, "Don't drive the car on the beach." I had that flash of me driving dad's car onto Barrington Beach.

I am now so down on my knees totally FORGIVING of my parents.

There had to be some sort of working LOVE there.

OCTOBER 1, 1996

I keep having the paranoid fearful feeling that I will discover something that will make my whole life A FAKE AN ACT, a big false lie and then I will have to change it all.

LADIES and GENTLEMEN, "THE FAMILY!"

OCTOBER 2, 1996

THE NEXT MONOLOG HAS TO DO WITH: THE TOWN, OUR TOWN, SAG HARBOR
for instance, where did the name "SAG" come from???

OUR HOUSE = "CHARM HAS ITS PRICE" said by the man who came to clean the windows.

For instance, the ORANGE PUMPKIN ON THE TABLE . . . just ON GOOD DAYS. ON GOOD DAYS, JUST THE SIGHT OF THE ORANGE PUMPKIN ON THE TABLE (THE SUN COMING THROUGH THE FRENCH DOORS) IS ENOUGH.

OCTOBER 7, 1996

Had dinner with Amelie *[the philosopher Amélie Rorty]*. She's very disarming and I still feel that she thinks the break-up with Renée was a great mistake . . . her reaction to the sad "line" that "Renée's bright lights will never shine on me again." She thinks that I think well in my work. The most disarming question that she asked was what did Kathie see in me? Also, she said ——→ you don't look for a pay back in your children—you just LOVE them and send them out into the world. YOU DO NOT LOOK FOR A RETURN FROM YOUR CHILD . . . this I guess is UNCONDITIONAL LOVE.

When I told her I needed to be alone (or is it really with a different woman every night) Amelie said, What better place to be alone than right in the middle of three children.

From November 2, 1996, to January 6, 1997, Gray performed It's a Slippery Slope *at the Vivian Beaumont Theater at Lincoln Center. In January, after the show closed, he began guest starring as a therapist on the actress Fran Drescher's television sitcom,* The Nanny. *(He appeared on the show sporadically until 1998.)*

On January 16, 1997, Russo gave birth to a second son, Theo Spalding Gray.

UNDATED ENTRY

I was fortunate to be there for the birth of my second son, THEO. It took place in the Southampton Hospital in Eastern Long Island. Kathie was in labor for 13 hours in the middle of the wild, wet north eastern. I helped as much as I could with the birth, holding her right leg up and back while a nurse guided her left. There was a strange turmoil in the air. It was not only the storm, but there had been an unexplained stillbirth that morning, which had left all the nurses somber. That was coupled with the memory in my mind of our first visit to the hospital for Kathie's amnio, which just happened to be the morning after TWA flight 800 went down. The whole hospital was on a very tense emergency ALERT.

When Theo's head first started to crown and I got my first real glimpse of the coming him, I thought Kathie was giving birth to a dead beaver and I kept looking at the doctor's face to try to read his reactions. He seemed fine and I had to trust that.

This was an unforgettable event for me. I had always heard that children come into the world with a great INDIVIDUALIZED personal character in tact and at last I had a chance to witness this. That old perplexed expression on Theo's face lasted for weeks and can still, at seven months, be seen. Holding him in my arms, I completely identified with that density of perplexity. As he looked up at me, he seemed to be asking over and over, Why this? Why something and not nothing? Why this glorious accident?

JANUARY 22, 1997

I'm in rainy L.A. again. I had a good flight out but drank too much so I don't know what all that scribbling is about.

THEO, our new baby was almost hit over the head from a piece of siding that fell down from the cupboard while Kathie was holding him in her arms. "It could have killed him," she said. The thought of it made me feel ashamed and angry. A stupid random death of a little angel.

Forrest took my heart by the way he arranged his little animals on the lip of my grandfathers bureau and how it gave a life history such a full dimension. THAT SACRED CHEST of drawers come to this . . .

JANUARY 28, 1997

Trying to get used to so many beings in the house. THEO makes it so much fuller. The other morning I was holding him in bed and Forrest came in and saw the windows . . . the bedroom windows reflected in his eyes and said, "THEO has windows in his eyes."

FEBRUARY 1, 1997

Austin Airport

DREAM: I was living by what seemed to be a kind of inland water-way. In this dream, I was doing most of my relating to what felt like ANOTHER MAN. This other man, who I could not see in the dream, owned a powerboat and I discovered that there had been some vandalism done to the boat and I was outraged by this and I kept telling him that he had to get out of such a place where people would do that to his boat.

Then I looked across the waterway canal where his boat was and saw that the whole place was like a huge MAUSOLEUM. And there all these soulless Mafia DONS standing like statues and staring out at me. And whoever I was with said, "These guys are buying us out." And I said, "Will I get a fair price?" And he said, "Yes." And I said, "Time to move. I've lost a house and I've lost a son. It's time to move on."

But I felt no remorse or sadness. I have no idea who I was talking to or what HOUSE or what SON I was referring to. It was a strange dream because it was so visual and so without feeling. It seemed to be about resolution.

Kathie got me . . . or helped get me out of New York.

FEBRUARY 3, 1997

I always thought I was too unstable to be a father. Now, just when I think the children will drive me crazy they make me sane. LIKE THIS MORNING when I was doing YOGA and Forrest came down with the "Where's Waldo in Hollywood?" book.

He was in such an unexpected good mood. Marissa has not gotten much better for me. Is so so confrontational but is so so good with the baby. She can rock him and sing him to sleep like no one else. So, there, WHAT A SURPRISE.

Last night I kept waking up to listen to THEO breathe and to hold his hand. I am the one that is getting so nervous about every breath. I am on the jitney now. On the move again. Will I ever slow down? I have to make CHOICE.

No real time at home. Frantic home. But first sex with Kathie this morning in over two weeks. Used a condom but felt like I was shooting bullets into a rubber wall. Not like I was shooting into her.

MARCH 4, 1997

I am not suffering from original SIN. I am suffering from "ACQUIRED SIN." It is after all an accumulation and I think what I may be forgetting is that I did have a kind of nervous breakdown and I think that I GET MISLED by the AUDIENCES' laughter at the report of this, and because they take it lightly, then I begin to take it lightly.

THUS THE NEED FOR A MORE PRIVATE NARRATIVE WITH MARTHA, in order to remember MY MADNESS. I'm not mad, I'm just anxious.

On March 19, 1997, the film of Gray's Anatomy, *directed by Steven Soderbergh, was released. "I saw the monologue and I think Kathie called and we discussed the possibility of doing it as a film," Soderbergh recalled. "The budget was really, really cheap. And this was on the heels of doing* Schizopolis *[Soderbergh's previous film], so I still had a crew, and it came together quickly. We shot it in this warehouse in Baton Rouge. It really was kind of like a group of people putting on a show . . . What was interesting about* Gray's *[Anatomy] was how easily Spalding could drop in and out of the monologue, since we shot completely out of sequence. It was astonishing to put it together and see how perfectly modulated it was. That was startling to me."*

Critics gave the film good reviews—though their tone was more often cheerfully appreciative than rapturous. "A chatty, colorful, nicely sardonic account of how this crisis led Mr. Gray to assess his medical state, consider his mortality and take one more funny, self-dramatizing look at the eccentric world around him," Janet Maslin wrote in The New York Times.

MAY 1997

MONTH OF MAY

DREAMS, SO MANY DREAMS OF THE WILD SEA, A WILD SEA ALMOST, ALWAYS ALMOST, SWEEPING ME AWAY.

The following are notes for Morning, Noon, and Night, *Gray's 1999 monologue leading his audience through a day in his life with his family in Sag Harbor. At this time, Theo was four months old, Forrest was four, and Marissa was nearly eleven.*

MAY 29, 1997

*MORNING CHAOS
MONOLOG MAY 29

Must do the CHAOS of me with THE KIDS in the morning.

"CRASH" the sound of glass breaking. "Dad, do you know that picture of George Washington dying in bed? Marissa just threw her shoe at it and it broke."

"I did not throw it. It came off. I'm not used to CLOGS."

"But those clogs are your mother's shoes. Why did you ever have them on?"

"I was dancing."

"But you are supposed to be eating breakfast. And you don't eat in here. I wanted to listen to *NPR* news. Since when do you dance to the news?"

"Spaldy what does SODOMY mean?"

"Why did you not even touch your oatmeal?"

"I thought I wanted it but I'm not hungry."

"Marissa, I cannot believe you broke that picture. Now there are shards of glass everywhere! It's all over the couch. Don't you know that's bad luck?"

"That's nonsense. In Colonial times the plantation owners tried to make their slaves and servants believe it was bad luck to break precious objects but you can't fool me. You can't repress and dominate me."

"Why did you kick that shoe? You must be angry about something."

"No, no reason."

"Don't tell me NO REASON. Maybe you don't know a reason but I'm sure there is one somewhere."

"Well if no one knows the reason does that mean the reason exists somewhere in the unknown?"

"And where is that?"

"HELP!"

(LOOKING NOW AT THIS PICTURE THIS PHOTO OF THEO. It is as though my father has been reborn and now I can kiss and touch him. And, touch his soft spot.)

Marissa goes out the door with a pocket book and high heels and says, "Goodbye you two losers. I have a date."

She comes back in and says, "Oh my God! It's a no man's land out there."

JULY 1, 1997

NEW MONOLOGUE

2 GIANT Horrors as I drifted off to that great undifferentiated void.

(1) That I was separated from Forrest FOREVER.
(2) That I could not tell you about it. I could not tell you how it felt.

NOVEMBER 5, 1997

The phone call from Kathie this morning and to hear Forrest's innocent voice of pure joy (Renée at her best) I just melted on the phone.

EACH TIME I try talking to myself there's no one home = AUDIENCE dear audience, it's you I'M TALKING TO.

JANUARY 19, 1998

Fabulous grass sex. I went twice again last night like old times but after I come, it does set off strong fantasies of wanting to escape but get out to where I wonder. Where would I run to this time? Good sex and happy children and Kathie being a good cook are all the GLUE and the STICKER that holds me here in this sweet grey town in SNOWLESS January.

JANUARY 27, 1998

MISSOULA, MONTANA

> What is important, Forrest? (THOUGHT)
> "Well, say if someone drowns . . . . ."
> (LONG PAUSE)
> "You've got to save them."

I had had a thought maybe I was stoned, I think I was. It went like this (somewhere in Montana)—the whole idea is to live the real life—the one that makes the unreal-real feel real.

God is something.

God is the thing that's not there when you need it.

MORNING, NOON, & NIGHT

I look at each book and try to remember what they say. Try to recreate a book report for each one. They seem to divide into EAST AND WEST. I think of Adam Phillips and BLOOM and "NEAR DEATH" experiences. I think of Martha and how I realized there could be no transcendent reconciliation with my mortality. Taking on THEO— for better or worse, was the only radical act for me to choose LIFE. TIBETAN DOGMA, the HIERARCHY of the priest that can only give you the good death. No wonder Kathie reads People Magazine to get to sleep.

MAY 1, 1998

A secret for me is like a black hole in which I feel myself disappearing. As in "this secret will never have a life." And that is where it gets a little destructive when I NEED to share all my secrets, secrets and fears and doubts with Kathie.

FORREST IS BECOMING AN INDEPENDENT "OTHER"
—MARISSA ALREADY IS. ALWAYS WAS.

Also, of late, THEO has reminded me of me—the way he has a real good time and then cries when it's not happening anymore as though there is no satisfying MEMORY TRACE.

JUNE 18, 1998

When I sat in the Captain Glover house *[a house in Sag Harbor that Gray and Russo considered buying]*, it was so nice to see the way one room would run into another, the way the house rambled but now back here at our "sweet little cottage" I see the whole setting; the whole landscape in which this house is set, also RAMBLES and goes in its own way from room to room, only the "rooms"; our outside: the yard, the cemetery, the glitter of the Lowell pool seen through the dapple of green trees. *[The house behind Gray's house in Sag Harbor belonged to Robert Lowell's stepdaughter Ivana Lowell. Lowell's third wife, Lady Caroline Blackwood, bought this house in 1987. When Gray discovered this fact, he told Russo he felt it was a sign that moving there was meant to be.]*

So, I am still happy with this place.

AUGUST 29, 1998

M. V. *[Martha's Vineyard]*

Theo running naked, running in circles into and out of the waves. A Perfect Moment. The end of another summer. The sad rhythm of the seasons.

Kathie constantly challenges the image I have of MY FRAGILITY so I keep asking. I don't know whether I'm having a good time or trying to kill myself and then, of course, there is that BORING IN BETWEEN.

OCTOBER 30, 1998

CAUGHT MY FIRST FISH

> savage eye of nature BLUEFISH.
> the silver shimmer of fish like a piece of the water itself
> like a part of the mother
> like a wild silver tear

and then the way the fish held still when I held as though it knew this game of
> being caught and thrown back in again

NOVEMBER 1, 1998

DREAM: That I was waiting in line to be guillotined, have my head cut off, and Woody Allen was the guy next to me.

NOVEMBER 18, 1998

I no longer know the difference between intuition and paranoia; the truth attacks the lie and the lie eats the truth; they are so close now they suck each other's tail soon to catch the body, eat it and become one.

DECEMBER 20, 1998

It's near Christmas and all the toys are talking. Ernie [*Gray's accountant*] gave Theo this FARM GAME type toy that just came in and said "good bye" to me as I went out the door. Also that Gorilla keeps going off with "HEY MAGDALENA." And then there is FLICK, the talking ant.

We all had a good time at "Babe, Pig in the City." We all went out to the South Hampton Brew Pub with Teresa and Sienna. THE FAMILY DRIVE HOME from the South Hampton Brew Pub . . . ⟶ we had Garrison Keillor on the radio and they were all singing Silent Night while I was secretly weeping. I mean the tears were just pouring down and at the same time I was crying, I was also ANALYZING why I was crying and just as I came into the clear and simple insight that it was not the actual story of the birth of Jesus that is depicted in Silent

Night ⟶ rather it is the history of that piece of music in my life. I mean it goes so deep, so very deep (like how I cried at the opening of the "Killing Fields" not FOR THE HISTORY DEPICTED but for the personal history behind the making of the movie).

AND THEN, right in the middle of my weeping, Forrest from the back seat said, "Mom, what does Gampa do for a living?" and Kathie started telling Forrest what LIFE INSURANCE was and I jumped in to tell him that if I died there will be enough money left for the family and Forrest just yelled, "YES!"

↓

And what did I say? I laughed. I really laughed and said, "Oh my God, I expected that not from you but from Marissa."

I thought I had an insight as to why I have felt that I've lived for such a long time in this family. It's because each year of the child's life seems so long and so different—so full of growth and change.

DECEMBER 20, 1998

SUNDAY

I don't know if I want to do a different monologue. Another. (Or this one.) Some part of me thinks I really wanted to step back then and settle in there but would the children be a surprise? "NO." That is the only way Forrest and Theo came into the world.

It was the way Kathie said to me in the canoe, when we were on mushrooms, and I told her that Renée had already ordered the wedding cake and Kathie said, "Oh, well, you could always give it back." I wouldn't care to know how to make up this situation in a play or fiction. I only care about it now, IN PRIVATE.

Liz, see if you can remember John Lennon and the reaction to his death.

JANUARY 1999

At parties I've run out of things to say I sit there stunned thinking of my sons and how
      TIME IS STEALING THEM AWAY.

FEBRUARY 1, 1999

These are good days. In spite of Forrest's irrational rage at his chicken salad sandwich today. (He stood in the yard and screamed)

I have, in spite of these little things; I have often thought that things will never be better than this . . . than these moments in our family life now. Last night I carried Theo home from the movies asleep in my arms under a full moon in this small sweet town.

FEBRUARY 12, 1999

Morning, noon and night went very well at Purchase, SUNY PURCHASE. The audience was really "up" at the end. Lenny and Marguerite Harrington gave me a ride home in their CLEAN Volvo. I could tell that they really liked the show. But on the way home in their CLEAN VOLVO, Lenny said something that kind of upset me. He told me that he got real angry about one section of the monologue—and at first he couldn't remember it. (INNOCENCE at all COST = THE PARENT REGAINS his innocence through the child) Then I helped him remember it. It was, of course, about the new section I'd written tonight—about how I told Forrest about death at an early age but—and I added this tonight—that I felt I saved him from THE FEAR by telling him that I loved him and that "Everything would be alright," that phrase, that phrase EVERYTHING WILL BE ALRIGHT. Lenny told me that he stopped being angry when I said that second part about "I love you" and I was thinking that maybe I don't say that enough to Forrest anymore. Then I had a sad flash of the preschool video of Forrest singing. My God! He was so THERE! Just so uncomplicatedly present. I wonder if Theo could ever be that way. And I also wondered if I helped take that innocence away from him. Lenny said his father told him completely honest answers to all questions and he resents him for that. He also said that Marissa wanted to spoil Christmas for Forrest and that was the first protective PANG I had about AIRING all our private stuff . . . that Lenny took it upon himself to say that Marissa wanted to kill Christmas for Forrest. THAT WAS WRONG.

Forrest really had an aversion to SANTA early on. "SANTA CLOCK SCARE ME." That was pre-Marissa.

When we, LENNY, M. and ME, drove up, it was raining and as we got higher up, the rain turned to snow. What a great homecoming for me. This nice white carpet of snow. It was just enough to change the whole yard. It is beautiful and I am sitting here getting drunk again. It is so beautiful outside.

THE CHILDREN ARE EVERYTHING FOR ME.

FEBRUARY 14, 1999

Sunday,
Valentine's Day

After BIG Valentine feed and funny card from Kathie I walked down to pond and heard the ice settle. WHAT A SOUND, and the STARS! And that tree down by THE BELL'S dock, how the branches went LIKE ROOTS INTO THE SKY—like roots into the ground.

BY THE LAKE TWO REALIZATIONS

(1) THAT I LOVED KATHIE FOR HER SPIRIT
(2) YOU CAN GO OUT OF HERE MORE CONSCIOUS THAN YOU ARE

I DID NOT ADD TO FORREST, NOT ONLY WILL WE HAVE TO DIE BUT WE WILL ALSO HAVE TO, IF WE'RE LUCKY, IN SOME CASES, GROW OLD FIRST

A FAREWELL TO THE MONOLOGUE
A MONOLOGUE IN 2 PARTS
GOODBYE MY FRIENDS
                    * KEEP GOOD JOURNALS *

FEBRUARY 21, 1999

Kathie is having a hard time. She feels a breakdown coming on. She says she can no longer do anything at 100%. She is too strung-out. She says that I still do my shows at 100% and it's true. That's true about my work. She is now talking about quitting her job.

[In September 1993, Russo went to work for Columbia Artists Management Inc. as a special projects coordinator; she also did booking

work for many of the clients there—Alvin Ailey and Twyla Tharp, among them. In 1996, she joined forces with a colleague from Columbia Artists and an independent commercial producer to begin their own New York management firm called Washington Square Arts. Russo was an employee at Washington Square Arts through 2007.]

When we all went all the way over to the river and then well into the woods to look at that house for sale, Forrest refused to get out of the car. "We already have a house," he said.

MAY 17, 1999

DREAMS
More dreams of a wild dark sea tearing me away from my night shore walk. Me trying TO GET MY ARMS AROUND THE ROOTS OF A TREE and knowing that it would be an easy thing to do, to just wrap my arms or hands around that root—making two interconnected circles but the dark waves came in and started to carry me out as I cried out, I think to Rocky, for help.

JUNE 9, 1999

DREAM—Last night I dreamed that Forrest, Theo and I went to look at a NEW LARGER HOUSE we were supposed to move into and some CULT had taken it over. Theo and Forrest went in and I was afraid to go after them lest I get BRAINWASHED.

JUNE 10, 1999

> We are innocent
> when we dream.

Forrest, the most any of us can hope for is to inhabit a few graceful moments in time and to recognize them as such. I am happy to say, we have already shared some of those moments together. The rest is an unsolved mystery.

JULY 9, 1999

THEO and I swimming out to the raft together. Theo jumping off the far side of the raft and then me helping him out of the water which feels like a kind of bullhorn with each time. Kathie swimming towards us, at a distance, THINKS, as she sees us: I made Spalding Gray a happy man.

JULY 1999

FRIDAY

THEN SURPRISE; I just got a collect call from Marissa, from a pay phone outside her camp in ITHACA and it made me cry. I could tell by her tone of voice how much she missed us and the other element that made me cry was how much she sounded like Renée when she would get in that sad 13 year old arrested development place that would make my heart go out to her and annoy and bother me at the same time. I wonder if that does not happen to me with Marissa so much because Kathie is in partner with me to help absorb so much of Marissa's need.

Kathie never gets that way with me she just says: "EAT MY SHORTS!"

JULY 21, 1999

The horror of the Kennedy plane going down [*John F. Kennedy Jr., piloting a private plane with his wife, Carolyn Bessette, and her sister Lauren Bessette on board as passengers, crashed into the Atlantic Ocean off the coast of Martha's Vineyard on July 16, 1999*], falling at a mile a minute and the way the press keeps reporting on the details makes it like a meditation on HORROR which reminds me of my RELIGION OF PARANOIA, my ritual of FEAR. Just this morning I found the seal on the milk had been broken and yet I went ahead and used it on my cereal. Then I began to imagine I'd been poisoned. I was even drinking as I held Theo in my arms. In the face of that mostly manufactured fear, LIFE SUDDENLY SEEMS SO PRECIOUS, so much like a rare gift. I think that is some of the fascination and the draw to the press reports of J.F.K. Jr. going down at that speed.

Kathie just called to tell me that they found his body.

AUGUST 4, 1999

[Martha's Vineyard]

I'm doing it again; after that wonderful day, our first real day here, with the long bike ride and Forrest in the ocean being knocked down by waves (Marissa refusing to go in) and Theo with his bat and ball, I discover this little spot on my right arm and begin to think: death by AIDS. It's my little punishment system for FEELING GOOD. MY SELF-REPRESSION.

It is such an OLD STORY but it's always or often in relationship to LOVE and INTIMACY. Sometimes when I look at Theo (mostly now, but still, often with Forrest) and I just can't stand it and then I look down at THE LITTLE SPOT on the inside of my right arm.

But we really did have a great time playing CHARADES which only Marissa could get us all to do and I was so HONORED that Forrest played me sitting in a chair at my table. I was so very touched.

SEPTEMBER 18, 1999

DREAM ———→ I am talking to a small group of people saying, as I hold one of my children in my lap, "Look even with all of this I still believe in THE LIFE ELSEWHERE."
And one woman, a therapist type, spreads her hands about 2 feet and says, "You realize you've only gone about this deep."
I said, "I KNOW."

OCTOBER 29, 1999

On the train back from Richmond now I am reading *[Mark Spilka's 1980 book]* VIRGINIA WOOLF'S QUARREL WITH GRIEVING which set me off to thinking about "Rumstick Road" and how that was my public grieving piece although Liz and I never discussed it. DIDN'T IT ALL START, in a way, WITH ME READING TO THE LIGHTHOUSE in Kashmir?

It makes me so sad to be happy.

NOVEMBER 5, 1999

TORONTO

I've always felt that I wanted to KNOW SOMETHING before I died, SOMETHING VERY HUMAN. And I have. I've come to know the love for my children.

Gray performed his monologue Morning, Noon, and Night *at the Vivian Beaumont Theater at Lincoln Center from October 31, 1999, to January 10, 2000.*

NOVEMBER 22, 1999

They're endless . . . the machinations of my paranoid mind are endless. Exhausted last night after a signing then a performance.

Even my show consciousness is being bombarded by inner fears that would throw me off like what if I found out I was dying? How would I do the show without that leaking through? Wanting always to confess to the audience about what's really going on but no one really wants to hear what's really going on.

I've gone through this before and it is difficult to explain to Kathie perhaps because she is so grounded in the immediate tasks of living.

NOVEMBER 27, 1999

The car ride to Brewster *[Gray also sometimes referred to Sedgewood as Brewster, as this was the name of the nearest train station.]* from Vermont was one of the most beautiful rides I've taken in a long time. Such constant, rural beauty even though my mind was so much in my intestines and I was anxious for much of the way.

Kathie wants me to be as mentally healthy as I sounded on *TALK OF THE NATION* talking to Melinda Penkava.

Renée would call it using people; as in I get bored with talking everyday chitchat to let's say Robby *[Stein]*—then when I have an obsessively hypochondriac need, I keep calling him in order to DUMP. My need to dump.

The well told PARTIAL TRUTH to deflect the private RAW TRUTH.

NOVEMBER 30, 1999

Ken *[Kobland]* is right about how the coming of the millennium has created an exaggerated sense of time in all our minds and for us older ones it has a "these are our last times" feeling.

Sitting in the car with Forrest just before school . . . he began to ask me about the millennium and when the next one would be. When I told him it would not be for another one thousand years; followed by, "I won't be here." Then I let it sit . . . I left it to him to say, "I won't be here either." And then for a moment we just sat there in that beautiful absurd silence and in all that beauty outside the car windows. It was that crazy, dizzy, unprotected feeling. That absurd vulnerable, totally unprotected feeling.

DECEMBER 21, 1999

I don't think that *Morning, Noon and Night* is a lie or an act or a front . . .

I think Theo got quite high from that bottle of coke I just let him have. He stretched out his arms and spun around and said, "I like this place. I like this whole place." As for me, I just had myself in the bathroom.

Yes, I am able to channel my anxiety in PERFORMANCE.

DECEMBER 31, 1999

LAST DAY OF THE CENTURY

Another big dinner party last night. The food and drink was fantastic. And then THEO. Just watching him dance is all I need.

Loving and loss go hand in hand for me. I can't see Theo and love him without that sense of loss. I'm past that with Forrest now. It has to do with their innocent VULNERABILITY?

2000–2004

BUT I STILL REMEMBER how my children have been a blessing and these memories burn in my heart like a religious icon.

A) Marissa toasting me on my birthday for bringing her brother Forrest into the world.

B) Forrest waking and kissing me in all my lost agitated state on the way to MV in the Ford Escort.

C) Theo's face at birth and the honest confusion it expressed. Kathie told me later how she had to hold him and comfort him and tell him it was alright.

Love is stronger than death, but life is stronger than love. (DARK, DARK, we all go into the DARK—ELIOT)

UNDATED FROM HIS 2000 JOURNAL

Gray was as content as he would ever be in the very beginning of this decade. His love for his family had given him an unexpected sense of appreciation and calm. Though even this proved challenging for him, as he would try to wrestle these moments to the ground in an effort to preserve happiness and would soon feel time rushing past again—the hours and days carrying life away. Thoughts of his own contentment were often accompanied by a mistrust of a mood that had so long eluded him. But a particular entry on January 21, 2000, stands out for its simple gratitude. "My cup RUNNETH over," Gray wrote. "Everything feels like more than enough today."

In the summer of 2000, Gray began rehearsals for a Broadway revival of Gore Vidal's The Best Man*—he played William Russell, the liberal candidate in a fictional presidential race. This re-ignited a sense of dread and anxiety. He worried about learning his lines, failing as an actor, shaming his family. Soon, he began to fret about his future work too: How could he do another monologue when he felt happy, of all things, living in the Hamptons with his family? Where was the story in that?*

"I think Spalding, as narcissistic as he was, also felt that sooner or later he would be revealed and someone would find out there was nothing there," Robby Stein theorized. "And so when he finished the monologue or the play or whatever he was doing, that was the end, because it was either he had exposed himself or exhausted the well."

After having enthusiastically revealed his new family in Morning, Noon, and Night, *Gray felt inhibited about returning to them for material. He'd become more careful about publicly unveiling his life as this now required unveiling the lives of his children as well.*

"After Morning, Noon, and Night, *I don't think he was sure where the monologues were going to go. An adult who gets involved with a performer is signing on for something, but the kids didn't sign on for this, they didn't have a choice," Steven Soderbergh remarked. "And I don't think he wanted to turn it into an Ozzie and Harriet thing. If you just start doing stuff in order to tell a story—that's cheating. So I have to believe he was really wondering, what do I do with this form now?"*

JANUARY 12, 2000

Yesterday was Kathie's and my TENTH ANNIVERSARY and today is the 10th anniversary of SEX together and it's snowing out. OUR FIRST SNOW.

 THE FAMILY IS THE STORY.
 THE STORY IS THE FAMILY.

JANUARY 16, 2000

THEO'S THIRD BIRTHDAY

On the way home from the party last night, Kathie reported that the Glover House has gone into contract. She feels she can let it go. Can I? But the view of the CEMETERY now in grey winter with its patches of white snow . . . is so lovely.

Kathie thinks the kids love our house because it's SUCH A NEST.

JANUARY 18, 2000

Woke at 3:40 NOT IN A SWEAT but then was so worried about falling into a sweat that I could not get back to sleep. Martha tells me that her husband also sweats if he drinks wine at night also THAT SHE HAS TINNITUS. We talked a lot about my little GUY that wants so much to regress and get into trouble. That little hungry cunt licking dog. He is all a big pant. Align yourself with Kathie, she said. Try to get over your anger for women and your need to punish them. And she's right about that RAGE.

> "Was it bigger, more important, worthier things that inclined others to a lifelong mate? Or at the heart of everyone's marriage was there something irrational and unworthy and odd?"
>
> ROTH
> [From American Pastoral by Philip Roth]

No, I know THE GUY that Martha is talking about . . . it's that panicked, paranoid hysteric that CHEWY DOG that Monster in a Box was really the apotheosis of. And I don't want him back. I know now because I am more conscious how to avoid setting it up.

JANUARY 19, 2000

I have been feeling bad about my old work. Thinking of it as MERE HYSTERIA and then last night a woman came up to me on Second ave. all smiles she started telling me how much she loved my Russian stories in "MONSTER."

JANUARY 21, 2000

The overwhelming love I felt for Forrest when the wind blew his hair up and just for a second I caught a glimpse of that moon face baby face I had mooned over myself as he slept by the old carousel in Watch Hill, Rhode Island. That oh so crazy summer of 1992?

My cup RUNNETH over. Everything feels like more than enough today.

JANUARY 24, 2000

Well-meaning FAN stops me on the street to tell me my monologues are too filled with laughter. TOO LIGHT. He likes the old dark days like with 'SWIMMING.'

FEBRUARY 19, 2000

CLEVELAND

I dreamed that I was collaborating with Laurie Anderson and she was naked in bed and looked great, young body going through all these fabulously contorted sexy poses. (Was Martha being seductive when she did that thing—those moves in the chair? Like Mom in that way? As in, "He could park his skis by my bed any day," she said once about *[Gray's childhood friend]* Roger Lund) And I was sitting on the edge of the bed so very, very frustrated because the audience was watching . . . I was also frustrated because I could not tell ART from LIFE.

APRIL 30, 2000

Back in N. Y. C. for an interesting meeting with Peter Greenaway *[a British filmmaker whose best-known film is* The Cook, the Thief, His Wife, and Her Lover*]* where he asked me who I wrote for when I did a journal. . . . well my audience of course. It is not enjoyable or easy for me to have a non-narrated private experience and I've always known that.

In May 2000, Gray was cast in The Best Man. *The play opened on September 17, 2000, with Gray and Chris Noth in the leading roles of competing presidential candidates. Gray played the patrician idealist, while Noth took on the self-styled, scheming politician.*

MAY 25, 2000

Back in Sag Harbor after N.Y.C. and saying "yes" to THE BEST MAN or rather, letting K. say "yes." And the big Harper's party last night and then Kathie and I made love for an hour just like floating on the top of all that sensual energy.

JUNE 6, 2000

A great birthday with K. Long x walk on beach. High breathing up into my chest. Splendor in the short grass, oh wow!

Kathie gave me a great, big party *[for his fifty-ninth birthday]*. Way too much food! I got so stoned with only three hits off of Donald's joint. And I had this great cuddling time with Theo in my studio. I held him and told him how much I loved him. Then he started this little litany of "What do you do out here dad?" And I'd tell him one thing and he'd say, "And what else?" I think his sly little question was all about finding K. and I naked under the sleeping bag.

NO FEAR, NO PAIN, NO THINKING on the trip, just sensation of being in it and of it. Perfect balance. My painful left shoulder felt so free as I flapped it like a bird's wing. Now this storm! And all the aches and pains and fears are back. It is as if this day is the opposite of yesterday.

JULY 4, 2000

Last night, I sat down and watched the tape of OUR TOWN and with all those years distance on it, I could see that I did a good job. Steady, slow and simple. Frank Rich was wrong!

JULY 29, 2000

[Brewster, New York]

The sun came out for a few minutes around 5:30 and I took Theo down for a swim. He can swim very well underwater. I pushed him on the swing for a long time and looked out at the lake saying my own silent farewell to another summer. How sad. And it was so, so short this time. It was for me a very beautiful moment, me pushing the swing from Theo's left so that I could see his face as he talked to me. Dragonflies darting over the lake all dancing in the reflection of the sun on the lake. We were almost the only ones down there and it did feel like a very early end to summer. Theo and I walked back together. Once again, he talked about angels playing FRISBEE and on the swing he asked me, "Who is Mother Nature's mommy?" Walking up the hill with me, he cried out, "Dad, I love myself!" "Very good," I said. "That's very good."

I have found that I like the fact that I have been writing everyday. I have been writing as though I was writing against a deadline and as I write now, I feel that good writing could help you to write your way out of almost anything, to spring you from the trap of not being.

To write well is to have POWER, GREAT POWER.

AUGUST 1, 2000

[First rehearsal for The Best Man*]*

It all felt a little unreal coming into the city after this much time out. First fight with taxi dispatcher and then some guy, who had observed it said, "Going to put that in your next monologue?"

We all met at 11:00 but did not do the read through until 3:30. I was very nervous but it went better than I thought it would and I liked the play more than I remembered . . . much more. I also like a lot of my scene. I think now that I can do it as in, BE CAPABLE but will I be able to hold up? That I didn't know. I did get tired today and every time the sky began to get bright outside, I would get distracted.

I have good first impressions of Gore [Vidal]. He's very ERUDITE and well read. I also like that my character looks at his K-9 teeth and that he is a politician from Rhode Island.

AUGUST 22, 2000

Tue.

I do not know how I am going to do it. I do not know how I will remember those lines each night, TO SAY EACH WORD RIGHT? Can you imagine it?

But memory turned me on and made me gleam. And it is also a body memory—in my upper back from lifting Theo up so that he could HOLD ON TO THE cable ride but the memory of him on that RAFT in his green suit, old before his time with a faded tattoo, saying, "Come on Dad, jump in, jump!" This little man, I can already see his age. His character in his mouth, in his teeth, and the way he directs those little asides to me. It's like he's already been here before and doesn't know that he knows it.

AUGUST 2000

SUNDAY 10:00 AM

I do have more than a perverse imp in my head. Just as I am relaxing a bit with my lines, the voices come, "You are no good. You are stiff and fake. You have AIDS. You are going to SHAME YOUR FAMILY!"

I am also starting to think a lot about my own work and how LUCKY I HAVE BEEN TO HAVE HAD IT and how I so very much want to do another GOOD and CONNECTED monologue.

Morning, Noon, and Night was so connected for me. I cry now at the loss of it AND THE LOSS OF THAT TIME IN MY LIFE.

And then, I think why didn't I do 8 shows of MN&N, and then I knew—I did not want THE SHOW OF THE FAMILY
    TO REPLACE THE FAMILY.

SEPTEMBER 7, 2000

THURSDAY

My life has been stolen from me by the play, the great Vampire. And Oh yes, how I long for my own work and the emotional connections I would feel when talking about Forrest but am I blind? Are those . . . were those only solipsistic, narcissistic states and I know that is a ludicrous fantasy. All I know is that they were transformative states that took me into another place. But when I am real tired and doing two shows those voices came to me on stage just before I have to say a crucial line.

"Eat pussy, snort a line, you can't do it, you're no good!"

Yes, my fear is that I will not be able TO MAINTAIN THE REALITY OF THE PLAY. That I will not care enough to do it. Oh yes I have the fantasy of being fucked but I'm not attracted to men or is it Roy* I want to want to fuck me. It is so very much that I want my ass to be an object of desire and I know that is a ludicrous fantasy and one I can hardly discuss with anyone even Martha but at least I am now willing for myself. It's only when the fantasy extends itself out or needs to be realized that there becomes a problem.

SEPTEMBER 10, 2000

SUNDAY

From the inside it often feels embarrassingly artificial particularly when I'm posing and "REACTING" and waiting for my Q's but I also understand IT IS A PLAY and the audience claps for the entrance and exit of cartoon PERSONALITIES and that's why I think Chris [Noth] gets longer applause, he is recognized as Mr. Big [on the television show Sex and the City] so he has a presence that goes beyond the play. Occasionally I will hear someone yell out "YEA SPALDING!" and that's nice.

SEPTEMBER 13, 2000

I WAS HURT, that LYNN REDGRAVE did not say "Good show" she said, "good to see you Spalding."

WHAT A STUPID POPULARITY CONTEST LIFE IS! And HOW DID I get in this show?

Ben Brantley's review of The Best Man *ran in* The New York Times *on September 18, 2000: "The casting is sometimes wonderfully apt, especially in the surprising case of Mr. Gray, best known as a self-searching monologist, as a Brahminlike presidential candidate a la Adlai Stevenson," he wrote. But Brantley also criticized the play more generally as lacking the "rousing, melodramatic vigor" it needed to keep it from seeming flat and dated.*

SEPTEMBER 30, 2000

Saturday

MONO
"WORK OUT YOUR OWN SALVATION WITH DILIGENCE" and also Freud; "every man must find out for himself in what particular fashion he can be saved." And that will most likely last a lifetime. For me, it has been THE FAMILY.

OCTOBER 8, 2000

THE UNOBSERVED LIFE DOESN'T FEEL LIKE LIVING. Once I no longer felt God watching, I began TO WATCH MYSELF

OCTOBER 12, 2000

Interviewing the audience is my SOCRATIC piece. It feels like the farthest I can go in making the public private and the private public.

Gray performs his breakthrough monologue, *Swimming to Cambodia*, based on his experience as an actor in *The Killing Fields*.

Gray on the set of Roland Joffe's *The Killing Fields*.

TOP In a helicopter with fellow cast member Craig T. Nelson (left)

MIDDLE With children in Thailand

BOTTOM Dressed as his character in the film, the assistant to the American ambassador in Cambodia.

Scenes from *Swimming to Cambodia*.
TOP LEFT The photo sent out as an invitation to the 1985 book party for the publication of *Swimming to Cambodia*.
TOP RIGHT On stage at The Performing Garage
BOTTOM Renée Shafransky with Gray on set for Jonathan Demme's 1987 film.

LEFT Gray with Shafransky in an undated photo booth session.
ABOVE Gray with Shafransky in his downtown Manhattan loft,
1986.

TOP Al Hirschfeld's caricature
of Gray drawn for the opening
of *Gray's Anatomy* at Lincoln
Center, 1993. This was
displayed along with other
drawings from the Hirschfeld
collection on the wall at Sardi's
restaurant in New York City.
BOTTOM Gray teaching a
storytelling workshop.

TOP Gray with his family: From left, seven-year-old Forrest (with a candy cane in his hand), Marissa, thirteen years old, and Theo, two, lying on Gray. Russo is reclining above them on the sofa in the living room of their first house in Sag Harbor, New York, 1999.

MIDDLE Gray and Russo at Sagaponack beach in Long Island, New York, 1999.

BOTTOM Gray with son Forrest, eleven months old, and stepdaughter, Marissa, seven years old, in Newport, Rhode Island, 1993.

TOP Gray with Russo at the
Sedgewood house in Carmel,
New York, 2003.
BOTTOM Gray with Theo in
Menemsha, in Martha's Vineyard,
Massachusetts, August 2002, slightly
more than a year after his car accident
in Ireland.

Annie Leibovitz took this photograph of Gray for *Vanity Fair* magazine in 1987.

NOVEMBER 4, 2000

SAT.

DREAMS OF THEO

In this dream I was shopping for RED WINE. And in this store the wine was all displayed in decanters and I had a sense they were all dessert wines, and too sweet. I went to talk to the wine woman, the shop tender and ended up having an erotic brush with her thigh. I remember the feeling of the contact and then I looked up to see that Theo—who was never visually in the dream—was gone. All I saw was a crowd of strangers and it was that old panic of loss again. That old; I cannot live without this child and even as I write this I know I am losing THAT CHILD, no so-called INNER CHILD could replace.

NOVEMBER 15, 2000

WEDS.

I am, for some reason, able to have a more subterranean life with Kathie than with Liz or Renée so I don't feel the same need for these SLEAZY ONE NIGHT STANDS

My subterranean ID finds an outlet with Kathie

NOVEMBER 24, 2000

DAY AFTER THANKSGIVING FRI.

We . . . Kathie and I took the boys to the big rocks in Central Park and then on to the Merry Go Round. The boys took a second ride alone and I thought what a great metaphor for the WHEEL OF LIFE AND DEATH. It's the great circle I anticipate the boys coming—ANTICIPATION—then I see them and they wave arriving in my gaze and then they are gone.

DECEMBER 16, 2000

Sat.

DREAM Kathie and I were being led to a very DIVEY bed and breakfast rooming house in an alley. Next scene, Kathie wakes up late real late (3:00) and in my old jealous and angry WAY saying, "What's wrong with you? Are you sick?" She has on old lady straw hat like Joan used to wear in Commune. Next scene, I am up on a high wooden walk way and in the yard below—its like a dirt corral like behind a ship and there are three young men getting all hot and bothered by Kathie who is dancing like a VIXEN in an open pit that looks like a fresh grave and Kathie has on these shorts and she is doing her vixen dance and I am up above getting all turned on by it and by the fact that the other men are turned on. I am getting a big erection in front of them all. Next scene, I am arguing with Kathie for being so seductive and then not coming in to bed with me and I am shouting at her and almost hit her. There is all this rage. Next scene, I am in bed waiting for her and I have this big erection and I have a tube down it and I am sucking up the sperm from deep in the base of my cock and it tastes good like sweet NOURISH-ING custard or cream.

DECEMBER 27, 2000

I watched TV until 1:00 AM. Starting with Ron Howard interview with C. Rose. And I had to face as I sipped my scotch on the rocks—that I am not, and never was, AMBITIOUS. It's a late day for my onstage fantasies that had I gone with CAA *[Creative Artists Agency, a power-ful talent agency that courted Gray in 1987]* I could have been my own vision of MALKOVICH. Ron Howard kept using that word for a qual-ity he obviously has, AMBITION.

JANUARY 2, 2001

While some others pray, I narrate and then I save it.

JANUARY 6, 2001

I am sitting in front of the fire with Theo. We have been listening and dancing to some very subversive music, Sargeant Peppers Lonely Hearts Club Band. It was snowing earlier in the evening and I couldn't wait to take Theo for a walk in the snow and maybe even go sledding but when I open the door to look out, it is raining a disgusting, slushy early spring-like rain. And I start ranting again. I start to talk about how it shouldn't be this way. How it's too warm for this time of year. How I remember the snow as a child in Rhode Island. I am suddenly in a foul mood and say, "Oh no Theo we can't go for a walk it's raining." And Theo replies brightly, "Let's go dad! I like to drink raindrops." Once again, one of my blessed children has delivered me from my bourgeois grumps, as I hold the small wet hand of my future generation.

FEBRUARY 9, 2001

[On tour with Morning, Noon, and Night *in Aspen, Colorado]*

Enforced day off from skiing. Oh God, I can hardly turn my back on these mountains. It's one of those perfect brilliant manic days. NEW SNOW & SUN! I can hardly think straight with those mountains reflected in the mirror as I write. Yesterday in that melancholy last run in fog and grayness I was the last one up to ELK CAMP and coming down SANDY trail, I stopped and tried to be still. It's not easy to stand still on skis because they are so built to go. But I stood there having that perpetual internal monologue. And I thought what I need a break from is that nonstop CHATTER narrative and I stood there long enough for it to stop and suddenly I had a split second moment of BARE AWARE-NESS where I saw only trees and they presented themselves and I got this whole tingle through my body from head to toe and then I felt it all just drop down into my balls and I felt this enormous SEXUAL CEN-TERING and I said, "I promise to give the narrator a rest."

Even though Gray had devoted a large portion of his monologue Morning, Noon, and Night *to his love of his Victorian green clapboard house in Sag Harbor, he and Russo began looking for a new home in or near Sag Harbor. Russo had suggested that the children needed more space, and Gray, despite feeling doubts, got caught up in the fervor of bidding on and buying a bigger place. In January 2001, Gray and Russo bought a new house in North Haven that, while only one and a half miles away, was no longer in the village of Sag Harbor. Soon there-after, in the period between buying the new house and actually living in*

*it, Gray began to write about his love for their Sag Harbor house and
his regrets about selling it.*

MARCH 8, 2001

And with this FANTASY of A MOVE all the panic holding on stuff
begins; that I will never be able to walk Forrest home from school again.

MARCH 11, 2001

Should I have OPTED, insisted on staying here? How can I get caught
in the flow toward the big house, THE GIANT HOME, THE LAST
SEA CAPTAIN.

But here I am a little bit drunk with THE BOYS; the place I seem to
always want to be without TV.

I am getting drunk, oh yes and the boys are dancing for me, dancing
to MOBY under the portrait of George Washington and in front of the
fire. It is so beautiful the way they dance together and Theo does this
great creative back up for FORREST.

MARCH 20, 2001

FIRST NIGHT OF SPRING

What is it? I keep wondering as I walk that makes this all feel so
familiar.

IN SHORT, I have never seen so many houses that I would like to live
in . . . that would give me great pleasure to live in.

OUR HOUSE AND OUR HOME AND THE FAMILY IS OUR CEN-
TER HERE

When I'm not working I get lost and then I begin to drift. Kathie wants
us to move to a new bigger house to contain my spirit.

I looked into Kathie's old sad gray eyes before we made love. I looked
into her eyes.

MARCH 23, 2001

Early fantastic spring light and big wind woke me up at 6:10 AM and oh wow! The view out each window and the way the rose light hit the top of the Lowell house. OH I WAS UP & HORNY!

I am running from window to window like a maniac. I feel like Emily in *OUR TOWN* when she comes back for her birthday and she gets SO ATTACHED; so very, very attached. I cry when I think of that scene. Like just now I could see the bay from Marissa's window and I saw THE BAY! Yes, for the first time in years and also how I inhabit this house in the most idealistic way whenever I perform the monologue.

MARCH 29, 2001

Did I see her? YES. Today. Renée in that blue Volvo and she didn't see me but I caught her in that bewildered vulnerable look. The same eyes I saw across the Studio 54 dance floor in 1979.

[Shafransky moved to Sag Harbor in 2001 and began a therapy practice there.]

MAY 13, 2001

MOTHER'S DAY

Nice sail and after dinner walk downtown. Forrest talked to me constantly about (like old days) and yes, how I will miss these walks to get ice cream; these philosophical walks but he started in on THE CREATION and how no one can know what happened because they were not there and this causes you to think about it and all this THINKING causes the feeling that ⟶ YOU BOTH KNOW AND NOT KNOW.

Also, yesterday at the beach, Forrest told Theo, Step in this water and you will be connected to all the oceans in the world.

MAY 21, 2001

Had the big CHAMPAGNE celebration last night at the new house. Robby somewhat less than enthusiastic but the new trees looked so good and the way that one cherry tree was planted right in the middle of those two dining room windows so you could see it from the hall by the front door framed in the window and those curtains. It looked like Chekhov.

On June 20, 2001, Gray took a trip with Russo and their three children, as well as their friends Barbara Leary (Timothy Leary's ex-wife) and her boyfriend, Kim Esteve; Tara Newman and her son Teddy Conklin; Carolyn Beegan and her boyfriend, Jake O'Boyle; and Gray's niece Amanda, to Ireland to celebrate Gray's sixtieth birthday. They'd been invited to the estate of John Scanlon, a high-powered publicist who worked with Monica Lewinsky in the aftermath of her affair with Bill Clinton. Scanlon also owned a house in Sag Harbor—he knew Gray from his performances and socialized with him on occasion in the Hamptons. More than once, Scanlon had offered his Ireland manor in the farm region of county Westmeath to Gray and Russo, explaining that he had many writer friends who used it as a retreat.

One evening, several months before Gray turned sixty, Russo was having drinks with Newman and Beegan, and they came up with a plan to take a group vacation at Scanlon's house to celebrate Gray's upcoming birthday. Russo surprised Gray with the trip a couple of weeks before they were to leave. Exhausted from touring with It's a Slippery Slope *and* Morning, Noon, and Night, *he was initially reluctant. But the next day, when Russo suggested that she go with the kids and Gray stay in Sag Harbor, he said he didn't want to be alone and worried he'd regret not going. So they went as a family.*

Scanlon died of a heart attack a month before Gray and the others were to visit his house in Ireland. But Scanlon's wife—now widow— told the group to go anyway. "John would've loved it," she said.

On their second day in Ireland, Gray and Russo went with Leary, Esteve, and Newman to one of Scanlon's favorite nearby restaurants for dinner. Afterward, it was decided that Russo, who'd only had one drink—a Bellini—would drive home. When they got into the car, Russo said, "Buckle up." No one in the backseat, including Gray, paid attention. "Yes, Mom," Russo remembered one of them saying. Just one mile from Scanlon's house, their car was struck by a veterinarian's van while waiting to turn on a small country road.

"Our car spun around three times, that's how hard he hit," Gray would later describe it in his 2003 monologue about the accident, Life Interrupted, "and he drove the engine right into the front seat of the car, where Kathie burned her arm. Somehow she got out. I thought Kim, who was next to her, was dead. His forehead was down on the dashboard. Tara Newman was yelling, 'The car's going to explode. Everyone get out!' I don't remember getting out, but the next I knew I was lying in the road next to Kathie, and she's saying, 'I'm dying! I'm dying!' and I'm saying, solipsist that I am, 'But I can't straighten out my leg!'"

Gray and Russo were taken to a local hospital. Leary and Esteve also went to the hospital but were released soon after—they were shaken but had not suffered serious injuries. Newman went straight back to the Scanlon estate after the accident to tell the others what had happened. Gray fractured his hip, which would leave him with a drop foot, a limp on his right side, and permanently in need of a leg brace in order to walk; he also suffered an orbital fracture—the orbit includes the eye and surrounding bones. Later, in surgery, hundreds of shards of bone were found lodged in his brain. Russo, meanwhile, got fifteen stitches in the back of her head where Gray had hit her with his own head when he flew forward in the accident. She had also bruised the tissues surrounding her heart. The hospital kept her for observation; they were concerned about the possibility of internal bleeding.

"We were both in dorm rooms with six beds in each one," Russo said, describing their hospital stay. "They gave us no hospital gowns, toothbrushes, or anything to change into because they said most patients 'bring their own,' as if we should have had an extra set of clothes in our car in case we were in an accident. There were two bathrooms in the hallway. I couldn't use the one that had a toilet and sink because there was shit all over the toilet. The other one had a bathtub with cigarette burns all over it; I would stand in it to go to the bathroom."

On her fourth day there, Russo walked out, even though her doctor wanted her to stay for further observation. She felt that she had to get back to the children—and that she was the only person who would be able to get Gray out of the hospital and under better care.

JUNE 24, 2001

[From notes Gray took two days after the accident while in the Midland Regional Hospital in Tullamore, Ireland]

THE ACCIDENT

The Hospital: that this one event could rule so, could change so much in one carnal-like image. The speeding little vet's assistant mini van hopping and popping over that crazy little road.

On this past tour *[of* It's a Slippery Slope *and* Morning, Noon, and Night*]*, we had stayed in more bed and breakfasts so when Kathie wanted to look at the Corwin house again *[the house in North Haven that Gray and Russo bought five months prior to this accident]* it felt more roomy like a Vermont B & B and I had been put in some instant head from traveling as all of a sudden you're here and it just falls in around you. I had lost my wider standing of reality of the slow reality of actual transformation how once you start to actually make the change from a place you have stabilized and perfected in your mind; how it rules, the object you're leaving takes on new and incredible detail as never seen before.

The American flag in the cemetery across the way when seen through a particular pattern, a frame of our Purist hedge was like a red, white and blue heart beating as it blew in the wind.

My self keeps shifting in relationship to these things but when the boys call me DADDY I respond.

When Theo stood there and said, "Are you going to be old now?" It broke my heart.

Forrest can't seem to express his emotions.

You eat the wafer in the morning, body of Christ; and in the afternoon you go 194 miles an hour and crash and in the evening you enter the glorious gates of heaven better than a famous life.

60—Yes, it all began with NO party which I thought was great. NPR made these announcements and Garrison Keillor once again ignored me and my three best male friends did not call, reminding me of Dad at 80.

Last night I woke and thought I was one of the many painful casualties on a civil war battlefield. I felt trapped in the pain of my body. A sound of crows and magpies all around.

If I was wearing a seatbelt I might have walked away from that accident and would have had a fun summer with Kathie, Marissa and the boys but instead there is this story and this advice. Always put your seatbelt on. First thing.

But I am alive and you are alive and we will now all go our separate ways until one day we stop and something else begins.

[Russo had Gray transferred, through the help of a friend who was the head of the Irish Arts Council, to an orthopedic hospital ten miles outside of Dublin.]

JUNE 2001

Have been moved to Dublin. I freaked when I was rolled into the windowless 6 bed room, all full. With suicide windows that just crack because someone did jump. How I resent that unknown suicide.

When the doctor told me that the nerve damage to my foot might not be permanent I said with deep feeling, "OH THANK GOD."

Would death be as simple as this blackout or is something contained in the still unconscious body and when it goes in it? A return to the nothing that was before something that was conceived by two,

"NO SEAT BELT
    NO EXCUSE"

LOVE = a misunderstanding between 2 idiots

BEGIN: I don't know where it all started. In Charleston when we saw those tombstones or in the hills of Ireland when we saw that sad crippled calf that couldn't get up and we hear a horticulturist to CALL THE VET.

So here's the little story I tell myself lying alone at the end of June in a dark hospital room at what is looking like the beginning of the worst summer of my life . . .
I say,
   Spalding, you're lucky to be alive. Give thanks.

The only healing cure I can think of would be to at last be able to TELL THE STORY.

They have come in and given me the PRE-THEATRE bath and suppository and pills *["pre-theatre" as in operating theater—Gray was about to get surgery on his broken hip in an effort to relieve his damaged sciatic nerve and drop foot]* now I am alone. (Why do I keep thinking of TIMOTHY McVeigh?) Am alone and thinking am I some sort of VICTIM? Am I the one chosen to suffer the most in these imperfectly annoying ways? The past five years of my life were very good. The best five years of my life and now this. I didn't want any more of this. I swear I didn't cause it.

2001

July 1 or June 30?

First time out into the hall and on the walker and realized I was crippled—my GREATEST FEAR and I started to faint and had to go back to bed.

A fear, this morning that I drank myself into the place I'm in. That the drink was my HOLLOW support system to get me wherever I am.

JULY 5, 2001

Just came back from my short walk on crutches and I am sweating wet from the humidity but I still prefer it to air-con, at least you feel the changes of weather. Kathie discovered a dent in my head and the doctor confirmed it this morning. This morning I woke up before 6:00 and then went back out by doing deep breathing and trying to flood my hip with positive energy but what is positive energy? If I try to fill my mind with good images from the past and think, say of that summer in MV when Theo was only two and me doing my catcher AQUA ACT of letting the wave sweep over me and letting him go to bob up above me. I feel also the sadness of the loss and how I NEVER EVER HAD IT. I was of the moment but never possessed it. I think what a sad thing it must be to die and how it all feels like a dream and I try to get back to this moment in the hospital but I can't stand to look out my window at the other windows and only to see the top of a dead tree. Why me?

"I can't remember being moved MORE by a book. *[Jonathan Franzen's]* "THE CORRECTIONS" saved me by lifting me out of my APRÈS car crash pain in a Dublin Hospital. It's a wonderful ~~story~~ book." *[Gray was drafting an endorsement for Franzen's novel,* The Corrections.*]*

I cried so at the end of "THE CORRECTIONS." I cried at my loss, of not sharing Dad's loss, of my not being there. How sad. And Dad was also like ALFRED, a lot about the great refusal. He found his strength in saying "NO" to so much so perhaps I'm crying for him, for his life.

JULY 7, 2001

SAT.

Even with this new information about my just discovered FRAC-TURED FACE *[Gray's orbital fracture caused his forehead to cave in]* I had one peaceful moment during lunch as I ate my garlic potatoes and green beans . . . everything settled down. It felt like that calm morphine state maybe 5 minutes of peace.

FEAR! All my life I have been afraid and all my fears culminated in this accident. I can say, "There, you see something bad did happen in this random world."

I'm afraid I will see the outside world as no longer one I can live with. And that I don't have any real friends, real close intimate friends, because I've isolated myself with my minor celebrity.

JULY 8, 2001

SUNDAY

Kathie seems not to accumulate. In most cases she is constantly LET-TING GO LETTING GO.

At this point it's hard for me to see Kathie as separate from THE BOYS. She is so with them all the time that they have become an extension of her. I am by nature more distinct. They are objects of mystery to me but they are coping well.

They are very flexible.

JULY 9, 2001

Went out for the first time. K. took me in a wheelchair. It was like a rebirth and would have been so ugly seen through other circumstances, me as a visitor, and I understood Kathie's depression. The revolving doors had Styrofoam packing chips with wooden reeds painted in gold paint, stuck in them. Outside a crow flew over and the SKY! Crane's Shopping Mall in the distance.

Gray went for a day of testing at St. James's Hospital in Dublin, where doctors told him he would need orbital fracture surgery. Gray and Russo decided to fly back to New York for the procedure. Because they had planned to stay at Sedgewood for the summer, they had rented out both their Sag Harbor and North Haven houses. Upon returning from Ireland on July 12, the family spent the week before the surgery at their friend Robby Stein's house in Wainscott, Long Island.

JULY 13, 2001

Friday the 13th

We are back at Robby's. It's beautiful. Clear, windy, almost more than I can take. It's odd but in some way the hospital room was easier because you could have your own selective fantasy of the outside world. Now I'm suddenly hit by life going on without me. I feel like a 90 year old man as I sit stupefied by the pool watching the boys play in it. Then there are sweet breakthroughs where I see the sun on the boys' bodies, broken and in motion through the slots of the picket fence by the pool and later when the boys played for hours with the CITRONELLA CANDLES as I lay on the bench and looked up at their faces illumined by the flame.

"When he came back from Ireland and stayed with me, we sat outside a lot and he was telling his mother's story," Stein said. *"This was a period where they hadn't moved out of the old house completely. The house had meaning to him, but what kept going in and out was his mother's story."* At this time, Gray began taking medication to help him cope with his growing emotional struggle. Over the next three years, he would try an array of mood stabilizers—Celexa, Zyprexa, Neurontin, Aventyl, and Lamictal, among them—in an attempt to alleviate his depression.

JULY 14, 2001

Robby had a date and K. went for a massage and T. took Theo out so I was all alone at COCKTAIL HOUR and it was not easy. Oh no, it was not. I tried to read that book on Depression and then I called Farley and then I just sat there with such bad thoughts. I still haven't done any FORMAL MEDITATION.

I remembered my first dream or first dream remembered.

DREAM: Renée was going in hospital and I was looking at all these stretchers to try to find her but she was AMBULATORY and walking into the hospital so I followed her and tried to wish her well. Then I was at a beach with the boys and there was a strange woman there lying on her belly and talking too low for me to hear and I was letting her know that I was not attached, no longer involved with Renée. I was free. Who was this woman?

JULY 18, 2001

I talked to Doctor Stieg *[Gray's surgeon for the orbital fracture]* and he told me that the nerve when damaged in that hip area does not often regenerate. This report took me way down and, in fact, I'm down there still.

(Robby just called to try to put my mind at ease to tell me that classical neurosurgeons do not know about nerve regeneration as much as orthopedic doctors do.) Kathie wanted to have sex last night and I was able to get on my knees and mount her from the rear and we did come together but my orgasm was still in slow motion. Like a leakage rather than a burst of pleasure.

I find it so difficult to have a positive mind when sitting still. POSITIVE = MOTION for me, my body in motion.

What is thinking positively maybe it's not telling people what Dr. Stieg said about my foot which I feel so sad for. But who do I pray to, to the QUARKS and the atoms, to the idea OF VIBRATING strings?

JULY 21, 2001

Depressed. I can't seem to keep it up. We had lunch yesterday at our new old house with the PHYSIO [physical therapist] who was from Wicklow, Ireland. Ken came out. It was good to see him even though he had a cough. Swimming in the pool was almost fun. I could tell Forrest was happy to see me swimming and Forrest swam beside me. (FATE FATE FATE) I just can't believe this is happening to me, that this is me and I should at least take joy in the good weather and the giant cherry tree. To be doing my exercises and see the birds with the sun through their wings . . . the sun through their feathers . . . but the discomfort at night just before bed is unbearable.

JULY 24, 2001

Spent a horrid day in the hospital. The trip down was THE WORST with the traffic and I kept breaking down and falling through the cracks and saying "NO, NO, I CAN'T" but then Theo broke down and started to cry because he found out we were not going to pick up Forrest but we were in fact going to another doctor and I find it hard to face Stieg because he was the one who said my foot would not come back but Theo pulled himself together. He got through it all and started playing with his toys or crashing them.

The nurses don't talk like in Ireland. There is no river of language, river of work to carry you on from one nurse to another save the blacks. The blacks are more likely to do it amongst themselves but not at work.

But the man who made my day and almost made me cry was the black attendant at the elevator who said, "Are you Spalding Gray? I love your work particularly 'Swimming to Cambodia.'"

"The operation lasts six hours. They cut me from ear to ear, peel down my forehead, and put in a titanium plate," Gray explained in Life Interrupted. *"More titanium plates in here; bone splinters are released into my frontal lobe—I think they have to try to pick those out—from the smashing of my head against Kathie's head. They sew me up; it looks like I've had a face-lift."*

JULY 28, 2001

SAT.

Theo never says tomorrow he says, "I'll see you after this night's over."

AUGUST 5, 2001

Sunday Aug. ?

Last night was the Sedgewood party. Liked the looks and sounds of our new neighbors. Good band. Hard to see.

K. and I slow danced on crutches. K. has to be taught how to slow dance. She starts out with a hyperness. She is not slow, languid or sensual but we did get into it. I wanted to dance and swim. I saw my other self there getting drunk and swimming and dancing.

AUGUST 7, 2001

TUE.

K. and I spent the day in three hospitals with three doctors yesterday. I seem to get most freaked out with Stieg. I hear him say things Kathie does not hear like how he damaged my nerve to my forehead so my forehead feels like a robot.

I am afraid. . . . I even find myself holding my breath when I am talking to people on the phone. I am so afraid they will describe some sensuous, sensuous summer scene to some idyllic spot or perfect moment.

Then when people say, "but just think, you could be worse off," I also think but that's down the road. This accident does not cancel out all the other slings and arrows of outrageous FORTUNE no no no. But be positive please be positive.

AUGUST 9, 2001

THUR.

Theo keeps asking me to tell him a "scary story" and at least I don't say, "LOOK around you. This is the scary story" but instead I tell him a story about PIRANHA FISH and after a while I say there are really no more stories it's only one story: "The fish are small and their teeth are sharp. When people or animals fall in and that school of piranhas comes there's a splashing and a thrashing and then there are bones."

AUGUST 10, 2001

It's impossible to be perky, manic or frantic on crutches. Every day starts in the same slow, OLD, creaky way. It's as though I grew old in a flash.

AUGUST 2001

SUNDAY

Theo breaks my heart sometimes. He picked a flower and brought it to me saying, "Here's a flower for the one who was hurt the most in the accident." I so often think that he doesn't notice me or that I have disappeared from his life and then he does something like that and it just blows me apart. Then our pretty next-door neighbors came down and disrobed and dove in and swam and that did me in. God how quickly the moments change sometimes.

AUGUST 19, 2001

Back at Robby's. I got through the first of the interviewing at Guild Hall. *[Gray did several shows of* Interviewing the Audience—*booked before the accident—at the Guild Hall theater in East Hampton, New York.]* It being taped by Barbara's crew *[documentary filmmaker Barbara Kopple filmed Gray for her miniseries,* The Hamptons*],* Don on camera, did help in the sense of making it all seem more important and it helped me come out of myself. Made me want to make a good appearance.

AUGUST 20, 2001

Monday

It's back to NOT BEING CONFRONTATIONAL I've not been with any one but the children not with Martha who is NOT calling me back which gets me depressed instead of angry but I can't I CAN NOT LET the children see me go crazy. I can NOT play that one act on them. NO big "NO." Because I am in the place of my mom now at home in hot non functional summer with thunder in the distance and me out in the woods with the deer groaning, on crutches, all three children are upstairs and Theo is screaming. I am sitting here with the distance of DEATH. I only long to be asleep or unconscious.

We live in between we live in the cracks of chance and disaster. The voices say, I won't get better and then they say oh yes you'll get better only to be sick again and die.

AUGUST 21, 2001

TUE.

Physiotherapy today. Kathie asked me if there was some part of me that was into being this way—THE VICTIM for people to feel sorry for? Oh God I'm afraid of that one!

AUGUST 23, 2001

Yesterday was the HARD one. K. and I drove to the city and dealt with DR. D'ANGELO [Gray's orthopedic doctor] and it was a strange office and he was odd and I freaked out in the exam room when he told me about the 30 to 40 percent chance the blood would not make into the bone depending on the nature of the break. He told me that it was lucky I didn't stay in the country hospital.

He said, "You are over 30, you're a mature man so I can tell you." No, no I say I'm twice 30 and I am not mature. I can't take any more. And of course he got down on me for dwelling on the negative and I told him that I always have. It won't work I think; we will never be able to do it.

AUGUST 24, 2001

FRI.

Kathie comes down late. I am frantic and need to go over the whole seat belt scenario again. This morning she put me at ease with "We were going slow. It was a back country road etc. . . ." She talked me down enough to have first GOOD SEX. I was actually kneeling and it felt alright I had a long full thrusting orgasm.

AUGUST 26, 2001

SUN.

It was like out of a BERGMAN FILM when that guy at the block party asked me if I had any children or he asked which were mine and I led he and his wife. . . . I led them on crutches to show them on there at the end of the docked framed by the rippling lake the boys Theo and Forrest were sitting together and it was the most idyllic moment of my life of this summer. It was a proud perfect moment.

Gray took Interviewing the Audience *to Bumbershoot—an art and music festival—in Seattle, Washington, over Labor Day weekend, September 1–3, 2001. He began the show with a short piece detailing the story of the accident and the many medical traumas that followed. This became the basis for his 2003 monologue,* Life Interrupted.

SEPTEMBER 4, 2001

What is Willem doing?

And John Malkovich?

What did Oliver Stone do on the fourth of July?

How long it takes to hitch Christopher Reeve up in the morning.

Distant love of 2,000 people. Cheering at an image they have of me. I raise my crutches and they scream.

Gray and his family moved to their new house in North Haven, an area just north of Sag Harbor, on September 12, 2001—a day later than planned. On the morning of September 11, when Russo told Gray that terrorists had flown planes into the World Trade Center, he thought she was making it up to distract him from his depression. And it did momentarily: Gray went to a vigil in Sag Harbor that night and wrote a short love letter to New York City, his adopted home-town. "I fled New England and came to Manhattan, that island off the coast of America, where human nature was king and everyone exuded character and had big attitude," he wrote. "You gave me a sense of humor because you are so absurd." (This was later published, posthu-mously, as a New York Times *Op-Ed under the title "Dear New York City . . .") But Gray soon returned with a new intensity to his misery about moving.*

He began to tell this story: Moving to the new house was a fatal mistake. His own mother had made the same mistake when she moved away from her hometown of Barrington, Rhode Island—away from the house that she loved with the restorative views of Narragansett Bay—to a secluded property in East Greenwich, Rhode Island. Now he, too, had left behind a beloved house to live farther from town, where Gray also felt isolated and uneasy. This story became his obses-sion, a mythic rant. He told it again and again as he tried to explain why he could not bring himself out of his black mood, why his thoughts had, as his mother's had, turned toward suicide.

"Quite a number of years earlier, he had flirted with the notion that there were potential parallels between [our mother's] life and his. That was built into his obsession with her suicide," his brother Rockwell remembered. "But he wove it in more toward the end and felt that he

was under a malign influence, that the stars were aligned against him somehow."

SEPTEMBER 12, 2001

MOVING DAY

All night I tossed and turned and dreamt that the whole move was a mistake and that in fact we could still stay in an old house. When I woke I felt like I was going to THE GAS CHAMBER.

No MEN I knew at the candle light vigil just Dan and Donald and then there was Renée who looked great. "Same old Spalding," she said. Yes LONG GUARDIAN ANGELS

FALL 2001

Kathie bought me this composition notebook last night in South Hampton. I'm afraid it's going to fall apart like every thing as in, "the center will not hold." The choice between moving into the new house and not is too ugly to face. The new house needs more light. I am on the ferry to try to go to work on my show. I am on Klonopin *[an antiseizure medication prescribed to Gray to treat his anxiety]* and worry about my liver and nerves. The sky over Conn. looked hazy and polluted. I flipped out this morning when the movers came. I must save Forrest but how can I?

I can't write what I'm thinking because it causes me too much FEAR, anguish. I don't have the courage to GO ON.

SEPTEMBER 18, 2001

I am far gone. The loss of the house and the neighborhood of houses is too much for me. I dull myself with champagne and beer and wake up in pure panic. What have I lost and how could I not see that all around me was beauty! But the saddest saddest thing that happened today was THEO broke down and started to cry and he cried and cried and said "Stop arguing." It was so sad. It was so very very sad. At first he went to Kathie and then he went to me. This is a very very sad time. Have I created this? The angel of our soul.

HOUSE

Things that might be helpful:

1) Sit still
2) Look into eyes

They're dark, the floors are darker than I had realized. Although I did catch a glimpse of them earlier on, I didn't realize it. Even though the house was bigger how could I have liked the wall tapestries? Last night when I went to bed it was difficult for me to face the windows.

I like Sag Harbor. I feel like I'm living in a house that was cast out of Sag Harbor and now we can't get back.

In October 2001, Gray began performing Swimming to Cambodia *once a week at the Performing Garage in order to rehearse for a reprise of the show at American Conservatory Theater in San Francisco at the end of December, another engagement arranged before his accident. "I saw him do* Swimming to Cambodia *at the Garage," said Eric Bogosian. "The performance was okay, but afterwards he was exhausted. It was the first time I'd seen him since the accident, and clearly he was not happy. However, he was interested in the fact that I thought it was a good show. I think he saw hope. I had the feeling 'Spalding is coming back.' He was fucked-up, but he was going to get better."*

OCTOBER 8, 2001

I can't stand the thought that there is no town outside. That I can't step out into THE TOWN. I have lost my sense of space.

Going to the old house today was some of the worst pain I felt since I broke up with Renée.

HELP!
I'm in suburbia!

OCTOBER 11, 2001

I am so unhappy and the family doesn't really understand. Kathie still thinks it's the accident and not the house. I feel like a ghost of myself. I don't want to lose the kids. They are so good! I loved my house, our house. I loved it. How could I kill the things I loved? Death is the mother of beauty.

OCTOBER 31, 2001

Halloween

This house is a piece of shit. I can't believe I bought it.

The sacred ABODE and the FIRE HAS GONE out.

I knew I can't live here. I knew I can't. I've never felt more crazed and it's a full moon. I will explode. Did some part of me choose this house to make myself insane?
    Or was it just lazy fantasy?

NOVEMBER 1, 2001

I'm a dead man; a ghost.

Ikea cupboards

From December 26 to 31, Gray performed Swimming to Cambodia *in San Francisco. He also told a fifteen-minute version of* Life Interrupted. *It did not lift his spirits to be in front of an audience again. "He wasn't excited about doing the show," Russo recalled. "And he didn't feel good about how it went afterwards."*
    Following his performances in San Francisco, Gray put on the same

show at the University of California, Los Angeles, in March. Later, he told Russo that he had considered throwing himself from the balcony of his hotel room. When she pressed him, he said he'd only imagined what it would be like, that he wasn't actually going to do it. The family met Gray in Aspen, Colorado, after his California stay for a weeklong ski vacation. Gray was meant to perform at the Goodman Theatre in Chicago, but Russo canceled the show because he seemed too depressed and was having trouble getting out of bed.

MAY 2002

Fear, fear that I am trying to imitate mom's route. Could not allow myself that steady state of happiness. Had to act out in front of the children.

Had a difficult visit with George *[Coates, an old friend],* who was full of questions as to why this and why that. Keeps wanting to know what my therapist says. G. has great recall of my life stories, remembering all the details. Calling Kathie a monster mom. I keep thinking about the bridge.

Can't seem to write because I keep going back to the house, which haunts me. I am not haunting a house. It's haunting me.

On June 10, 2002, at the suggestion of Gray's psychiatrist, four friends—Ken Kobland, Howie Michels (Francine Prose's husband), Paul Spencer (Gray's creative consultant on It's a Slippery Slope)*, and Donald Lipski (a sculptor and friend from Sag Harbor whom Gray met through Kobland)—along with Russo, confronted Gray in his doctor's office and convinced him to commit himself to a psychiatric hospital. With some coaxing, Gray agreed to go.*

A week later, Russo and Kobland took Gray to Silver Hill, a hospital with a forty-five-acre campus in New Canaan, Connecticut, specializing in treating mood disorders and substance abuse. (Billy Joel was a patient at the time Gray checked in; later, Gray would interview

Joel about their time together there for a theater magazine called Show People.*)*

"*We had to take him to the area of the building where there is a lockdown—the doors are locked and the rooms are suicide-proofed, there are no lights,*" *Kobland recalled.* "*And he freaked out . . . The idea was that he'd go through this for a week until he was examined carefully and then he could be put into a more hotel-like room, which was like an inn where you could be in your own room and go to dinner. You didn't have the kind of restrictions that you had in the first building, which was like a twenty-four-hour watch . . . He just said, 'Please don't leave me here. I'll never get out.' We left him there. But he couldn't be alone in the street. I mean he would have been arrested at some point because sometimes he would act so crazy. I apologize to him eternally. I wish there was a place he could have lived at that point.*"

After a week in the locked ward, Gray was moved to "the country club," as Russo later wryly described it. Gray stayed in Silver Hill for a month. He did not write in his journal while he was there.

JULY 2002

Last night Kathie once again read the riot act to me and gave me five weeks to shape up and I keep saying I don't know how she thinks Silver Hill should have taught me how and I just sit, going back to all those places in the past where I could have stopped the sale of the house which is what I'm doing now and I hear myself say "cosmetics? This place needs a major, major face lift."

If I had written yesterday it would have been a long suicide note to all I love including Ken.

Today, we are fighting a lot. So what's new? "I can do it" Kathie says to me, "it's an act" "snap out of it." We went out in the kayak and fought always in the kayak. She called me a "loser" and I agreed. Left over grief growing. Virginia Woolf oh yes.

AUGUST 3, 2002

Saturday

Really bad morning where Kathie lit into me. I was lamenting the house and she said that I rushed into buying it, which is unbelievable but true. It was not thought out at all (concrete thinking?) I was in such a state. I don't know if I only have a few days to live or not. It's up to me. I love everyone, all my friends. I do feel love for my family and friends. I can hardly stay awake with these thoughts in my head all the time.

At the end of August 2002, Gray traveled to Martha's Vineyard to perform Interviewing the Audience *at the Vineyard Playhouse.*

AUGUST 2002

Tue.

Interviewing the audience did not go very well. I, of course, was bringing up the house in my mind. I'm choosing the house over almost every other reality. Wine at the Bebe's dinner party. Not good I know, pouring gasoline on the fire.

SEPTEMBER 20, 2002

I'm starting to get more and more insane. I'm sitting here thinking about walking Forrest home. The old walk and how I was the stage manager of OUR TOWN right next to the cemetery and how Greg Mosher had rented that very house and wanted to buy it. And I think how I threw all of that away to move out of town. It was those walks and talks with Forrest that I loved. NOT RIDING IN THE CAR! Oh my God help me please help me. I have made such a great mistake.

If it means not meeting Forrest and walking him I should have said "No! I won't do it!"

The whole thing feels like some humble set up. The way I act things out in my life on such a real life scale. I have moved out of the town I love just like Mom.

double vision rotting truth. I don't want more trees. I wake and I see the house and the street and lights.

I feel like I'm going insane. Nothing will get better until I do anything but obsess on the house. I'm in a vision's loop. It is relentless. It takes all my energy to relate to the boys. I feel trapped here and dependent on a car. There is nothing more to say. It was the sale of the house that did it.

In dreams, a house is often your body.

We were blessed and I complained and now I am paying for it.

On the afternoon of September 29, 2002, Gray paced back and forth on the Sag Harbor bridge—which connects Sag Harbor and North Haven—hyperventilating. He told a stranger that he planned to jump off. A woman who witnessed the scene called the police. By pure coincidence, Russo, driving over the bridge after a doctor's appointment, saw Gray huddled with the police. She stopped, and the police allowed her to take him home. She called Gray's psychiatrist—the same doctor who had recommended the intervention that brought Gray to Silver Hill—who advised her to take him into Manhattan immediately and admit him to New York University Langone Medical Center. Gray voluntarily committed himself to NYU and spent four days there. The hospital did not take his insurance, though, so he was moved to Payne Whitney Psychiatric Clinic on the Upper East Side. Marilyn Monroe, Mary McCarthy, and Robert Lowell, whom Gray had so long admired, were all once patients there. Gray remained at Payne Whitney for a little over four months.

"We had to ring a buzzer and a guard came, searched our bags, and let us in. There was a communal room as you walk in where most patients are watching TV or playing cards. In the center was the nurses' station—they only spoke to the patients by microphone because they were behind protective glass," Russo said. "The first time the kids came, we brought their artwork and a ton of photographs and covered an entire wall in Spalding's room with it to make it cheerier. The kids would only visit on the weekends because of school, but after

about a month of this Forrest [who was ten years old at the time] broke down and said he couldn't do it anymore. It was too depressing. Theo was very young [five years old] and would go anywhere I went at that point, and Marissa was a teenager, so she had her own social thing going on at home."

Spalding's younger brother, Channing, and his wife also visited Gray. *"There was a large waiting room where the patients sat with a nursing station that formed an island in the center,"* he recalled. *"Spalding was walking at full speed with his bum foot about twelve hours a day. In order to talk to him, I had to pace along with him. His hair was all disheveled, and he was in his pajamas. He really looked bad. I had a fair number of conversations with him about the house . . . It was regret, which is a tough one, it's like anxiety . . . His psychiatrist would say, 'That house is just a pile of sticks, it's nothing, you can get another one.' But it was an illness, an affliction."*

In Payne Whitney, with the reluctant consent of Russo, Gray received electroconvulsive therapy [ECT], also known as electroshock treatment, a last resort for patients with severe depression. Russo remembers his having a total of twenty-one treatments. Initially, ten were done on one side—they were hesitant to administer bilateral treatments because to the metal plate in his head—but when the unilateral approach failed to bring him out of his depression, eleven more were done bilaterally.

"After the first few treatments," recalled Kobland, *"there was a noticeable—to me, to many people—improvement. He was more cogent, more relaxed, more stable, less repetitive. But it didn't last. He drifted back to the kind of crazed suicide desire."*

Many, including Russo, now believe that Gray wasn't able to come out of the obsessive torment he felt about the house because he had some kind of brain damage. *"This last breakdown was different . . . There was something implacable there. When I was helping him in other times, there wasn't that wall, that very hard presence,"* Bill Talen said. *"When I used to go and sleep next to him on that braided carpet in the lockdown, he would go into his looping conversations, looping phrases about his old house. And that had a much scarier aspect to me . . . He had lost control of his thoughts. They were just going round and round. I thought, 'Oh my God, how can you get out of this?' It was a mechanical breakdown, it was a brain injury."*

Russo was unhappy with Gray's treatment at Payne Whitney and requested his release after six weeks. The hospital, she said, asserted that he was still a threat to himself and did not release him until three months later, in January 2003. Throughout his stay, Gray's friends wrote letters to the hospital, advocating for him to be discharged. In one of the letters, a friend complained that he felt the staff neglected Gray, not giving him his medications at the proper times, failing to provide him with physical therapy or even change his bedding. He was, another friend wrote, "treated like the cranky village idiot."

Through Gray's literary agent, Suzanne Gluck, Russo had met Peter Whybrow, director of the Neuropsychiatric Institute at the University of California, Los Angeles, who sent a letter as well. "I agree that Mr. Jones [Gray had checked into the hospital under the pseudonym Edward Jones] has been in the grip of a severe melancholia for several months," he wrote. "His psychic self-flagellation surrounding the family's house purchase, his loss of weight, the contraction of his intellectual facility, all reflect this severe melancholic state which by history appears to be super imposed upon a bipolar mood disorder." Whybrow suggested that Gray be allowed to leave the hospital and engage in cognitive therapy, which he believed would help "break up the ruminative thinking."

OCTOBER 20, 2002

[Written at Payne Whitney]

THE SIN

TO SELL A HOUSE
YOU LOVE

FOR MERE PROFIT???

HOUSE OF FAMOUS
WRITER

When we left and had the accident, accident Oh my God of course
NO ONE WAS HOME TO PROTECT

The house. Oh my God help me! I am seeing too much into it. Help me! I'm having too much insight! Help me

"When good ghosts turn bad, and then turn good" Forrest said that was the title

THE SIGN KEPT DISAPPEARING and I know it was the ghosts

That's the triumphant story yes!

Walk away from $700,000 yes, yes!

Help me please. This is not the story I want to tell. No, No, No!

When Gray was released from Payne Whitney at the end of January, Robby Stein took him away for a weekend retreat at Francine Prose and Howie Michels's country house in Krumville, New York (the same property where Gray and Shafransky had once rented a cabin), along with their friend Donald Lipski.

"Spalding seemed to be in free fall—sliding down an actual slippery slope toward suicide," Michels described it. "It was as if this house had become a symbol of his state of mind before the accident . . . That weekend, you could watch him play a kind of morbid movie in his head in which he could walk slowly through the old house. He could hear the creaking floors, touch the banisters, and look out the windows. He did this every time he got too close to the realities of what would happen to his children, his career, and the joys of life that used to exist for him."

Gray had also begun to believe supernatural forces were at work: he was convinced the realtor he had used was a witch and there were ghosts in the old house that had compelled him to sell it in order to drive him to suicide so that he might join their spirit world.

"We tried to break apart some of the more psychotic thinking that was organizing him, the whole issue around the house or his helplessness," Stein recalled. "We would both verbally and physically challenge him, push him, try to bring him back into the world. It was almost like a 1960s encounter group. Get him involved. Cook dinner with him. Resist him falling out. After maybe a day, he all of a sudden said that he wanted to make pea soup, which was his favorite thing—it

felt like a kind of breakthrough. We all got in the car in the middle of the night trying to find the ingredients for split pea soup. He made the soup, we all ate it, and it was delicious. You didn't get a feeling that he was well, but you got a feeling . . . I don't know if I'm projecting hopefulness on it, but I think we all felt that there was some possibility that could be built on."

A little less than a month after Gray had been released from Payne Whitney, he performed It's a Slippery Slope *in Boulder and Steamboat Springs, Colorado. The family went with him. The performances were surprisingly good, according to Russo; he received a standing ovation at one of the shows.* "Spalding was having a great time with the kids. He even got into the pool with them at the hotel. He was engaging with them in a way I hadn't seen in a long time. I had a sense that he was getting better," *she said.* "To be clear: he was never happy again after the accident, but there were degrees of depression. On this trip, he only seemed to be mildly depressed."

Gray traveled from Colorado to Houston, Texas, to do Interviewing the Audience *for a sold-out performance in a thousand-seat theater at the Society for the Performing Arts on March 21, 2003.*

"This very scruffy-looking man came in the stage door," *recalled Toby Mattox, then the executive director of the Society for the Performing Arts,* "and I thought he was a homeless man from the street because he was rumpled and his hair was askew and he had that scar on his forehead. He really looked unkempt." *Gray and Mattox had known each other since 1992, when Gray began performing at the Houston theater. That evening, when Gray was onstage,* "he was not the bright, on-top-of-things artist that he had always been. He stumbled in his words, he lost track of what was happening, he even started a confrontation with one or two of the audience members," *said Mattox.* "I think he was saying unkind things about George Bush [and the U.S. invasion of Iraq] and you know this is Bush country in Texas, by and large . . . People started talking back to him, and he got heated. In fact, it was so confrontational that people got up and left. I would say ten or twelve people left. I went out into the lobby to get their names and numbers, and they demanded their money back . . . It was so sad to see that he had deteriorated to that extent. Those people in the audi-*

ence were his fans, and all of a sudden he had turned many of them against him."

MARCH 2003

Oh god where has the year gone?

All I have left to keep me afloat is FANTASY of the old house. And yes I've gone a little mad and procrastinate. I'm not happy man and it's driving Kathie crazy. I'm not trying to do it on purpose . . . I've become my damn own worst enemy. I can't stand this person I've created for myself and canceling the good man and I wearing the sweat shirt and DESTINY comes to mind. Destiny and how I used to scoff at it scoff it off. I didn't want to move why did I move? Oh help, I'm going in circles again.

MARCH 2003

Monday

Its one long farewell that's all I can write in my mind, it keeps going farewell to all of you. It's so hot here today. The house and the loss of it has my pain so tight. Farewell to everyone. This is the way it should . . . has to be. My handwriting is so awful. Farewell. It's so hot and I can't stop the house from loving me if only, if only. I can't go back. I'm dying. I feel it. I'm not strong enough to go on living not strong enough. Never was but Kathie, it's better for you if I do take my life. You are so good at making things work out. Today, I miss our old guest bedroom so much it affects my heart. Heartache. I can feel it in me that room. Almost taste that room. Oh God.

In April 2003, Gray went to Sagg Main Beach in Sagaponack, New York, taking his journal along with him. While there, with a crowd of onlookers on the beach, Gray waded into the ocean fully clothed. (A woman who witnessed the event found Gray's diary in the sand

and returned it to him later.) Someone contacted the police, and they picked Gray up. "They brought him to the house," Russo said. "He was dripping wet. We talked, and they said, 'He seems okay, we're not going to take him away' . . . They didn't feel it was a full-fledged suicide attempt. But after that, he made numerous attempts to take his life." He also began leaving suicide notes on the kitchen table only to return home again, unable to go through with the act.

In one such letter, Gray wrote: "This was the most courageous way out for me. It has taken courage to face death and you, in time, will understand how there could be no other way. I don't want to be the lonely old man I find myself becoming. I grow older each day. I feel the lonely old man came into me. I can't wish, ski, swim, walk, make love. All my power and pleasures are gone. All that gave pleasures and meaning in my life are gone. I can't get to you kids. I feel cut off by the house and how much I hate it."

In June 2003, at the recommendation of Whybrow, Gray checked into the psychiatric hospital at UCLA for nearly two weeks. There, doctors determined that he was suffering from both bipolar disorder and brain damage, which was due to either the head injury he sustained in the car accident or the surgery following it, and that a temporary assisted-living environment might be necessary until he responded favorably to treatment. It was also recommended that Gray continue "pharmacological intervention" as well as cognitive behavioral therapy, that he quit drinking, attend rehabilitation sessions at a traumatic brain injury center, and be monitored for "recurrent suicidal ideation."

The following month, Russo met with Oliver Sacks, the well-known neurologist and author, whom Lipski knew through a friend. Sacks agreed to take Gray on as a patient. They saw each other for five months, until December 2003.

AUGUST 13, 2003

I can't believe I did this to myself so much so that at this distance it feels like it never happened. Kathie said unless I change now that she has had it with me, need to have sex this morning but all I could think of was my old house. What a life.

Wake this morning in innocent forgetfulness then it marked down on me.—Our home was gone.

Gray wrote the following obituary for himself in his journals; he was drafting it for the television and radio host Larry King for a collection called Remember Me When I'm Gone: The Rich and Famous Write Their Own Epitaphs and Obituaries.

"He didn't get the irony," Russo said. "He was too deep into his depression to see how strange it was that he had been asked to write his own obituary."

SPALDING GRAY 1941.
He was a good and devoted father and a legal husband but most of all he was known for his autobiographical monologues in which he would sit on stage at a table with a glass of water and tell true stories from his life. He could capture the details _____ of his _____ and slightly eccentric life in a way that caused audiences to laugh and relate.

Also known as the talking man, he was an American original and will be deeply missed.

On September 9, 2003, Gray went to Lenox Hill Hospital on the Upper East Side of Manhattan for a second hip operation, an attempt to regenerate nerve growth. According to Russo, she was to pick Gray up on the following Saturday, but the night before, she received a phone call from a nurse at Lenox Hill to let her know that Gray had left his crutches behind. "I asked her what she was talking about," Russo recalled, "and she said he'd called a car service and left. There had been strict instructions for them not to let him leave without me, but they let him go." When Gray left the hospital, he told the nurse he was going to take a bus back to North Haven. Russo called the Hampton Jitney office and was told that there was a reservation under "Gray" for a 7:00 PM bus. Hoping this was her husband's reservation, Russo waited at the station, but he never arrived. (Gray did not have a cell phone.) She checked the messages at the loft in Manhattan and heard Gray's voice. "I'm sorry, I'm going to do it," he said, crying. "I'm going to jump from the Staten Island Ferry." Russo left immediately. "I was screaming in the car," she remembered. Russo drove to Tara Newman's house, where she'd been for dinner prior to driving to the bus station. Lipski was also there. He listened to Gray's message and called the police. An hour later, the police responded, saying they'd found Gray sitting on the ferry, riding it back and forth. Russo asked them to take Gray to the nearest hospital, informing them that he'd left her a phone message threatening suicide. The police took Gray to St. Vincent's Hospital on Staten Island. Gray stayed there for a week, while Russo talked to Sacks about what to do next. Sacks suggested that Russo check Gray into the Kessler Institute for Rehabilitation in West Orange, New Jersey, which provides services for those suffering from brain injuries, among other physical traumas. Russo had Gray admitted to Kessler; he stayed there for nearly three weeks, until October 4.

SEPTEMBER 21, 2003

[Written at the Kessler Institute]

SUNDAY

Kathie,

I told you yesterday that I could no longer live a joyless life. I don't want to drag you down anymore. You'll never know how much I love you and the children. Please forgive me.

Love,
Spalding

When Gray and Russo first saw each other in the hospital after the car accident in Ireland, they had vowed they would get married. Now with Gray's numerous suicide attempts, "I didn't know if he was going to live or die," Russo explained. "I felt like the end was imminent, and I wanted to have that experience with him, no matter what the circumstances were, since we had been through so much together as a couple. That surprised me because I hadn't seen the importance of marriage prior to the accident."

Their friend John Perry Barlow, a Universal Life minister, officiated at the ceremony in Gray's hospital room at Kessler. Gray sat on the bed with Russo next to him, holding his hand. "It was not a particularly romantic setting," Russo said, "but it felt right."

During this time, Gray also wrote and mailed a letter to each of his three children, telling them individually what he loved about them. He expressed his desire to come back home and be their father again. But on the day he left Kessler, as he and Russo sped down the Long Island Expressway, Gray admitted he'd tried to slit his wrists in the hospital. "What are you trying to do to me?" Russo yelled, pulling the car over. "You don't tell the doctor this, and now you want me to take you home?" Gray sat silently, staring ahead.

Less than two weeks later, Gray was performing again. He did two shows of Life Interrupted, on October 15 and 16, at a downtown Manhattan theater, P.S. 122. Later that week, however, he jumped into the water from the Sag Harbor bridge; he was rescued by a man who swam out after him and brought him back to shore. The police took Gray to Stony Brook University Medical Center, with Russo's consent. Gray was released after one night of observation.

In November and December, he continued to perform Life Interrupted twice a week at P.S. 122. "It seemed with the last monologue, he had gone over to the other side," Bogosian recalled of this performance. "It wasn't going to be fixable, no matter how much you looked at it or thought about it or dialogued about it or monologued about it or told jokes about it, it still was an unsolvable problem and there was no answer."

"I think, in the end, when he felt he could no longer do it—that he couldn't save himself with another monologue about this disaster," Kobland said, "he was lost."

Only you can decide
What is important to you
Lucky numbers 3, 8, 12, 23, 32, 42

[Gray occasionally taped messages from Chinese fortune cookies in his journal.]

Beginning on December 18, Gray carried a tape recorder with him everywhere he went for several days. Sometimes, he plainly described the details of their day—dropping off Forrest at school, visiting a possible new house to buy, talking about the upcoming holiday. Other times, he recorded conversations between him and his family. "At first, I thought he was documenting something, maybe gathering material for a new monologue. At least it was different. It was more interesting than sitting in his chair every day," Russo said. "I thought it was a positive sign." The following is an excerpt from this recording. The events lurch between the everyday and the dramatic frequently. At one point, Gray goes to bed, finding Russo there reading Rick Moody's memoir The Black Veil. *They discuss Gray's mood, his inability to read long books anymore, whether Russo had read to Theo when she put him to bed. (She had.) Finally, Gray makes an out-of-the-blue comment that this is his last tape.*

"Fuck you," Russo says, suddenly fierce. Gray backs down a bit, stammers.

"The last tape you'll ever, ever make in your life?" she asks in a gentler tone.

"No, no," Gray says, laughing a little. "I've run out of things to say."

After his death, Russo found this recording in Gray's desk drawer with a label that read "My Last Tape."

So it all started with Kathie and I—we were skiing in Colorado, and she said, "I saw this house for sale. It's outside of the town. It would make a wonderful family compound, and we could put a pool in the back." At any rate, when she told me this, I was seized with this immediate compulsion to try to get this, if it was a good deal, if they'd lower the price, whatever. I don't know what that came out of, you know, when I look back on it. Because I had no intentions of moving, I didn't want to move. I was happy where I was. I was honestly happy where I was. And we got back, and we had been staying at a lot of bed-and-breakfasts, and we got back. I feel like I've told this story to so many therapists. I think in the past two years I've had . . . oh, at least ten therapists. Maybe more. Including the psychopharmacologists. Which I've had three.

I'm talking to the boys now: you guys, Forrest and Theo . . . what happened to your grandmother Gray, my mom, was that she too moved out of a house that she loved 'cause it was right on Narragansett Bay and she used to love to walk along that bay, that shoreline. And when my father sold the house and they moved across the bay into the woods which is where we are also, in the woods, she flipped out. And they tried to buy the house back. And they couldn't—they wouldn't sell it back to them. And they said, I'm sure, that, you know, Mrs. Gray—my mom—has other problems about the house, it must be symbolic of something, that same old Freudian rap, you know, sometimes a cigar is just a cigar, sometimes a house is just a house. She missed the house. It wasn't symbolic of something, she really missed walking along the sea. I miss walking in the village, I miss the cemetery, I miss hundreds of things. But boys, listen: when you get to that point, where you have been driven so crazy by something, like for me, when I think about the house, it's not me thinking about it, it's thinking me. In other words: some people live in houses that are haunted. In this case, the house is haunting me. I left it, I don't know why. And now it's haunting me to the extreme.

Forrest, Theo, I love you. What more can I say? I—I am terrified of dying. I don't want to be driven by ruminations and I know that you guys are fed up with it and bored with it. So, going on with the history of how we came into this place, I can remember Mom and I coming home from skiing—I don't know where you guys were or Marissa, I don't remember—but, when we walked into our house, she said, "What do you think?" you know, our old house, and I said, "It's little, it's small." And then we came down here and this was bigger, twice the size. But not twice as nice. And at the same time, I at first sight asked how much it was and was ready to bid on it before we'd even had an engineer's report. And that's what I will never understand. And Kathie said to me maybe a week or two after, "I hope you're not buying this house for me." And I said, "No, I like the house." And I don't. And I didn't then. But I said to her, "No, I like the house."

And I just can't face . . . dying. Forever and ever and ever and ever and ever and ever and ever and ever and ever and ever and death. Forever and ever and ever and ever and ever and ever and ever and ever and ever and ever and ever and ever. Forever and ever and ever and ever and everevereverevereverever. Oh, help me help me help me help me help me help me help me help me help me help me there's nothing to be done, there's nothing to be done, there's nothing to be done. I hate this place. I hate this place. I can't even go up to bed because I can't stand the floors. I can't stand the bathrooms. I can't stand the lights in the bathroom. I can't stand to see my face in the mirror. And I can't stand taking off my shoes to reveal that horrible brace. And there's nowhere to go, there's nowhere to walk to in the neighborhood because the neighborhood is . . . the neighborhood is a suburban dump. And the woods with the deer and the deer and the deer and the deer and the darkness and the darkness and the deer and the darkness.

Anyway, what I'm saying is you just don't know what condition people are in to drive them to suicide. Virginia Woolf was hearing voices, you know? And what, put her away? She doesn't want to be put away, she'd rather drown first. So that's the choice she makes. To try to get some relief. I think it is about getting relief. For Sylvia Plath, it was the same. I don't think that I'm in any place to judge these people. And my mother as well.

I never knew we'd come to such a diminished state. Kathie
fights to go on. She is such a fighter. She is just . . . she won't
give up, and I admire that in her enormously. She is a great-
spirited woman. I wish that I could match that in some way.
I can't. I don't. I'm not . . .

When they took me into the hospital, they said, "So what
prevented you from jumping?" And I said, "It was fear." Not
thoughts of what I would miss, but just plain out-and-out fear.
And that's . . . that's what has people in institutions. The people
that are in institutions are the ones that are afraid. Afraid
of suicide. Or can't figure out how to do it, just aren't clever
enough.

*Over the Christmas holiday, a week later, Gray's brother, Rockwell
and his wife, Madeleine, visited the family in North Haven. "He was
utterly out of it. He sat by the fire in an armchair and closed his eyes.
He ate dinner with us, but it was like being with a ghost," Rockwell
said. "I felt I'd really lost him . . . 'What am I supposed to do now?'
Kathie asked me. 'Am I supposed to let him go on this way talking
about suicide?'"*

*At the end of December, Gray and Ken Kobland made a plan to see
each other in the city. "We went over to his loft and had a beer," Kobland recalled. "He was saying what he always was saying, you know,
that he just wanted to end it and he can't stand it, he has no life. And I
was—I wasn't bored, I was hopeless. I said, 'I don't know what I can
do, Spald, for you anymore. But please don't because you'll hurt me.
Please think of us. I mean sacrifice yourself, just stay around and be an
idiot.' But it was like asking him to torture himself . . . I don't remember the talk as much as I remember the image. He was standing over
by the bookcase. I was at the table with a beer. And there was no point
in talking about anything anymore. There was nothing else to say. So I
just gave him a little hug and left. And he was a statue."*

*Shortly afterward, Robby Stein and Gray saw each other in Sag
Harbor. "He asked me if he could meet me for lunch, so we met and he
said, 'You know I'm going to do this,'" Stein said. "He never used the*

word 'suicide' with me, it was always the act itself: 'I'm going to jump off a bridge; I'm going to jump off a ferry.' He was very, very calm this time . . . I said, 'I understand, Spalding, how you feel, but as hard as it is for you, it is going to be harder for everyone else.' He said, 'Just promise that you'll take care of the boys.'"

The following morning, Gray traveled to Manhattan to meet with a psychopharmacologist whom Sacks had recommended. He told him he was looking forward to an upcoming ski trip. (As a gift, Russo had made reservations for him at a ski clinic in Aspen, Colorado.) In the afternoon, Gray met with Theresa Smalec, a New York University graduate student who was writing her thesis on Ron Vawter. Later, she wrote an essay about this interview in which she described finding Gray in his loft "lying on the couch, very still." He remained in that position throughout the interview.

That evening, Russo, Theo, and Marissa arrived to join him at the loft. (Forrest was staying with friends on Shelter Island.) Gray was not there, but he'd left a message on the answering machine saying that he was out for a drink. Later, Russo found out that he was actually riding the Staten Island Ferry back and forth. When Gray returned home, he took the kids to Bubby's, a restaurant in lower Manhattan. Russo went to a business dinner. This particular weekend, the Association of Performing Arts Presenters was holding its international booking conference at the Hilton in midtown Manhattan. Russo had to attend this event throughout the weekend.

After dinner, Gray put the kids in a cab and said that he was going to walk home, even though it was ten degrees below zero outside. Once again, he went to the Staten Island Ferry. When Russo returned home that night, Gray was already there, asleep.

"My mother used a trope very regularly: 'That which I have greatly feared has come upon me.' It was a form of some biblical phrase. Behind it was 'You've got to avoid being afraid. You will get what you worried about. If you worry about illness, you'll become ill.' I see that as woven into those later stages [of Spalding's life]," Gray's older brother, Rockwell, said. "Of course, the whole thrust of Christian Science is that it is in your hands. If you want to know the truth, you can be saved. But if you don't, you're just going to bring trouble on yourself. It was a very angry notion, and I think that Spalding was working out some adult form of that."

On January 10, 2004, at six in the morning, Gray left for the ski clinic in Aspen. "I walked him down and helped him with his bags," Russo remembered. "Before he got in the car, he gave me a kiss and said, 'Thanks for the trip, honey.' I said, 'You never call me "honey."'" He smiled.

Gray went to the airport and discovered his flight was canceled. When he was offered an alternative flight with another airline, he didn't take it. He called Russo and said his flight was not taking off but that he would leave the following day. That evening, while Russo was at a theater showcase at the Poetry Project at St. Mark's Church in-the-Bowery, Gray took Marissa and Theo to see Tim Burton's Big Fish, a film about a son trying to re-create his father's life as his father is dying. The film ends with this line: "A man tells a story over and over so many times he becomes the story. . . . In that way, he is immortal." Gray had gone to see the movie without knowing it would cut so close to the bone; they'd chosen the film because Theo had seen a preview with a parachute scene that had intrigued him. Gray cried throughout.

When they returned to the loft after the movie, Gray picked up the phone and, speaking to the dial tone, pretended to make a plan to meet his friend Larry Josephson for a drink. He left without his wallet or his keys. When Russo called from a taxi on her way home at midnight, Marissa told her of Gray's plans. Russo immediately called Josephson, who said he'd never spoken to Gray. When she arrived home, Theo reported to his mother that Gray had called him about 8:30 PM—later, the police discovered this phone call was made from the Staten Island Ferry terminal—to say that he loved him and would be home soon. Despite the frequent letters in the past detailing Gray's intentions to end his life, Russo could find only a blank legal pad with the imprint of "Dear Kathie" pressed into the page from a note he'd started and torn out. The police embarked on a two-month search for Gray, during which Russo received reports of sightings of him all over the country—in Grand Central, at a Hallmark store in Florida, walking in Venice Beach. Finally, on March 7, 2004, Gray's body was found on the waterfront near the Greenpoint neighborhood of Brooklyn.

Perhaps, on that freezing night in January, Gray gambled with fate and lost. "I think Spald was experimenting with how far he could step over the line . . . Just as before—how far could he go without losing it? How far could he go with affairs? How far could he go with what he could tell his audience? With his fears? What if I dropped the baby? I think he tried to go too far and he lost his balance and control," Kobland said. "At that point, it's too late. He made himself available for suicide. He experimented with it, and he accidentally completed it."

Or perhaps Gray created his fate by telling a story.

I BEGAN TO REALIZE I was acting as though the world were going to end and this was helping lead to its destruction. The only positive act would be to leave a record. To leave a chronicle of feelings, acts, reflections, something outside of me, something that might be useful in the unexpected future.

1970

ACKNOWLEDGMENTS

I AM DEEPLY grateful to the Estate of Spalding Gray. I'd like to thank
Kathleen Russo, in particular, who first offered me the opportunity—
and the privilege—of reading the journals of her late husband. I admire
her courage and determination.

At Knopf, Robin Desser not only brought passion and insight to the
project but always offered wise and steady counsel. Sarah Rothbard
and Anke Steinecke were also strong and dedicated forces in bringing
this book into being. I would also like to thank Ingrid Sterner, Carol
Carson, Victoria Pearson, and Maggie Hinders for their careful attention and excellent work.

I am so thankful to those who shared their time and reflections with
me: Channing Gray, Rockwell Gray, Ken Kobland, Elizabeth LeCompte,
Clay Hapaz, Willem Dafoe, Richard Schechner, Eric Bogosian, Suzanne
Gluck, Robby Stein, Francine Prose, Howie Michels, Jonathan Demme
(and Shane Bissett for helping to connect us), Gary Fisketjon, Steven
Soderbergh, John Perry Barlow, Bill Talen, Toby Mattox, Tara Newman, and Peter Whybrow.

My gratitude to literary agents Suzanne Gluck and Kim Witherspoon for leading the way. To Jan Constantine at The Authors Guild for her good advice. To Glenn Horowitz for generously inviting me to work in his offices while the journals were there. To David Olson for helping to document the illustrations. To Helen Adair for her guidance at the Harry Ransom Center and to Jean Cannon for her stellar research assistance. To Ron Jenkins for his thoughts on the history of solo performance. To Andy Young for keeping the facts straight. To Maury Sullivan and her family for hosting me in Austin, Texas, and Connie Casey and Harold Varmus for offering me a quiet writing retreat in Chatham, New York. To Rozália Szabó for keeping our children—and us—such good company throughout. As always, my heartfelt gratitude to my beloved friends and family, most especially to my husband, Jesse Drucker, and our two children, Hank and Eve, for so joyfully carrying me through.

Above all, I am indebted to Spalding Gray.

PHOTOGRAPH CREDITS

Unless otherwise noted, all photographs are courtesy of the estate of Spalding Gray. We have tried to identify copyright holders for the photos from Spalding Gray's personal collection; in case of an oversight and upon notification to the publisher, corrections will be made in subsequent printings.

INSERT I

Page 3 (bottom): *Times-Union*, Albany, NY
Page 4: Sharon Walker Boyd
Page 5: Clem Fiori
Page 6 (top), page 7 (top): Ken Kobland
Page 7 (middle): © Copyright by Marianne Barcellona, All Rights Reserved
Page 7 (bottom): Nancy Campbell
Page 8: Bob van Dantzig

INSERT II

Page 1, page 3 (bottom), page 4 (right): Ken Regan/Camera 5
Page 3 (top left and right): Nancy Campbell
Page 5 (top): © Al Hirschfeld. Reproduced by an arrangement with Hirschfeld's exclusive representative, the Margo Feiden Galleries Ltd., New York. www.alhirschfeld.com
Page 6 (center right): Ken Regan
Page 6 (top): Nicole Bengiveno/*The New York Times*/Redux
Page 8: © Annie Leibovitz, 2011

Printed in the United States
by Baker & Taylor Publisher Services